Boston Free Religious Association

Freedom and fellowship in religion

A collection of essays and addresses

Boston Free Religious Association

Freedom and fellowship in religion
A collection of essays and addresses

ISBN/EAN: 9783337263720

Printed in Europe, USA, Canada, Australia, Japan

Cover: Foto ©Lupo / pixelio.de

More available books at **www.hansebooks.com**

Freedom and Fellowship

in

Religion.

A COLLECTION OF ESSAYS AND ADDRESSES

EDITED BY A COMMITTEE

OF

𝕿𝖍𝖊 𝕱𝖗𝖊𝖊 𝕽𝖊𝖑𝖎𝖌𝖎𝖔𝖚𝖘 𝕬𝖘𝖘𝖔𝖈𝖎𝖆𝖙𝖎𝖔𝖓.

BOSTON:
ROBERTS BROTHERS.
1875.

Copyright, 1875,
By Roberts Brothers.

Cambridge:
Press of John Wilson and Son.

CONTENTS.

	PAGE
INTRODUCTORY. THE RELIGIOUS OUTLOOK	1
THE NATURE OF RELIGION. By David A. Wasson	17
THE UNITY AND UNIVERSALITY OF THE RELIGIOUS IDEAS. By Samuel Longfellow	46
FREEDOM IN RELIGION. By Samuel Johnson	93
RELIGION AND SCIENCE. By John Weiss	135
CHRISTIANITY AND ITS DEFINITIONS. By William J. Potter	178
THE GENIUS OF CHRISTIANITY AND FREE RELIGION. By Francis Ellingwood Abbot	222
THE SOUL OF PROTESTANTISM. By O. B. Frothingham	265
LIBERTY AND THE CHURCH IN AMERICA. By John W. Chadwick	299
THE WORD PHILANTHROPY. By Thomas Wentworth Higginson	323
RELIGION AS SOCIAL FORCE. By Ednah D. Cheney	338
VOICES FROM THE FREE PLATFORM	355

INTRODUCTORY.

THE RELIGIOUS OUTLOOK.

THAT religion still occupies the thoughts of men as a great human concern need not be argued. It may be said to occupy them as it never did in times when it claimed an interest on grounds of its own, wholly separate from other human affairs. The religious question now makes a part of every question. There is scarcely a concern of any moment in which religion does not hold a conspicuous rank. It is debated in the highest places; it is the business of empires; it occupies the thoughts of princes and administrators; politicians make account of it; statesmen and demagogues alike take bearings from it. It haunts the scientific mind; literature cannot leave it unrecognized; philosophy finds it mingling in all its problems. The social questions that vex our age address themselves to it less directly indeed, but no less earnestly, than of old. They who talk of the declining interest in religion cannot be close observers of the times. The forms the interest takes may have changed, but the interest was never so vital before.

The religious aspect certainly has changed. The theological epoch draws near its close. Fifteen years ago, Mr. Buckle called attention to this, and supported his position by quotations from eminent authorities of the English Church. The impulse given in the reign of Charles II., when the Royal Society received its charter, — an impulse clearly understood as committing the English mind to natural studies as distinguished from supernatural, — has gone on with accelerating motion ever since, until now the books on natural science outrank in power, if they do not in number, the works on theology. The great writers in dogmatic and speculative theology are of the past. Warburton, Cudworth, Barrow, Taylor, Hooker, are little read; and such interest in them as remains is due rather to their rhetoric than to their reasoning. The human mind has abandoned that province. The press of England and America still pours out pamphlets and booklets, expository and polemical, with a persistency born of ancient habit; but the tractates are written for the most part by divines who like to see themselves in print, and, having nothing vital to talk about, talk about the doctrines of the church. The quality of the literature — if literature it can be called — is thin, weak, sentimental; its readers are the personal friends of the authors, or the pensive devotees of the church in whose interest they write. The working mind of the age turns from theological questions with a kind of disgust; and as no great thinker engages in obsolete or unreal speculations, the literature of theology languishes. To one who remembers the place it held but half a century ago, this fact is of profound significance.

The disposition to discuss religion in its political relations is another sign of a new era. This disposition has been gaining force for two centuries and more, — from the reign of James I. Dr. Arnold called attention to it in his lectures on modern history. In our day the fact declares itself in a way not to be misunderstood. It implies that religion must justify its existence to society, must meet the human mind on its natural plane, must accept the methods of science, and secure its title to support by the cordiality with which it accepts the conditions of ordinary life.

The establishment of the scientific method is another fact of vast moment to the religious world of our generation. Scientific men no longer apologize: they assert with an emphasis the theologian cannot surpass. They have their dogma; they lay down their law; they speak with an authority that carries weight from the power of their achievements, as well as from the splendor of their talent. Their audience is immense, intelligent, enthusiastic: it comprehends the strongest thinkers and most earnest workers. Their literary performances are marvellous for copiousness and brilliancy: they compel attention and enforce the necessity, if not of accepting special results, at least of adjusting beliefs to a new method.

Christianity is now on trial at the bar behind which it had sat as judge for a thousand years; and the judge on the bench is the scientific spirit it had so often remanded to the dungeon or consigned to the flames. Its dogma is discredited in the high places of thought. Repeated modifications, definitions, restatements, made for the purpose of readjusting it to the human mind, have so far impaired its integrity, loosened its compactness, and thinned its substance, that even in its private haunts, among its most staunch friends, it is no longer what it was. Of its great cardinal doctrines, some — like trinity, incarnation, atonement, depravity—have been explained till they have scarcely more than a name to live; others—like election, predestination, the damnation of the unbaptized, the endless torment of the unbelieving—have been, in their dogmatic sense, repudiated. Millions still profess them, but millions do not; and the millions who do not are the most intelligent portion of the human race.

In the old world the church of Rome is engaged in a struggle for existence, and is losing. In Italy, the government, though exceedingly moderate in its measures, under the lead of a king, himself a Catholic, and a ministry scarcely aggressive enough to meet the wishes of the people, gains steadily on the papacy, and pushes reforms in the papal city that cause the ecclesiastical powers to shudder. In Rome, where the traces of Protestantism were wiped out with a swift hand, the Evangelical Alliance has proposed holding its next meeting. In Germany, the battle with the empire, under the lead of Bismarck, goes heavily against the Pope. Catholic Austria modifies her school laws in the interest of secular education. In England, Mr. Gladstone has succeeded in unearthing and exposing the pretensions of the church. The equivocations of Archbishop Manning and of Monsignor Capel confess the truth of the charge they try to evade. None appear in open defence of the position which the ex-premier assails. There is indignant protest, holy horror, honest denial; but of manly championship there is none. The discussion, which is carried on mostly by Catholic writers, reveals differences of opinion that may easily ripen into dissension. The enormous sale of Mr. Gladstone's pamphlet shows that the English people are interested, but there is no evidence that they are afraid; and the tone of the press foreshadows with terrible decision the attitude Englishmen would take if Rome should ever interfere as a dominion with the organization of their political or social life. On that issue Romanists themselves would fatally divide. If in the reign of Elizabeth such interference was resented and resisted, in the nineteenth century the bare suggestion of it would excite only derision.

This question has not come up in America, and probably never will; but it may. Mr. Gladstone reminds us that "even in the United States, where the severance between church and state is supposed to be complete, a long catalogue might be drawn of subjects belonging to the domain of competency of the state, but also undeniably affecting the government of the church; such as, by way of example, marriage, burial, education, prison discipline, blasphemy, poor relief, incorporation, mortmain, religious endowments, vows of celibacy, and obedience." More than once we have been made uneasy by the possibilities of Catholic meddling with our public affairs. More than once we have suspected officious dabbling and intrigue in elections. It is notorious that the Roman Church has received large endowments from the state, and that it has obtained them through political influence. That this church has heretofore kept up affiliations with existing forms of despotic power is undeniable; that these affiliations were not incidental is reasonably believed; that, from the nature of things, spiritual despotism must be in league with political, is a rational persuasion; and, though in America the elements of political despotism, instead of being organized as in Europe, are continually shifting from party to party, and undergoing perpetual transformations, still they exist, and maintain their characteristic features; which are ignorance, prejudice, pride of race and class, intolerance, and contempt, — in a word, inhumanity, under one or another guise.

The decline of the temporal power of Rome may be assumed as an event accomplished in modern history. But it is not generally perceived that the decline of the temporal power involves the decline of the spiritual. The religion must follow the fate of the empire. Rome sees too clearly that the fair vision of increased and increasing sway over souls that is promised as the reward for laying down her imperial sceptre is baseless. By a strong logic she was impelled, as early as Constantine's day, to apply her principle of spiritual authority to all matters into which moral considerations entered; and perceiving, as every intelligent person must, that such considerations enter into all concerns whatever, public and private, social and domestic, judicial and administrative, she asserted her paramount right and duty to interpose in the regulation of the social condition, on the whole and in all its parts. The claim of spiritual authority is idle breath without this solid burden of inference. The power that controls conscience controls society. On that point Archbishop Manning is in full accord with Mr. Gladstone. They differ in this: that whereas Archbishop Manning believes in the existence of a visible power divinely authorized to control conscience, Mr. Gladstone does not. But if the power to control conscience implies the power to control society, denial of the power to control society involves denial of the power to control conscience. Take away the temporal power, and you take away the very throne of power. You reduce the church to an organ of teaching and of influence on individual souls. The right to dictate opinion, to direct principles, to impose rules on conduct, to fulminate edicts against misbehavior, to visit moral offences with civil or social penalties, to use the confessional for other than strictly sentimental purposes, is taken away. The greater part of her machinery falls instantly into disuse. She is shut up within the limits of reason, imagination, and feeling, where other forms of religion compete with her with more or less of success. She would, thus limited, be less than the shadow of what she was.

We are told that facts do not bear out this prediction; that, on the contrary, the increase of the Catholic religion has kept pace with the shrinkage of political power. It is said that in 1765, England and Scotland contained but 60,000 Catholics; in 1821 there were 500,000; in 1842, 2,500,000; in 1845, 3,380,000. The Catholics boast of 600 conversions a year; and claimed in 1873, 1,893 priests, 1,453 churches and chapels, 86 convents of men, 268 convents of women, 21 Catholic gymnasiums, 1,249 schools, 20 dioceses, 33 Catholic lords, 77 baronets, 6 members of the Privy Council, and 37 members of the House of Commons. But neither figures nor facts explain themselves: there are causes behind them that are not easily interpreted or analyzed. It certainly would be rash to conclude that these facts and figures report a genuine spread, to such an extent, of the Catholic faith. The essential Romanism of the English Church, which leads the most severely consistent of its members directly back to the older communion, accounts in considerable degree for the success of the Tractarian movement. The passion of the wealthy, idle, and aristocratic class for pomp and the prestige of antiquity; the proclivity of the same class, among the women especially, to sentimentalism; the conservative love of order; the dread of infidelity, and the social revolution associated with it; the reaction against scientific rationalism, — are circumstances that will explain a great deal. Add to all this, the singular activity of the Romish priesthood, their devotion to their work, the intense earnestness apparent in their lives, the unwavering character of their beliefs, and the tone of authority they use, and the increase of Romanism in England is justified without supposing any deep spiritual change in the popular heart. Mr. Mill, in a recently published essay, dwells forcibly on the power of mere authority to carry crowds away; but the crowds so transported are liable to be swept back, or borne in a different direction, by the first strong wind from an opposite quarter.

The ingenious Father Burke told the enthusiastic Irish of Cork that there were 9,000,000 Catholics in the United States, at a low estimate; while at the time of the Declaration of Independence they counted but 25,000; and then he went on, with true Irish fervor, to state the details of this amazing spread. The number he gives is probably something more than three times the actual sum. But, supposing it were correct, it must be admitted that they are almost wholly composed of the different branches of the Celtic race, which is Catholic wherever found; and that from the numbers of that race in America must be deducted the hundreds of thousands who have simply been transferred thither from the old world, chiefly from Ireland. It is not fair to count even Catholics more than once. The established habit of doing so at the polls must not be permitted to disturb the axioms of arithmetic. The Catholics of intellect and culture — lawyers, judges, men of letters, physicians — are, with few if any exceptions, of Irish extraction, — Catholics by tradition of race. The Spaniards of New Mexico are Catholic, of course; so are the Italians; so, in a less proportion, are the French. The aristocratic class, or a portion of it; the lovers of form and ceremony; the reverers of authority; the admirers of fixed beliefs; the sentimentalists; the alarmists; the doubters, who refuse to be tormented; the believers, who refuse to be disturbed; the worldly, who regard religion as a police force to protect respectability, and therefore advocate the strongest church, — are Catholic in America as they are in England. But such converts are to be counted, not weighed. Between the indifference of the educated Catholics, whose faith is a sentiment or a tradition, and the stupidity of the uneducated, whose faith is a remarkably disreputable superstition, there is not much room for vital belief. The evidence that the Catholic religion gains ground where it is least implicated in the concerns of the state, is very slight indeed.

No doubt, the Catholics are making prodigious efforts in the old world and the new. The old Catholics of Germany are trying to recover lost ground, by disengaging themselves from the papacy. The new Catholics of America are trying to revive the ancient system, by disengaging themselves from the traditions of Europe. But it is probable that the unity of the church suffers as much as its superficial area gains by these diversions. Instead of one church, there are many:

its moral integrity destroyed, its power disappears. Judged by its spiritual — that is, by its intellectual or rational — influence alone, we are not warranted in conceding to the Catholic religion as much sway as the largest single sect of Protestantism exerts.

The weakness of Protestantism, so openly and plaintively confessed at the recent sessions of the Evangelical Alliance in New York, is attested by numerous signs. In England, there is lamentation over the falling off in the number of missionaries, — a lamentation rendered more agonizing by the admission that in quality, as well as in quantity, the new recruits are inferior to their predecessors. The Episcopal Church there is disturbed by controversies that increase in bitterness, and show results in secession. The debates on the subject of ritualism, at the late conference in New York, disclosed an unsuspected gulf of separation. The departure of Dr. Cummins with a large following is ominous of dissolution in that communion.

He that would study the fate of Protestantism has but to ponder the history of the Evangelical Alliance. The very existence of an organization, avowedly formed with the object of beating back menacing and dangerous foes, — Romanism on the one hand, and Rationalism on the other, — is an indication of acknowledged infirmity. The difficulties experienced in forming the league, the concessions that had to be made, the lukewarmness that had to be surmounted, the appeals that had to be issued, betrayed the extent to which sectarian divisions, dogmatic prejudices, party jealousies, had demoralized the churches and disintegrated the faith. The disproportion of the result to the plan — three or four sects only entering into the conspiracy, and they held with great labor to their allegiance — was a confession of weakness it is surprising that far-sighted men should have made.

The Christian unions which put on so brave a look, and call attention so vauntingly to their breadth and earnestness of spirit, their willingness to sacrifice incidentals to essentials, and the deepening of their Christian faith, are rendered necessary by the pressure of rationalism. The sects draw together for mutual support, surrendering outworks of belief they can no longer hold, and consenting in the occupation of the last trench. They admit as many as they can, that they may present a good front to the besieging foe. The liberalizing of creeds, the allowance of different interpretations of book and article, the relaxing of definitions, are suggestive of decaying bonds. Great boast was made of the expanded temper of the orthodox churches, because Dr. A. P. Peabody gave a course of lectures in a Presbyterian Church on the Christian Evidences. The enlargement was not remarkable; for the lectures might have been delivered fifty years ago in any place less liberal than a Jewish temple, and, if read by a Baptist or a Romanist, would have excited no comment. But the willingness to listen to a so-called Unitarian really proved no more than the readiness of orthodoxy to reckon on all the forces it could call in. On the other hand, the huddling of the Unitarians of Saratoga behind the old defences showed the fear lest longer exposure in the open field might be fatal to existence. When vitality retreats from the extremities, dissolution is commonly supposed to be near. When the garrison retreats to the citadel, ultimate surrender is predicted.

To say that the modifications in the statements of Christian theology are merely adjustments of the faith to the devout intelligence of modern times, is to concede the whole case. The devout intelligence of modern times does demand precisely this, — the indefinite modification of the Christian theology; and it will press the demand till every vestige of the theology is swept away, and reason is alone and supreme in the domain of truth. Enthusiastic believers inside of Christendom rejoice to see their religion overpassing its ancient close boundaries, and cordially meeting the human mind on its own ground. But, to the cool observer outside of Christendom, it looks rather as if the human mind had overpassed the boundaries fixed by church authority, and was driving the religion back. Christianity is at bay within Christendom. The "Christian world" contains more non-Christians and anti-Christians than Christians, more unbelievers than believers, more unworshipful than worshipful, more lukewarm than ardent, more irreverent people than reverent. The naturalists outnumber the supernaturalists. The rationalists carry more weight than the fideists. This is so, at all events, in the centres of thought; and the centres of thought are the fountains of thought. The live mind of the world — meaning by live mind inquiring mind — is deserting Christianity for philosophy, science, and literature.

But a more decisive indication of the decline of the Christian system as interpreted by Protestants of all degrees, from Lutheran to Universalist and Unitarian, is the all but complete divorce of the system from popular life. Its influence on the practical concerns of men is scarcely perceptible. The politician sets up rules and standards of his own; the lawyer obeys the precedents of his profession; the merchant complies with the regulations of trade; the financier consults the principles of social economy; ladies and gentlemen conform to the precepts of fashionable etiquette; men and women of the world follow, without hesitation, the maxims of the community they live in. Human existence, in all its departments, goes on unconscious of the presence of a law that rebukes its whole spirit and practice. This point has been keenly touched in a little book entitled "Modern Christianity a Civilized Heathenism," by the piquant author of the "Fight in Dame Europa's School." The argument, as he puts it, is conclusive against the vitality of the Christian system; but he might have pressed it further without exaggeration, and shown an equal incompatibility between modern life and the faith and ethics of the New Testament. The teachings of the Sermon on the Mount are as irreconcilable with the cardinal principles on which modern society is based as are the implications contained in the Thirty-nine Articles, or any other Christian confession. Society drives neither coach nor cart over that road.

If Christian professors and divines exhibited in their own daily habits the power of the faith they contend for, so that the Christian life confronted the world with a majesty undaunted by insult, and a sweetness unruffled by neglect, the assertions just made would be deprived of their pertinency: for then a prospect of ultimate victory might be entertained by the men of faith. But this hope is not granted. Christian believers make strenuous efforts to defend and spread abroad their faith; the spirit of consecration is active;

the number of earnest, devoted men and women in the various communions is very large; examples of heroism and saintliness, of the pure Christian type, are presented by refined people in the heart of worldly cities: but they are not sufficient to create or keep alive a body of opinion; they are exceptions to the rule, even among gospel people; indeed, they are, by all admission, very rare. Their separate brilliancy only serves to reveal the density of the surrounding darkness. They confirm the condition of things which they deplore: they convict the age of a stubborn, deep-seated, ineradicable fidelity to the law of reason, so far as revealed.

The chaotic state of opinion on religious questions is simply the result of the general breaking up of the Christian system. Intelligence, being thrown upon its own resources to find a path over heaps of ruin, looks in every direction for an issue out from the falling city. Spiritualism, materialism, atheism, positivism, sentimentalism of every mode, fanaticism of every phase, mark the efforts that are making to overleap, burrow under, dig through, blast away the piles of ignorance, dogma, tradition, that cumber the ground. They are efforts of the human mind to come to an understanding with things as they are.

The faith that such an understanding can be reached gains in force every day. The destructive period has about passed by; the constructive period has begun. In science, the greatest men are distinguishing themselves by positive generalizations. In philosophy, the lines are converging towards certain central principles. The outlook of Mr. Herbert Spencer's system is prefigured in John Fiske's "Outlines of Cosmic Philosophy," — a remarkable book, which, if it establishes nothing, indicates some of the highways that the future intelligence will tread. Lewes's "Problems of Life and Mind," and Strauss's "Old Faith and New," are contributions to the structure that is rising on the ruins of the old creed.

To those interested particularly in religious speculation, cheer comes from Owen, Müller, Lubbock, Rawlinson, Legge, Muir, Elliot, Tyler, Ellis, Newton, Oppert, Dillman, Weber, and the noble fraternity of scholars who are showing the identities and sounding the unisons of faith in all ages of mankind, and are laying the foundations of a religion inclusive of all special faiths, and more intellectual, more spiritual, more uplifting and commanding than any one. The beautiful idea of the sympathy of religions has already become familiar, and not to "rational" thinkers alone. No less eminent a person than Arthur Penrhyn Stanley, within the solemn walls of Westminster Abbey, has countenanced the noble conception, not in so many words, but in sentences of grave admonition to Christians, and honorable recognition of the merits of those whom Christians go forth to convert. Up to this time, outside of Christianity the intellect has had the field of religious inquiry mainly to itself; as was fitting, seeing that the need of criticism was the most imperative. For a long time yet, the relentless armor must be worn, and the pitiless weapon kept sharp and bare; but sentiment and imagination, recovering from the shock occasioned by the fall of their old idols, are rallying courage to do their part in peopling the new heavens with worshipful ideals, and clothing in robes of glory the august forms which the seraphs at the gate of knowledge allow passage to the upper skies.

This volume of essays, printed under the auspices of the Free Religious Association, written by different minds, in different moods, for different occasions, working without the least reference to one another, and associated here by no other bond than that of a common feeling of intellectual need, a common persuasion of their personal responsibility to meet it as they can, and a united conviction that sooner or later it will be met adequately and triumphantly, — is thrown out as their contribution towards the religion of the future.

O. B. F.

FREEDOM AND FELLOWSHIP IN RELIGION.

THE NATURE OF RELIGION.

By David A. Wasson.

IN the productive order of nature, nothing is sudden, there is no break of continuity; between lower and higher runs ever a thread of relation. Hence the principles that flower in the consciousness of humanity are not absolutely new; already, before the advent of man, Nature has had them in use, and wrought them into the structure of the world. Religion, accordingly, though as a conscious principle it is peculiar to man, has already a clear anticipation in the forms of life that lie below him. To find it in that depth of relation will assist toward an understanding of its nature; this, therefore, will be first attempted.

The growth of a plant may be regarded in three several aspects. In the lowest and most limited view, it consists in the formation of minute organic cells. From one tiny cell another proceeds; from these, others; and the result is, now a grass-blade, and now a California cedar. Cell-formation, an exceedingly small process, always and everywhere the same, is that which clothes the fields, builds the forests, makes the earth green. Such is the atomistic view of vegetable growth, — taking *atomistic*, of course, in an approximate, not the strict, sense. It is not, however, the less true, nor should be the less interesting, for being such. Smallest and greatest are wedded in nature ; and a well-balanced mind will be as little disposed to overlook the one as to *underlook* the other.

This view, nevertheless, is no complete one. Besides this small process, and above it, there is a structural idea,— an immanent, artistic genius, one might almost call it, — which assures to every plant an entire characteristic form. I remember walking, many years since, over a hill in Maine, and seeing the first buttercup of the season ; and the question rushed upon my mind, What, then, builds that ? I stood astonished to the heart before an object so familiar, looking down through it into the great deeps of natural mystery ; and the accompanying thought, new then, but never afterwards to be overcome, was: The miracle is natural order, not its interruption. But what builds that ? who can answer ? This alone we know: the idea of the plant, as an individual whole, is there from the first to make it a whole. A mass of clay is formed by the mere putting together of parts ; a pine is likewise formed by the addition of cell to cell ; but in this case there is something more: the whole is there from the outset, — only ideally, if you will, but effectively one sees, — to preside over that process, conduct it; and, were it not there, no such process could take place. The tree is — in a low sense indeed, but a real one — an individual; were it conscious of that individual unity, it would be also a person; and the notion of individuality is this: an ideal unity of parts and members; an ideal whole, which presides over, and remains identical with, its own realization.

Again, every plant stands in a system of universal relations, strictly necessary to its existence. That one grass-blade may grow, there is needed at least a whole sun and whole earth: a sun capable of shining with a given power, and of holding the planet in its orbit by a given force of attraction, therefore having the constitution and dimension of that one which actually rules in the heavens; an earth holding a spheric ocean of fire in its bosom, with a solid crust formed from this and floating upon it, with a certain chemic force of its elements, with water and evaporation, and seas to supply evaporation, and the flowing air and vapors to temper it, — in short, that one blade of grass may grow, this sun and this earth are required, with all their physical history, and all that system of relations which their existence implies. The plant, therefore, has not merely its physical roots, ramifying through some few inches or feet of soil, but also its unseen roots of vital relation; and these extend through what a space in the present, through what a depth in the past!

The husbandman that awaits the coming of the vernal sun, then casts the seed into the earth, making it over, in the hope of harvest, to the care of its cosmic relations, might well find matter for thought in his simple, customary act. The act says that the universe is a party to all vital formation within it; and that activity, power, function, proceed from the great whole to each particular existence. Does not that already suggest a religion? If the tree were conscious, it would be a sun-worshipper surely! With consciousness of vital relation on that scale, must come some response of feeling to it; and that response, — were it not a worship?

Well, a conscious being is indeed here, and with relations out of measure higher and finer. To him, accordingly, we turn.

On the lowest scale, man is not conscious. Interior physiological process — which, though in him it includes more than mere cell-formation, may be taken here as represented by it — goes on without immediate report to the mind. One has no direct knowledge of his own anatomy; of the blood's circulation; of the formation and elimination of tissue; of the functions assumed by the stomach, liver, brain, and so forth. Concerning all this one must learn by observation as of external objects. So far man is indeed to himself an external object.

It is at the second degree of the scale that human consciousness appears. The tree is an individual whole, and knows it not; man is such, and does know it. The ideal unity, which in the lower organism remains dark, silent, becomes luminous in the higher, becomes vocal, and says *I*. This consciousness — to the unthinking not wonderful at all, to the thoughtful just *infinitely* wonderful — is the root of personality; and there are two questions about it to ask, two facts about it to determine, if possible, here.

First, What is that which says *I?* The answer to this question will be found through another: What is there *to* say it? Something recognizes, enunciates itself as pure and constant identity. If we find somewhat which could so speak of itself, and speak truly, it may be regarded as clear that this is indeed the speaker. Well, we have already found it, even in the plant. The tree, it was said, has individuality of a low order, but unmistakable. Now, *individual* means " what cannot be divided," indivisible unity; and the characteristic unity even of a tree is, indeed, indivisible. The body, the matter of it, may be hewn in pieces: but hand a bare chip from it to the woodman, he will at once name the whole tree, oak, larch, pine, cedar, birch, maple, as the case may be; and in doing so will name an assemblage of characters that are simply inseparable, — one there, all there. It is an ideal unity always whole, whole in the seed as in the tree; and, though its physical realization is to tower a hundred feet, amply accommodated, it may be, in a seed no bigger than a pin's head. Now, if that ideal unity should, in the tree or in a higher creature, voice itself as such, it would clearly speak truth. The fact is there, even in a plant; and it is here, a hundred-fold more emphatic, in man, and it may justly call itself what it really is. I know of nothing else in man which could say, "I am oneness, and always the same oneness," and not speak falsely. Self-consciousness is, therefore, *ideal unity recognizing and enunciating itself.* The fact affirmed is older than man, — old as organic being on this globe; there is, there could be, no vital formation without it; but in man alone does it become to itself known, and find a voice.

Secondly, Can consciousness be, with any show of propriety, described as a material manifestation, or must we define it as a spiritual fact? What is matter, and what is spirit? Matter is all that we see, hear, touch, taste, or smell; and all effects of which we learn by the senses are physical effects. That is the widest possible definition of matter and material effects. No materialist will desire one more liberal, since the materialist assigns the same limit to all knowledge whatsoever. Now, consciousness can neither be seen, heard, touched, tasted, nor smelled. It escapes the senses utterly. When, therefore, one describes it as a material manifestation, he speaks neither from understanding nor to it. It is as when one declares that he believes in contradictories; the statement is one to which no mental conception does, or can, correspond. We should say that one spoke absurdly, should he call a horse a bald eagle. Yet the eagle, like the horse, has body, weight, feet, eyes; the blood circulates, the formation and deformation of tissues go on, in both; they have really much in common. But when that is called a material manifestation, which to the senses does not exist, the words mean simply and absolutely nothing intelligible. We see light, hear sound, feel gravitation and electricity, observe physical laws in their outward effects; but personal consciousness is that which, never to be reached, never approached, on this road, *reveals itself to itself.* That which does so, I define as spiritual. If any one thinks the word a bad one, let him find a better. But let him not fall into sheer unintelligibility, by saying *material* where no mental conception does or can accompany the term.

But, further: it has been seen that the vegetable organism has, besides its individual wholeness, which in man becomes conscious of itself, also its system of inter-relation with the great whole of nature; and in this fact a religious suggestion has been recognized. Man has, of course, the like, but incomparably higher and finer; and he has it with consciousness. By that relation, and in it, he lives, moves, and has his being: it gives him a body, and affords to it nourishment; it makes him a thinking mind, and furnishes this with matter of thought; it endows him with a moral soul, and supplies this with a field of action. His debt to it, in short, equals the entire worth of his being, be that more or less. One's life is not in himself alone. In himself alone! — what paltrier conceit could a human head ever harbor? Humanity, therefore, even in awakening to itself, awakens also, and with awful emotion, to a sense of that supreme relation; and with some greatest word, Jehovah, Brahma, God, or whatever else, with hymns also and invocations, and with that manifold gesture, faintly signifying the unspeakable, of primitive worship, it responds to that illimitable whole by which it feels itself creatively and sustainingly embraced. "I am a son of the universe," the primitive man would say, and speaks really but a little *toward* the fact, in a symbolical, faintly approximative way, that to another age may seem quite too ineffectual, or even seem an idolatry. Speak, think, the great fact completely, no man ever did or will; but recognize it with feeling, every one may.

Religion, then, in its broadest, simplest definition, is the consciousness of universal relation. A sense of subordination, "sense of dependence," goes with it, in which Schleiermacher and others would see its first principle and nature. Other accompaniments vary from man to man, or from one stage to another of human culture. Here it is attended by abject fear, there by ennobling awe; now by that superstition of self-interest which Coleridge wittily described as "other-worldliness," again by heroic loyalty and an inspiration to act in the spirit of that large reception. The principle generates ever its worship of one sort or another; but the sorts vary extremely, from mere howling exuberance, as of animalism fermented, to sentiments that surpass every symbol, every word, and shrine themselves in a hidden place of truth and duty. As lust is the villain-relative of love, so there is a lust of religion, bred backward, so to speak, from its principle. But for this the principle is not responsible, as pure love is not for its graceless kinsman. What were the response of a healthy soul to the fact signified, one sees.

The definition here given will not, at first sight, satisfy all, even of those whose mental conditions are such as one would wish to satisfy. It is religion, some will say, with God left out. But is that indeed the case? If God *can* be left out of a system of universal relation, — such relation, too, as inducts and sustains the being of man, — what place for theism more? The ground is surrendered. It seems not advisable to make such an admission hastily. Nevertheless it is clear that not enough has been said, and we proceed to determinations more definite.

And first, this: the universe is *one*, and there is but one universe: it is a system, not a jumble, and it is the all-embracing system. There is nothing outside it, it has no outside: and there is no absolute cleft, no final discordance, within it; for, if so, it were no unitive system. To sustain this statement, in a mere rapid sketch like the present, by any extended deduction, is, of course, impossible; nor is it, perhaps, at all necessary. A divided, discordant universe were simply no universe, and were self-destructive; it is inconceivable. Nor is it to be supposed that the imagination of two or several universes, standing quite out of relation with each other, and liable, or, in the measureless course of time, certain, to come into collision, with mutual wreck, will be entertained by any sane mind. This universe is therefore one; the absolute universal is absolute unity; and in this unity it comprehends all. There can be, then, in the most extended view, no relation with a part of the universe and not with the whole. As every needle on the pine, every cell within it, is related to the whole structure, so here relation is with the universe as one and whole.

Now, this matter of a *comprehending* unity is of peculiar interest to man; touching in him, I know not what central, sympathetic chord. Perhaps the secret of its suggestiveness and charm is that he is such himself: the aspect of it represents to him the identity of consciousness in the manifoldness of experience. That unity of the manifold is harmony in music; it is indispensable to delight in any work of art; it begets admiration in the study of vital organisms, with their numerous parts and processes consenting to a common end; and it is at the root of that interest with which every man contemplates a complex, perfect mechanism. Hence, every fresh discovery of this in nature is like new blood in the veins. What an impulse did Newton's great discovery give to the modern world! It brought out the unity of near and far, — of laws familiar to us as our hats or hands, with the laws by which worlds move in their orbits. So when Goethe saw, as none had seen before, into the unity of vegetable structure, and announced it in his "Metamorphosis of Plants," the fact was as a melody to the mind, fitly told in verse. This it is that draws the scientist, as he traces the great roadways of law through the world. And what a magnet it is! To what patience of pursuit, to what silent, unseen fidelity of labor, does it inspire! Is there in our time any class of men who do more from a pure, unworldly interest than the men of science? See, too, to what they condescend. No mother or maid in the nursery accepts more of what were drudgery and disgusting service, but for the lofty interest that consecrates it, than the naturalist; and, like the mother, he has no sense of condescending. The great fact he seeks is great enough to dignify all it inhabits. Let him but find that, were it in a frog's foot, in the interiors of turtles and clams, in snakes, spiders, or mud-worms, and he feels himself looking upward. He is, indeed, looking upward. Cosmic unity, law that expresses it, — you touch there a string that vibrates melodiously, sweet and awful, through all worlds. Physical science has indeed its customary limitations, — has, as I think, its blind eye, — and looks for the whole truth there where the *whole* truth is not; but it has the merit of believing with understanding, which is no small one; and, moreover, by the fact it pursues, by the object of its devotion, it is in unison with the principle of religion. Unity in the great whole; religion says that, and science *sees* it — part way! Half a loaf, however, is better than no bread and may be better than an entire loaf, if the former is white flour, while the latter is much mixed with bran, bitter seeds, and earth, — as the whole loaf of traditional religion unhappily is.

The universe is one: Of what grade is that unity? To point the question: Is the great whole, as a whole, mechanical only? Is it dead or living, a machine or a self-active organism?

The strong tendency of our time is toward a material and mechanical conception of the cosmic whole. On the contrary, however, it seems not overbold to say that the universe is, must be, a self-active organism. A machine requires external propulsion. It can propagate force, not produce it. That is the iron limit of all mechanics. Speak that word, and spontaneous activity is excluded. What, now, is external to the universe, which should propel it? What assumes for it the part of the boy at the crank of a grindstone, or of the falling water which drives a mill-wheel? The notion is self-contradictory. If such be at all the posture of affairs, there is *no* universe; unity is destroyed, absolute dualism confessed, and the very spinal cord, not only of religion but of reason as well, is broken. When it is asked, indeed, What is outside and at the crank? the old theologians answer readily, "God is the motor." But the Paleynotion of a God appended to the universe-machine, and only now and then breaking in, by way of miracle, to do a little on his own special account, is one that may here be regarded as obsolete. It served in its day as an approximate expression of religious feeling; but it gradually ceases to serve even that purpose, while, as a mode of dualism and clearly recognized as such, it is to thought only an affliction. Meantime, the mechanical philosophers, religious in their way, cling — or would cling — to the clew of unity, and admit no such *deus ex machina*. What, then? An outside propulsion cannot be admitted; no machine propels itself; whatever does so, is by the fact taken out of the category of mechanical structures; and yet the world moves. It is therefore self-active. Can the conclusion be avoided? But, with this attained, much is left behind, if much yet lie before.

A living universe, therefore, not a dead one. But, again, of what grade? Happy he who is permitted to answer that question in silence, as he can, to his own heart! But if the privilege of silence may not be claimed, let speech go only so far as indubitable fact goes with it.

Now, here is this fact, quite indubitable: the universe brings forth man and comprehends him. Does it bring forth its own superior? Is the product of a higher nature than the whole nature which produced it? But superior to it man surely is, if his mind and heart are his alone. Tell us not here of mere space, size, and power. What are these in comparison with thought, love, loyalty, honor? The volcano, vomiting lava, buries a thousand human homes; but in one mother's heart is that which is not only greater, but incomparably, unspeakably greater, than all volcanoes. Were some brute leviathan, big enough to fill the ocean's bed, the equal of one baby Shakespeare? The universe is the mother of mind, of reverence and pity, of the love of justice and truth; is it, can it be, the mother of that which is foreign to itself? It is an old question, and old enough to have been answered as the believers in a dead or brute universe would have it, were it answerable that way.

But, farther: man is comprehended in the unity of the all. Now, the higher may thus comprehend the lower, but not the lower the higher. Thus the organism of man includes that of the ape; it is all that and more: but the converse is not true. The larger circle is clearly not to be drawn within the lesser. An ape-universe, or one rounded in unity at that degree, could not comprehend in its unity the mind of Newton, the heart of Jesus.

The point can perhaps be more clearly put before the eye, if a somewhat grotesque illustration be permitted. The anaconda is a unitive organism of a certain grade. Imagine that to this organism, just as it is, a human head were somehow added. The total thus formed were no organic whole, no unity for the mind; but a mere monstrous conjunction of incongruities. Well, if we assume an infra-human, brute universe, — whole indeed, but in its principle of unity below man's degree, — the appearance of a human head *there* would be in like manner incongruous. *In* such a universe, indeed, in its idea, in its unity, a human soul were not, could not be. Man is to be conceived of, were that assumed, as a capable, wonderful parasite, wandering and building on the surfaces of a cosmos to which he does not belong, which knows him not, nor corresponds in its principle to the genius that animates and illumines him. And, nevertheless, this same alien universe, this same wholly foreign Nature, is his mother! In short, the assumption of a universe merely brute in its all-comprehending unity is, to my mind, a plunge into a bottomless abyss of unreason, where thought can think only its own contradiction.

It is like coming from a pit into clear air and out upon the sunlit world, when we turn from these confounding imaginations to that which the religious consciousness ever affirms, — a luminous, spiritual whole, open and akin to the mind of man. Religion has represented the great whole under a human form, recognizing this as its largest symbol. That is the "anthropomorphism" nowadays so much complained of. Of course, the complaint is not ungrounded. When there is set before us, as the object of worship and symbol of the great whole, some celestial Squire Weston, — a particular individual, and with his full share of individual limitation; when, moreover, this county potentate is taken, not as merely symbolizing the universal whole, but as the fact itself, — then the cry of anthropomorphism is quite in place. But when the representation of the universe under a human form is cried out upon because one believes it infra-human, inhuman, brute, then the occasion has come for discrimination both ways. The ancient, world-old worship of human gods signifies the immanent persuasion of man, that the universe is not infra-human, — that its principle of unity is spiritual, lying rather above man than beneath. Religion has said that: Can reason say less? I see not how, — with what adherence to itself. The universe is not a house divided against itself: it comprehends man in its unity; the lower does not, cannot, thus comprehend the higher. Can the mind think otherwise without unthinking itself?

And, indeed, the unthinking of reason by reason itself is the latest method of escape from the great conclusion here indicated. The intellectual, moral, civilizing genius of man is serenely set aside as merely "subjective;" that is, in plain terms, as a fiction that concocts itself in his breast, a congeries of unreal images that plays itself off in his consciousness. Reason, therefore, is good for itself, but has no validity as representative of universal fact. As when a little girl imagines that her doll sleeps, wakes, listens, takes food, and does so with a half-sense of reality, these fancies are good for the fancy which begets them, so the conscious intelligence of man is to think of its thoughts. When the light of thought has thus dishonored and denied itself, then it may be assumed that the universe really is, not what it seems to thinking mind, but only what it is found to be by the unthinking senses. Then religion also goes, of course, into the same limbo of subjective illusion, of self-concocted fiction. That is the newest fashion of enlightenment, — cherished, too, by good men, sincere, patient inquirers, able, instructed teachers, from whom I gladly learn. But what wise man shall teach us the wisdom of unthinking thought, and reasoning reason itself down?

Who shall do so while the fact lies before the eye, that it is the objective, true universe itself which brings forth the supposed fiction, and as its highest product? It flowers in the consciousness of man, so much is certain. Flowers in fiction, in unreality, in falsehood, shall we say?

The plant, observe, puts its principle at the top, rounds itself there into the unity of the seed. Man is the summit of natural process: is the unitive principle, the little whole, not also there?

Religion is the sense of universal relation; and not merely of dissolute relation with this, that, and the other, but with the universe as *whole*. That whole comprehends man: it is therefore not less, but greater; not lower, but higher. Therefore it is living, spiritual unity. The question of grade is answered so, if it is to be answered rationally.

This consciousness first makes man indeed a citizen of the universe, and at home there. He may feel that he is really *in* such a universe, and not merely *on* it. As a kindred whole, it rings to his heart in tones that invigorate, vitalize, inspire; and the heart rings response, for it is also whole; and its resonance is the bibles of the world, or say rather the one great, ever-proceeding bible of man's worthy thinking, doing, and being. And so it is that nature is ever vocal to us with a language not unintelligible nor unmoving. We touch the earth, and cannot feel that it is but a clod beneath the feet; we look up to the heavens, and see not merely a gas mingled with vapors; the sun is more ever to man than a mere ball of fire; daisy and grass-blade, wood, hill, and river, breathe suggestion, without voice but significant. For in all lives, in all speaks, the spiritual whole, not unheard. To every human soul this is indeed a *speaking* universe. What if it were not such? Then man himself were dumb; and dumb not of tongue alone, but to the core.

It is perhaps bold, but I think not too bold, to say that religion is, as in this view it should be, the root of all civilization, all human culture. That civilization began with it, is certain; it is the historical root, if no more. Auguste Comte, who would limit all knowledge to the mere surface of nature, and make man but surface even to himself, — a man, however, who thought largely and with method, — not only recognized this fact, but gave it an especial prominence. As is generally known, he found in the history of civilization three great epochs, of which the first was characterized as the "theological." The initial, genetic epoch is theological? Civilization, thought, begin there? It is significant surely! Comte himself, indeed, though professing for observed fact a respect not only profound but exclusive, had no use for this one. He simply and serenely threw that epoch away. It signified to him only so many centuries spent in making an encumbrance for later ages to get rid of. Is that the wisest way to contemplate and treat history? A parallel case will perhaps show. There was a first epoch in human development, which might be called the linguistic, — the period when language was forming. This passed, and men ceased to be, in a considerable degree, makers of language. What, then? Had speech become superfluous? Were language and the period which produced it to be simply thrown away? The making of language came first, because it was of primal and perpetual necessity. The summary throwing away of what has the first place in a process of world-growth is of more than doubtful propriety.

World-history is psychology, — is the natural history of mind, written large. He that will hold fast to that clew, may spare himself much wandering and groping. Necessary bases in history are bases in the mind for ever: it is the great law of unity in yet another aspect. Find the order of development in humanity, and this represents the dependence of powers in the mind. Metaphysic might learn more, did it pore less over its distressingly fine print, and read now and then the large letter-press of that open book. The precedence, therefore, of religion in civilization may be taken as a hint which it were well not to neglect.

Meantime the propriety of Comte's terminology may be doubted. The primitive ages were occupied with the suggestions of religion, but clearly not with theology. Moses and the singers of the Vedic hymns were not theologians; Jesus was no theologian. Theology, properly so called, comes later; and of this there may be a superfluity. Religion, then, is initial and genetic in civilization; but the theologic scholasticism, that accrues upon it, is put grossly out of place when to it a like antecedence is attributed.

And now let us see, by an instance or two, how this principle, with its grand key-note of unity, is implicated as radical in what chiefly ennobles man.

I. It is the radical principle in morals. For what do morals exact? Justice, adjustment, right unity between men. The underlying truth is the one spoken of old: "We are all members one of another." Love, justice, truth, loyalty, pity, are terms of community, — of a cordial, faithful holding together; hatred, envy, injustice, egotism, treason, falsehood, are terms of disintegration and disunion.

What, now, is the principle of morals? "Utility," say some. Utility may be accepted as the practical criterion of morals: what is in the highest sense useful is moral; that is, it is moral to do good, and immoral to do mischief. No moralist disputes that, nor can it be regarded as a recent discovery. But the producing principle of morals in man is one thing, and the outward practical test another. Why *must* one do good and not evil? What says that, and enforces it, in the mind? The ideal exaction comes from that law of unity, which may well speak sovereignly in man, since it is sovereign in the universe. Meantime a right holding together, a true faith, with others, is equally a holding together with one's self. He that acts with a vicious intention, acts against his own better knowledge, — knows one way and wills another. He violates thus the unity of his own being. Conscience is the vital ligament between conviction and volition, knowing and willing; and he who cuts that, falls asunder.

II. Rational thought has the same interior chord of world-unity. It is curious and significant, in reading the beginnings of Greek philosophy, to find it occupied with the question, What is the universal principle? what contains and explains all the rest? But why assume such at all? Why suppose that it at all exists? Simply because reason, to be such, must assume, what religion asserts, the interior oneness of all manifoldness. How is one to think rationally and not think this? Will he reason of causes? Cause is the law of unity in the successions of things. Will he reason from analogy? It is obviously to follow the same clew. Does he reason from various phenomena to their law, after the manner of inductive science? The assumption that they necessarily have a law is the very one we speak of. Why should there not be phenomena without law, without cause, without connection? The imagination is lunatic, but indulge it a moment; suppose such a witch-welter of things, then put reason in the midst of it, and where is it? In an exhausted receiver. It can think nothing, for there is nothing to think, nothing but contradicts all thought. The wholeness that religion affirms is the faith of reason, without which it ceases to be such.

III. Again, one sees what a part is played in the productive genius of humanity by the consciousness of freedom. There is, indeed, a false conceit of liberty, and there has been, within a century, so much of windy mouthing in the spirit of that conceit, that a reaction has set in. Those who talk of liberty most, scarcely believe their own words; while it has to many become a recommendation of the mechanical philosophy, that it denies the fact altogether. As when in a season of drought a gusty wind blows up the dust in dense clouds, men shut the eyes, and refuse for a moment to see, that they may save sight, so in this case: the mind closes itself to a fact about which such a dust of demagoguery, sentimentalism, and mock philosophy has been raised. But, on the other hand, banish from man's breast all consciousness of freedom; let him really feel himself a machine and no more, — and what must follow? Duty, responsibility, heroism, become empty syllables, signifying nothing; honor and shame, self-blame and self-respect, turn to smoke. George Washington and Aaron Burr, Luther and Tetzel, St. Paul and Dr. Titus Oates, become moral equivalents; that is, one and all equivalent to zero. Admiration dies with the notion, the possibility, of human worth; and meantime a vital incitement, an inspiration of personality and of history, without which they were to the moving spectacle of life what dead ashes are to flame, would be then no longer. Be it that the consciousness of freedom is an illusion, man would lose his human genius, his human soul, with it. Those, therefore, who had proved it fictitious, would have next moment to turn around and say, "Fiction is the better fact: by fiction man lives and is man!" Who could wish to see himself placed in that too equivocal attitude? Just what had been for ever disgraced as truth, must be cherished as practical necessity, and preferred before truth. But how in a world of law is freedom possible?

The divine universe, it has been said, with brief assignment of reasons, is a self-active whole. *It* is therefore free, not as being lawless, but as generating its own law. It itself, in its wholeness, makes and is the law which it, the same universe, in its parts and particulars, observes. Were it a machine, externally moved, then indeed freedom were possible neither for it nor for any thing within it. But, as purely self-moved and self-ruled, it cannot possibly be otherwise than free. Now, this free whole is productive, as we see. Does it, can it, never bring forth, as the flower of its expression, some image, some reflection, of itself? Wonderful, if in a process of ascending production, extending through incomputable periods of time, it could arrive at nothing which should represent its own nature! Wonderful, if pure freedom must for ever bring forth only its own contrary! These generalities, however, will not satisfy the doubt, or rather overcome the necessarian dogmatism, now current. How can one be free, say our philosophic friends, seeing that he is operated by motives? But *is* one operated by motives? Addressed, incited, by them one is, indeed; but operated, turned as with a crank, by them? Does *motive* signify *mechanical motor?* Look and see. A wise man does not of necessity, nor habitually, follow the first motive which addresses him: he detains it, says "I will think about that," considers what were best, and then acts. Now, this power of detaining motives, of deliberating upon them, weighing them, even of waiting for the possible appearance of such as are not immediately before the mind, *is already freedom.* Has the machine any such power? Can that, when a motor really capable of moving it has been applied, suspend its own motion, and wait to see if another, stronger motor, will not appear to overrule the one already present? When that self-suspense of the will, perfectly familiar to us all, has been accounted for on mechanical principles, then, and not till then, the necessarian hypothesis will be admissible.

Freedom, so far, is conditional only, I grant. This is indeed a world of law; and a final liberty against law there cannot be. If the determination arrived at run counter to the self-affirming and self-enforcing law of the great whole, then it is under correction, and certain not to escape correction. Otherwise, the sovereign freedom of the universe were not such; it might be contradicted, and the contradiction be sustained; then it were already under constraint, already mutilated and undone. That nation is not free as a whole to govern itself, in which all laws are at the mercy of every lawless will; on the contrary, it has as a nation, in its unity, *no* freedom. But, on the other hand, good laws take away the liberty of no good man. If he may not disobey them, neither would he do so: he wills the law, is for it, not against it; and because he is not against it, neither is it against him. He wills his obedience; how can what is with his will be against his liberty? And thus it is that in a universe of law, man may be, to the extent of morals, free, not only conditionally or provisionally, but finally and wholly. Rational duty that makes itself, is free in obeying itself. Without, there is nothing to correct it; and it is a law to itself within. When the soul of man spontaneously generates that same law, which springs eternal in the universe itself, then is it also a free whole, inwardly ruled, and not outwardly overruled. Now, duty *does* make itself in the human soul; that is clear. How else did it get there? It was never foisted upon humanity from without.

We say, then, first, that the power of the will to suspend its action while motives are weighed, or even waited for, is — to look no farther — a freedom of the will, but not final: there is a subsequent adjudication; secondly, that the power of the human soul to produce spontaneously the law which it ought to obey, opens to it a freedom which *is* final. This is the great style of liberty, and I trust it will one day be better understood. Duty is the all-emancipating human word, and in the sufficient making of that lies the superior freedom — the only one that should be named, moral or political — of individuals and nations alike. And this freedom is that of the great whole, *repeated*, — springing in man from its native sources, and making him lawgiver, that he may be free as the subject of law.

Such, then, is religion; and such are some of the relations in which it stands. It is the sense of relation, of unity, with the infinite whole; and morals, reason, freedom, are bound up with it. If all this has been but hinted, how could it be more under the conditions? Time is limited, and the ground so large!

Religion, as actually represented, has indeed ugly

and odious manifestations. The best historical religion in the world is many times more stained with crime than infidelity ever was. Unbelief has no inquisition; if it does not honor the cross, neither has it consecrated the rack and the fagot. It was a pope's legate, and not d'Holbach or La Mettrie, who was one morning seen upon his knees tying the shoes of the king's strumpet, the infamous Du Barry. Voltaire lied at discretion; but when Archbishop Manning flatters, for a purpose, that religious liberty of England which his pope damns openly, and himself secretly, is he an honest man? Too often, moreover, has the Christian church — which nevertheless is the best church — made itself the champion of moral and intellectual barbarism. In the last years of the seventeenth century, Balthazar Bekker, of Amsterdam, himself a preacher, pure beyond reproach in character, and perfect in all decent orthodoxy, was thrust by Protestant religion from the pulpit, and with cruel persecution harried out of the world, for not believing in witchcraft and possession by devils. In 1612, the Protestant consistory at Stuttgart issued its solemn reproof to the great Kepler, bidding him bridle his frivolous curiosity, and no more vex the church of Christ with vain subtleties; and he, under the ban of religion, must pursue his grand labor in circumstances of poverty, almost of misery. But why enter farther upon the long, disgraceful chapter? It is unreservedly acknowledged, that is enough. Well, under the laws of growth in the vegetable kingdom, noxious weeds, the deadly nightshade, poisonous fungi. are brought forth: who, therefore, accuses the laws of growth, and the productive energy in nature? Culture and classification are needed in religion, as in all that pertains to man. If there be much of mischievous false reasoning, is that an argument against reason? It is an argument only for a wise, capable culture of it. If there be false conscience, shall we therefore decide to banish the sense of obligation? Religion is not worse represented than any other great principle of man's being. It were well to be sane here as elsewhere.

Let religion have air. It has been kept too close, — kept in that "house of God" that derives from the mason and carpenter, and thereby kept, so much as may be, out of that limitless house, eternal on earth and in the heavens, which was not made with hands. It needs, as preliminary to all else, the air of understanding. We have now, not only to feel it, but to think it, — think it out of that supposititious connection with nasal tones, cut of a coat, verbal formularies, recited gestures, which has so almost fatally disguised its nature, and think it into all the largeness of morals, politics, science, art, industry. I do not mean that we should proceed to tag these severally with words, phrases, formularies, called religious: if they need the tag, then they are already not religious. Purity in morals; true faith of man to man in politics; in science, the devoted pursuit of law, the recognition of a speaking universe ; in art, truth; in industry, a due giving for all taking ; and acquiescence in that order which is for the health of the whole, — these *are* religion, as whatever is which expresses a living, cordial, ordered, productive wholeness, — a unity which is first human that it may be divine.

There are many to cultivate religion in a sort; there are some whose clear calling it is also to clarify, to interpret and apply it rationally. These are far from having occasion to blush for their work, if not for the manner of doing it. None is greater, none answers more to the needs of this age and of all ages. One is here at the root of high effects ; and though, in the long seasons of the world, he may not live to see the fruit of his labor, yet every drop of water, fitly poured, finds its way, and is sweet in the ripeness of the fruit at last. And, whatever the special tendency of the present, let such workers be sure that to this radical, nutritive mother-principle, the world will again come cordially, and with new intelligence ; since, for the healthful union of men in societies, — for that prosperity of thought without which man is dehumanized, — for the vitalization of morals, the maintenance of progress, and the ennoblement of character, — in short, for the sustenance of every high faculty, and the inspiration to every memorable achievement in history, this principle of religion, taken in the fulness of its great import, must ever remain, as it has ever been, the first necessity and resource of humanity.

THE UNITY AND UNIVERSALITY OF THE RELIGIOUS IDEAS.

BY SAMUEL LONGFELLOW.

THE old definition of Catholic Truth was, "*Quod semper, quod ubique, quod ab omnibus,*" — what has been believed in all times, in all places, by all men.

It would be easy to catalogue the *diversities* of the religious conceptions, the moral practices of different times, places, nations, and to emphasize the contradictions, until it might seem, as some, indeed, believe, that there is no truth attainable by man, — nothing but notions and opinions, fancies, errors, and superstitions, perpetually changing, and alike futile. Till it might seem, as many believe, that nothing but a miraculous intervention from heaven could at last reveal the truth and the way, and bring any order out of this chaos. I do not believe either of these conclusions. And it is my undertaking in this paper, to show a unity and universality of truth existing in spite of all these diversities, and under them all; to show the elements of truth existing beneath all errors and superstitions. I take the errors and superstitions not to refute, but to bear testimony to, the reality of the truth they have so poorly, yet so really, represented. These are the witnesses. Superstition declares an impulse in man to religion. Idolatry establishes the inborn impulse to worship. Polytheism reveals the native instinct in man to conceive of mysterious power above man and nature. Necromancy involves a belief in immortality. These are the rude beginnings, the imperfect, sometimes monstrous, growths. But where there was all this smoke, there must have been some fire; where there was all this manifestation, there was something seeking expression. That something was Religion: man's native sense of somewhat within him and beyond him other than the visible; the sense of the unseen and infinite and perfect haunting him, now in rude and incoherent dreams, now in clearer vision; but from which he could not free himself. He tried to name it, and he stammered. He tried to reach it, and he stumbled. But still it stirred within him, and would not let him alone. Still it shone before him and beckoned him on. That, in spite of all unintelligible and absurd beliefs, in spite of all burdensome and monstrous and cruel practices, in spite of all tyrannies of priestcraft and church authority, nearly all nations of men have remained religious, is to me a most striking proof of the reality and indestructibility of the religious element in man's nature.

We must keep in mind the distinction between essence and form, — between a ground-idea and the outward conception in which it shapes itself. The conception varies, as the idea works itself out in more or less clearness and force.

The diversities, however great, need not disturb our faith in unities of idea. But the diversities have been much exaggerated. The unity is found again and again, not merely in the underlying idea, but in the very expression of the truth.

The great religious ideas are these: God, Duty, Benevolence, Immortality. And these are universal ideas. They have been believed in all times, in all places, by all peoples. You cannot travel so wide but you will find temples, or the ruins of temples, altars, worships. You cannot read so far back into the history of men, but you will find men thinking of God, praying to him, trying to do right, loving their kind, looking beyond death to follow the souls of their friends into an unseen world. The forms which these ideas have taken have differed, and do differ: depending upon national character, upon race, climate, degree of civilization; sometimes buried under superstitions, sometimes coming out in simple forms and clear thought; clothed in one form of words in the imaginative and dreamy East, in another in the practical West. In all ages, too, and peoples, the more enlightened have held the popular faith under a different aspect from the ignorant. In all ages and peoples there have been individual men who have been above the level of their time, superior to the limitations of their race in a degree, though never entirely free from them; men of finer organization, wiser mind, more sensitive spiritual perception, keener moral instincts; lofty and saintly souls, who have striven to draw men away from superstition to truth, from baseness to virtue, — to awaken them to a more living faith in God, duty, immortality. These men have been reverenced as prophets, have counted themselves sent of God. They have been looked upon as his special messengers. About them generally after their death, the reverence of men, and the imagination and wonder of men, have gathered legends of miracles; have attributed to them supernatural birth and supernatural powers; have believed them incarnations of a descended God, or have raised them to demigods, and worshipped them.

I.

The first great religious idea is the idea of God. It is the idea of a mysterious Power superior to man, — creative, retributive, beneficent. With this idea the mind of man has always been haunted and possessed; and growing intelligence has not destroyed it, but only modified and elevated the forms of it. The *idea* is germinal in, and native to, the reason of man; but his understanding, sentiment, and fancy have embodied it in many varying *conceptions*. We trace its presence and unfolding through the forms of Fetichism or Idolatry, Sabeism or Nature-worship, Polytheism, Monotheism, to pure Theism, the conception of one universal infinite Spirit, whose immanent presence is the perpetual life of all things, whose infinite Personality includes and inspires all persons, while it transcends them: the "one God and Father of all, who is above all, through all, and in us all."

Behind all idolatries and image-worships there has always been a sense, more or less recognized, of an Invisible which they represented; and the more intelligent have declared them to be only symbols, — a condescension to the senses and imagination. Thus an English missionary relates that, standing with a venerable Brahman to witness the sacred images carried in pomp and cast into the Ganges, he said: "Behold your gods; made with hands; thrown into a river." "What are they, sir?" replied the Brahman, "only dolls. That is well enough for the ignorant, but not for the wise." And he went on to quote from the ancient Hindu Scripture:— "The world lay in darkness, as asleep. Then he who exists for himself, the most High, the Almighty, manifested himself and dispelled the gloom. He whose nature is beyond our reach, whose being escapes our senses, who is invisible and eternal, — he, the all-pervading Spirit, whom the mind cannot grasp, even he shone forth."[1]

In like manner, wherever Polytheism has prevailed, there has been a vague sense of unity accompanying it and growing clearer with growing intelligence. One of the gods comes to be re-

[1] *Laws of Manu*, I. 5.7.

garded as supreme, and the others to be but his ministers or angels. The Jehovah of the Jews appears at first to have been conceived of as not the only God, but the special god of their nation, superior to the gods of the other nations. Thus even in Homer we find a tendency to gather up into Zeus, as centre and source, all the functions of the other divinities:[1] a tendency which afterwards developed into the faith expressed in the magnificent Hymn of Kleanthes. The Egyptians believed in a "first God; Being before all and alone; Fountain of all." A very ancient inscription upon the tomb of Mentuhotep speaks of " Tum, the one Being, the great God, existing of himself, Creator, Lord of all gods."[2] In the " Rig Veda," the most ancient collection of Hindu Hymns, we read: " They call Him Indra, Mithra, Varuna, Agni; — that which is One the wise call in divers manners." And again : " The poets make the beautiful-winged, though He is One, manifold by their words."[3] So the later " Bhagavad Gita " speaks of " the Supreme, Universal Spirit, the Eternal Person, divine, before all gods, omnipresent. Creator and Lord of all that exists ; God of gods, Lord of the Universe."[4] And the " Vishnu Purana " says, " The one only God, the Adorable, takes the designation of Brahma, Vishnu, or Siva, accordingly as

---

[1] See Denis : *Histoire des Théories et des Idées Morales*, I. 7.
[2] From the translation of Lepsius.
[3] *Rig Veda*, I. 164, 46 ; and X. 114, 5. See Müller, *Chips*, I. 29.
[4] *Bhag. G.* ch. X.

he creates, preserves, or destroys. He is the Supreme, the giver of all good."[1] The Aztecs of Mexico, with their more than two hundred deities, recognized one supreme Creator and Lord, whom they addressed in their prayers as "the God by whom we live," "omnipresent, that knoweth all thoughts and giveth all gifts," "without whom man is as nothing," "invisible, incorporeal; one God, of perfect perfection and purity."[2] So the ancient Peruvians had their "Creator and Sustainer of Life;" the American Indians, their Great Spirit, "Master of Life;" the Scandinavians, their "All-father."

In the Masdean, or Zoroastrian, belief, Ormuzd (Ahura-mazda) is spoken of as "omniscient, omnipotent, and omnipresent; formless, self-existent, and eternal; pure and holy; Lord over all creatures in the universe; the Refuge of those who seek his aid." He is invoked as "the Creator, the glorious, majestic, greatest, best, most fair, mightiest, wisest, highest in holiness; who created us, who keeps us."[3]

And where the forms of polytheistic mythology occupied the popular mind, the intelligent and philosophic have always regarded these as but shapes of the fancy, and taught a pure doctrine of the unity and spirituality of God. Xenophanes, as Aristotle relates, casting his eyes upward to the heavens, declared the One is God. He condemned

---

[1] Wilson's Transl., I. 41, 43.
[2] Prescott: *Conquest of Mexico*, I. 57.
[3] *Avesta:* Yaçna, I. 1, 2. Bleeck's Translation.

the prevalent mythologies and the notions of gods in human figure, and severely blamed Hesiod and Homer for their scandalous tales about the gods. He taught that "there is one supreme God among beings divine and human. . . . He governs all things by power of reason." The Pythagoreans taught the unity of God, and compared him to a circle whose centre is everywhere, whose circumference nowhere. "There are not different gods for different nations," wrote Plutarch. "As there is one and the same sun, moon, sky, earth, sea, for all men, though they call them by different names; so the One Spirit which governs this universe, the Universal Providence, receives among different nations different names."[1] "There is but one God, who pervades all," writes Marcus Aurelius, the Roman Emperor.[2] "In all this conflict of opinions," says Maximus Tyrius, "know that through all the world sounds one consenting law and idea, that there is one God, the King and Father of all, and many gods, the children of God. This both the Greek and the Barbarian teach." And again he says, "I do not blame the variety of representations: only let men understand that there is but one Divine nature; let them love one and keep one in their thoughts."[3]

Upon a temple at Delphi was the inscription *EI* = Thou art. And upon this Plutarch writes, "We say to God, Thou art: giving him thus his

---

[1] Cit. by Denis: II. 224.
[2] *Thoughts*, VII. 9.   [3] *Dissert.*, 38.

true name, the name which belongs alone to him. For what truly *is?* That which is eternal, which has never had beginning by birth, never will have end by death, — that to which time brings no change. It would be wrong to say of *him who is*, that he was or will be, for these words express changes and vicissitudes. But God *is :* He is, not after the fashion of things measured by time, but in an immovable and unchanging eternity. By a single *Now* he fills the *Forever*. For Deity is not many, but that which is, must be one." [1]

Again, after denying the fable of the birth and education of Zeus, Plutarch says: "There is nothing before him: he is the first and most ancient of beings, the author of all things: he was from the beginning; too great to owe his existence to any other than himself. From his sight is nothing hid. . . . Night and slumber never weigh upon that infinite eye, which alone looks upon the truth. By him we see, from him we have all which we possess. Giver of all good, ordainer of all which is, and which happens, it is he who gives all and makes all. In him are the beginning, the end, the measure, and destiny of every thing." [2]

We are sometimes pointed to Buddhism as an instance of a religion without a God. That its primitive teaching was such, I suppose must be admitted; perhaps it was a reaction from the excessive devoteeism, or the corrupted worship, of the

---

[1] On the word *'EI*, 17, 19, 20. [2] Cited by Denis, II. 225.

Brahmans. But it was not long before the Buddha himself became an object of worship. And there is ample evidence that in our day the three hundred millions of Buddhists are not without a belief in God. In a Buddhist tract we read : " There appears in the law of Buddha only one Omnipotent Being. . . . He is a Supreme Being above all others ; and, although there are many gods, yet there is a Supreme who is God of the gods." [1] Huc relates a conversation with a Thibetan Lama, who said to him, " We must not confound religious truth with the superstitions which amuse the credulity of the ignorant. There is but one sole sovereign Being who has created all things. He is without beginning, and without end : he is without body, he is a spiritual substance." [2] And Schlagintweit says, " In face of all these gods, the Lamas emphatically maintain monotheism to be the real character of Buddhism." And again he speaks of a chief Buddha, *Adi Buddha*, called " Supreme Buddha," " the Being without beginning or end," " the Supreme Intelligence, God above all." [3] So that evidently the statement, " that a third of the human race have lived and died without a belief in God," is altogether too strong.

With the idea of God we find united the idea of providence, beneficence, and friendly care toward

---

[1] Upham's *Sacred Books of Ceylon*, III. 13. In some of the tracts of this volume the existence of a Supreme Being is denied.

[2] *Journey through Tartary, Thibet, &c.*, I. 121, 122.

[3] *Buddhism in Thibet*, p. 108.

man. And from this, joined with a perception of a moral likeness between him and man, sprang naturally in the heart and mind of men the conception of his fatherhood. This thought of God as our Father is often represented as the peculiar revelation of Jesus. But it was known and taught long before and far beyond Christianity. We find the name of Father familiarly given to the Supreme in India, Greece, and Rome.

Thus we read in the "Rig Veda," "May our Father, Heaven, be favorable to us. May that Eternal One protect us evermore. We have no other Friend, no other Father." "The Father of heaven, who is the Father of men."

"Father of gods and of men," says Hesiod of Zeus. And "Father of Gods and of men," echoes Homer; and again, "Zeus, most great and glorious Father." "Father omnipotent," is Virgil's phrase, and "the Father." In Horace we find "Father and guardian of the human race;" "the Parent who governs the affairs of men and of gods;" "the Father." Plutarch declares that "Zeus is by nature the Father of men; and the best men he calls his sons."[1] "He, the glorious Parent, tries the good man and prepares him for himself," writes Seneca.[2] "God, of all things which are Father and Maker, more ancient than the sun; whom no voice can express, no eye behold," says Maximus Tyrius. And Epictetus, "If what philosophers say

---

[1] *Apophthegmata.*   [2] *De Providentia*, I. 6.

of the kinship between God and men be true, . . . why should not a man call himself a citizen of the universe? why not a son of God? . . . Shall not having God for our Maker, Father, and Guardian free us from griefs and alarms?" And again, speaking of Heracles, he says, "He knew that no human being is an orphan, but that there is a Father who incessantly cares for all. For he had not merely heard it said that Zeus is the Father of mankind, but he esteemed and called him his own Father, and in the thought of him performed all his deeds."[1]

Philo, the Alexandrian Jew, says that "he who regards the whole universe as his country, feels bound to seek the favor of its Father and Framer:"[2] and again, "God, whose most fit name is Father;" and "One Creator, one Father."[3] And in the Talmud we read, "Every nation has its special guardian angels: Israel shall look only to Him. There is no mediator between those who are called his children and their Father which is in heaven." "As long as Israel is looking up to its Father which is in heaven it will live." "If we are called servants of God, we are also called his children."[4] In every synagogue in Judea and Galilee were recited at each service these sentences of prayer: "Be thou merciful unto us, O our Father, for we have sinned." "Most merciful Father, pardon us." "Bring us back, O our Father, to the keep-

[1] *Disc.* I. 9 : III. 24.   [2] *De Monarchia.*
[3] *Confus. of Lang.* 33.   [4] *London Quarterly Review*, Oct. 1867.

ing of thy law." And daily in the temple was spoken the prayer, "Bless us, O our Father, all even as one, with the light of thy countenance."[1]

II.

The second great religious idea which I named is the Moral Idea; the idea of Right, of Duty; and the sense of the obligation of the Virtues. I call this *religious;* I know it is often called "only moral." But if by moral be meant any thing deeper than mere custom or habit or external good behavior; if it go down to principles and laws felt to be of a creation and an obligation superior to human will, — then we are in the realm of the invisible, the eternal, in the realm of religion. Therefore I call righteousness an essential part of religion. To some men, who have little of devout sentiment, or who have speculative difficulties about belief in God, or in *a* God, morals or righteousness is the substance of their religion; and, if it gives a sacred sanction and an immutable ground of nobleness to their lives, it is truly a religion. To the devout mind, the sentiment and idea of right become identified with the will of God. Obedience to the law of our own being is obedience to his law; his service is therefore perfect freedom, and finds its sacred sanction in likeness to him.

We ought not to be surprised to find that the idea of right and wrong has been universal among

[1] See Prideaux and Lightfoot.

men. That is but saying that men have always been men; have always had consciences, as they have always had senses, affections, language, society. We ought not to be surprised that the virtues of justice, honesty, veracity, purity, have been inculcated and practised under all forms of religion. Yet there are those who, on account of superficial diversities and differences of development, deny any universality in the moral ideas. They point, for instance, to the immoralities attributed to the gods in some of the polytheistic mythologies. But the wiser men in these nations disbelieved and denounced these fables. Thus we find Plato in his "Republic" at great length blaming Hesiod and Homer for attributing low morals to the gods, and declaring the falsity of such notions.

But even among those who currently believed these things of the gods, the practice of them was not justified or approved among men. There was thought perhaps to be a different law for the Immortals, or only their own will. Just as, in Christendom, God's mere will is thought to be for him the only law of right. In Christian churches it is currently taught that he may justly do what in man would be monstrous cruelty. God is believed to spend eternity in burning alive those of his children who have disobeyed him, or who have only not accepted his conditions of salvation; or in subjecting them to tortures of which burning alive would be a faint symbol. But the same act would not for a moment be justified, or be judged as other than monstrous cruelty, in a man. In the decadence of Rome, it became a fashion for the dissolute young men to take the names of the several gods, and addict themselves to their special vices; but of course in that there was no serious belief of any kind. And precisely in these periods of corruption we find the wiser and better men lamenting the prevalence of vices, inveighing keenly against them; in the name of religion urging a pure morality, endeavoring to awaken the sense of personal virtue, and working reforms in morals and manners.

But it is urged that practices condemned by the conscience of one time and religion have been approved or commanded by that of some others. Doubtless these diversities in the *application* of moral judgments have existed, and do exist, according as the moral sense has been more or less enlightened and cultivated. I am not declaring the absolute *uniformity* of the moral — or the religious — conceptions or practices of men; only the virtual universality and essential unity of the idea. Doubtless the diversities exist. But they have been exaggerated. And the difference is often on the surface, — in the form of the act, and not in its quality or motive. Thus human sacrifices, so prevalent in primitive worships, are held up as instances of sanctioned cruelty. So they would be for us; and always they mark, of course, a low state of religious and moral perception. But they were never offered in a *motive* of cruelty. A religious feeling overrode the natural sentiment of humanity; that sentiment was sacrificed in what was erroneously deemed a higher feeling: as in the tale of Abraham offering his son. Moreover, under the practice of human sacrifices lay the true idea of *offering to God that which was most precious.* Doubtless the young men who, among the Aztecs, were every year selected and prepared for the bloody rites of the god, counted it a glory to be so consecrated, and went to the *teocalli* with something of the exalted sentiment with which a youth devotes himself to death in his country's defence. But the same religions which enjoined these bloody offerings to their gods, enjoined among men the obligations of kindness and humanity. The Christian church proclaims daily the acceptableness to God of the great Human Sacrifice, pictures the body torn upon the cross, and dwells with earnest iteration upon the efficacy of the *blood* shed on Calvary, and its necessity to appease the wrath of God. But it inculcates at the same time on *men*, pity, compassion, and justice. A sincere but mistaken religious sentiment blinds it to the essential cruelty and injustice involved in God's acceptance of such a sacrifice as it depicts.

With all the differences, then, in the culture of the moral sentiments, and in the application of moral judgments, we are justified in declaring the universality of the moral idea. In no age or people has any thing been approved *because* it was unjust, or that was seen at the same time to be unjust.

More than this: we find, in widely different nations and times, the continual recurrence of the same moral injunctions, the inculcation of the same virtues.

In the "Vishnu Purana," a Brahmanic scripture, we read: [1] —

"The earth is upheld by the veracity of those who have subdued their passions, and, following righteousness, are never contaminated with desire, covetousness, or wrath." "The Eternal makes not his abode in the heart of the man who covets another's goods, who injures any living creature, who utters harshness or untruth, who is proud in his iniquity, and whose thoughts are evil."

"Kesava [a name of God] is most pleased with him who does good to others, who never utters calumny or falsehood, who never covets another's wife or another's goods, who does not smite or kill, who desires always the welfare of all creatures and of his own soul, whose pure heart taketh no pleasure in the imperfections of love and hatred. The man who conforms to the duties enjoined in the Scripture is he who best worships Vishnu [God]: there is no other way."

"The duties incumbent alike on all classes are the support of one's own household, marriage for the sake of offspring, tenderness toward all creatures, patience, humility, truth, purity, freedom from envy, from repining, from avarice, from detraction."

[1] Transl. of H. H. Wilson, Vol. III.

"Know that man to be the true worshipper of Vishnu, who, looking upon gold in secret, holds another's wealth but as grass, and directs all his thoughts to the Lord." "The Brahman must look upon the jewels of another as if they were but pebbles."

The five commandments of the Buddhist religion, which dates six centuries before the Christian era, and counts among its adherents more millions than any other church, are these: 1. Thou shalt not kill. 2. Thou shalt not steal. 3. Thou shalt not commit adultery, or any impurity. 4. Thou shalt not lie. 5. Thou shalt not intoxicate thyself with drink.[1]

I need not occupy space with quotations of moral precepts from the ethical writings of the Greek and Roman philosophers. A single sentence of Aristotle sums them up: "In all times men have praised honesty, moral purity, beneficence. In all times they have protested against murder, adultery, perjury, and all kinds of vice. No one will dare maintain that it is better to do injustice than to bear it."[2] So we find in Cicero, "The true law is everywhere spread abroad, it is constant, eternal. It calls us to duty by its commandments; it turns us away from wrong-doing by its prohibi-

---

[1] Upham's *Sacred Books of Ceylon*. Sometimes five other commandments are added.

[2] *Topic.* VIII. x., cit. by Boutteville, "*La Morale*," p. 542. So Plato: "He who commits injustice is ever more wretched than he who suffers it." *Gorgias*, Bohn's Tr. I. 177.

tions. We can take nothing from it, change nothing, abrogate nothing. Neither the Senate nor the people have the right to free us from it. It is not one thing at Rome, another at Athens; one thing to-day, to-morrow another. But eternal and immutable, the same Law embraces all times and all nations. There is one Being alone who can teach it and impose it upon all: that is God."[1]

This same religious sanction of right doing we find in various writers, urged with the motive of likeness to God. "God is just," says Plato, "and there is nothing that resembles him more than the just man."[2] "The temperate (virtuous) man is dear to God, for he is like him."[3] Zeno taught that "men ought to seek after perfection; for God is perfect."[4] Epictetus says that he who would please and obey God must seek to be like him. "He must be faithful as God is faithful; free, beneficent, noble, as God is; in all his words and actions behaving as an imitator of God."[5] "Love mankind: follow God," writes Marcus Aurelius.[6]

There is a celebrated moral rule which is called the Golden Rule of Christianity. Confucius, some five centuries before the Christian era, was asked, "Is there one word which may serve as a rule of practice for all one's life?" The Master replied,

---

[1] Cited by Denis: *Théories Morales*, II. 16.
[2] *Theætetus:* Bohn, I. 411.
[3] *The Laws:* Bohn, V. 140.
[4] Cited by Boutteville, p. 531.   [5] *Disc.* II. 14.
[6] *Thoughts*, VII. 31.

"Is not *reciprocity* such a word? What you do not wish done to yourself, do not do to others."[1] Thales, first of the Greek philosophers, taught: "That which thou blamest in another do not thyself to thy neighbor;" and Isocrates: "Thou wilt deserve to be honored if thou doest not thyself what thou blamest in others."[2] "Let no one treat his brother in a way he would himself dislike" is a Sabean maxim, preserved by El Wardi. In the fourth chapter of the so-called "apocryphal" book of Tobit, among many other excellent precepts, we read, "Do to no man what thou thyself hatest." In the Jewish Talmud, also, we find, "Do not to another what thou wouldst not he should do to thee: this is the sum of the law," given as one of the teachings of the Rabbi Hillel, who died when Jesus, according to the common reckoning, was ten years old.[3]

It is not merely external rules, nor outward good conduct alone, that we find inculcated in these universal morals. The wise and good in all times have looked within the heart for the motive and quality of right action. Confucius continually urges the "having the heart right." "I keep pure my thoughts," says a Parsee hymn. And throughout the Zoroastrian scripture "good thoughts" are always joined with "good words and good works." "Seek to converse in purity

---

[1] Legge: *Confucian Analects*, XV. 22.
[2] Cited by Boutteville, p. 533.
[3] *London Quarterly Review*, Oct 1867.

with your own pure mind and with God," says Epictetus. "The first and highest purity is that of the soul." And he warns his disciple that he should not even look upon the wife of another with an impure thought.[1] So Ovid: "It is not by locks and bars that a woman ought to be guarded, but by her own purity; she who does not sin only because she is unable, has really sinned; her heart is adulterous."[2] And Juvenal: "He who in the silence of his own thought plans a crime has upon him the guilt of the deed."[3] "The good man," says Cicero, "not only will not dare to do, he will not even think, what he dares not proclaim."[4] "Keep thy divine part pure," writes Marcus Aurelius; and again, "Look within; within is the fountain of good." "That which is hidden within, — that is the life, that is the man."[5]

So we shall not be surprised to find that not only the conspicuous virtues are inculcated by the so-called "heathen" teachers; the lowly and the passive have their place and commendation. "Whoever wishes to be happy," says Plato, "must attach himself to justice, and walk humbly and modestly in her steps. He who lets himself be puffed up with pride, devoured by ambitious desires, and thinks he has no need of master or guide, God abandons him to himself. He ends by

---

[1] *Disc.* II. 18; IV. 11.　　[2] Cited by Denis, II. 124.
[3] *Satires*, XIII. V. 209.　　[4] *De Officiis*, III. 19.
[5] *Thoughts*, III. 12; VII. 29; X. 38.

destroying himself."[1] "Do what you know to be right without expecting any glory from it," is given as a saying of Demophilus, the Pythagorean; and " Keep thy life hid " is said to have been one of the great maxims of the Epicureans. " Dear to all hearts is he whom lowliness exalts," is a Persian saying;[2] and another, " Make thyself dust to do any thing well." " He who knows the light, and yet keeps the shade, will be the whole world's model," said Lao-tze; and again, " He that humbles himself shall be preserved entire, — that is no vain utterance." " To attain God, the heart must be lowly," is a Hindu maxim. " Patience and resignation is the one road: Buddha has declared no better path exists," says a Chinese scripture. It has indeed been objected that Buddhism unduly exalts the " passive virtues." " Who is the great man? He who is strongest in the exercise of patience, he who patiently endures injury," is a saying attributed to the Buddha himself. In the Brahmanic " Vishnu Purana," " Tenderness toward all, patience, humility," are named among the " duties incumbent on all." Humility is said to have had only an ignoble meaning with the Romans; but Epictetus,[3] who may have learned the lesson as a slave, recommends to his disciple to " train and perfect his will and render it noble,

---

[1] Cited by Boutteville.

[2] This and the following sentences are from Conway's *Sacred Anthology*.

[3] *Disc.* I. 4; II. 8.

free, faithful, *humble*." And elsewhere he says, "Such will I show myself to you, faithful, *modest*, noble, tranquil, since Olympian Zeus himself does not haughtily lift his brow." In his imperial palace Marcus Aurelius could say to himself, "Take care that thou be not made into a Cæsar. . . . Keep thyself simple, good, pure . . . kind, affectionate." Again, "Make thyself all simplicity."[1] He everywhere praises modesty; and commends the "sweetness" and "patience" of Antonine. "The more exalted we are, the more lowly we ought to walk," said Cicero.[2] In the Talmud we read, "He who humbles himself will be lifted up; he who exalts himself will be humbled." "He who offers humility before God and man shall be rewarded as if he had offered all the sacrifice in the world." And again, "He who gives alms in secret is greater than Moses."[3] So Seneca wrote, "That which is given to infirmity, to indigence, to honest poverty, ought to be given in secret, and known only to those who are benefited by it. . . . Such is the law of benefits between men, — the one ought to forget at once what he has given, the other never to forget what he has received."[4] And Plutarch, "The virtuous man buries in silence his good deeds." "All thinking beings," says Marcus Aurelius, "have been made one for the other; they owe patience one toward another." "'T is against nature to cherish ill-will

---

[1] VI. 30; IV. 28.
[2] *De Off.* I. 26.
[3] *London Quarterly*, Oct. 1867.
[4] *De Beneficiis.*

to him who is your neighbor, your kindred, your brother."

III.

And so we strike upon the sentiment of benevolence, the virtue of disinterestedness, the idea of Brotherhood. We shall find the inculcations of Love as widely spread as those of Justice. While inhumanity has always existed in the world, and selfishness and cruelty, certainly not yet outgrown, in all times there have been protests against them from the lips of the good, from the better heart of man. Always there have been kindness, forgiveness, charity, and the inculcation of them. Those sweet waters have flowed ever from the perennial springs in the heart of man and of God, to refresh even the most desert places. "He who injures any living creature, does it to God," says the "Vishnu Purana": "He is most pleased with the man who does good to others; who bears ill-will to none." "The Brahman must ever seek to promote the good of others, for his best riches are benevolence to all." "He who feeds himself and neglects the poor and the friendless stranger needing hospitality, goes to hell." "He who eats his food without bestowing any upon his guest eats iniquity." The Pythagoreans taught that the old ought to treat the young with benevolence; and men, to be kind to children, remembering that childhood is especially dear to God. We must bear one another's burdens, they said, but not lay burdens on any.

Justice, they said, is the beginning of political equality, but brotherly love is the completion of it. If disputes or anger arose between any of his disciples, their master taught them to be reconciled before the sun should go down.[1] Iamblichus tells us that, "Pythagoras taught the love of all towards all."[2] In Confucius we find these noticeable words: "My doctrine is simple and easy to understand. It consists only in having the heart right, and in loving one's neighbor as one's self."[3] And when one asked him about benevolence, he answered "it is love to all men."[4] "We are by nature inclined to love men," says Cicero.[5] "Take away love and benevolence, and you take away all the joy of life."[6] "Kindness, justice, liberality, are more in accordance with our nature than the love of pleasure, of riches, or even of life." And he quotes with approval the maxim of the Stoics, that "men are born for the sake of men, that they may mutually benefit one another."[7] "What good man, what religious man, will look upon the sufferings of others as foreign to him?" writes Juvenal.[8] "Is there a better sentiment than compassion?" says Quintilian, "or one whose source

---

[1] Denis, I. 15, 16.   [2] Boutteville, p. 381, note.

[3] Pauthier's Transl., p. 130. He declares his version to be exact. Legge renders more verbosely and prosaically: "to be true to the principles of our nature, and the benevolent exercise of them to others." The two Chinese words, he says, mean literally *centre-heart* and *as-heart*. *Analects*, IV. 15.

[4] *Analects*, XII. 22.   [5] *De Leg.* I. 15.   [6] *De Amicitia.*
[7] *De Off.* III. 5; I. 7.   [8] *Satires*, XV. 131.

lies more in the most venerable and sacred principles of nature? God, the author of all things here below, wills that we should help one another. . . . If I have given bread to a stranger in the name of that universal brotherhood which binds together all men under the common Father of nature, would it not be a good deed to have saved a soul ready to perish?"[1] Menander, the Greek dramatist, has these beautiful sentences: "To live is not to live for one's self alone. Let us help one another. Let us learn to have pity upon the sorrows of others, that they may with cause have compassion upon ours. Help the stranger, for thou mayest one day be a stranger. Let the rich man remember the poor; for the poor belong to God."

"Will you not bear with your brother," cries Epictetus, "who has God for his Father, his son as thou art, of the same high descent?" Notice this religious motive urged for brotherly love. And again, "Will you not remember over whom you bear rule, that they are by nature your kindred, your brothers, offspring of God?"[2] speaking of slaves. Epictetus had himself been a slave. The poet Terence, who had known the same hard experience, had plucked from it the same flower of sympathy for his fellows. His sentence, "I am a man, nothing human can I count foreign to me," has become almost a proverb. Menander, before

---

[1] Cited by Denis, II. 156.   [2] *Disc.* I. 13.

him had said in almost the same words, "No man is a stranger to me, provided he be a good man. For we have all one and the same nature, and it is virtue alone which makes the true kindred." So Marcus Aurelius: "The good man remembers that every rational being is his kinsman, and that to care for all men is according to man's nature." "We are made for co-operation: to act against another, then, is contrary to nature." "We are created especially for the sake of one another." "It is the proper work of a man to be benevolent to his kind."[1]

The doctrine of the Brotherhood of Man has been declared to be found in Christian teaching alone. It is difficult to find it in the Gospels; the single sentence usually quoted having reference only to the small company of Christian disciples. Paul states it in one passage: "God has made of one blood all the nations of men." But the idea was already familiar to the heart and mind of good men. Denis, in his learned and interesting work on the "Moral Theories and Ideas of Antiquity," from which many of my quotations have been gathered, says that "Diodorus proposed to himself to write a universal history on the ground that *men everywhere belong to one family.*" Plutarch speaks of "that admirable republic imagined by Zeno, the founder of the Stoic sect," which shows us "that all men are our countrymen and

[1] III. 4; II. 1; VIII. 56, 26.

fellow-citizens;" and he adds that "Zeno left this description as the dream or imagination of equity and of a philosophic republic; but what he taught, Alexander realized. Conceiving that he was sent of God to unite all together, he formed of a hundred diverse nations one single universal body; mingling, as it were, in one cup of friendship the customs and laws of all."[1]

"The love of mankind,"—*caritas generis humani* — is Cicero's beautiful phrase;[2] and the expression "the fellowship of the human race" often recurs in his writings.[3] "A man must believe himself born not for himself, but for the whole world," writes Lucan; and he foretells the time when "the human race will lay aside its weapons, and all nations will love each other."[4] "We are members of one great body: nature has made us kindred . . . and implanted in us mutual love," — these are the words of Seneca.[5]

But this is not all. We find among the writers of "heathen" antiquity, not merely the inculcation of kindness, compassion, benevolence: these find their highest expression in the doctrine of *forgiveness of enemies*. No doubt we find the *lex talionis:* the Greek Eschylus, with his "evil for evil," matches the Hebrew "eye for eye." But it was also a Hebrew proverb, "If thine enemy hunger, give him bread to eat; if he thirst, give him water

---

[1] *De Fort. Alexand.*   [2] *De Fin.*
[3] *De Off.* I. 44; III. 6. *De Amicitia.*
[4] *Pharsalia,* II. 383; VI.   [5] *Epist.* 95.

to drink."[1] The Pythagoreans taught, that if in the state the law recompensed evil with evil, private men ought, on the contrary, to injure none, but to support patiently wrongs and insults.[2] Pittacus, one of the seven wise men of Greece, taught that clemency is preferable to vengeance, which brings remorse; that "it is better to pardon than to punish;" and said, "Do not speak ill of your friends; no, not even of your enemies." So Cleobulus said that "we ought to be kind to our friends, to make them more our friends; and to our enemies, to make them our friends." Confucius thought that we "ought to repay injuries with justice, and kindness with kindness;"[3] but his countryman Lao-tze had said, "The wise man avenges his injuries by benefits."[4] Plato reports Socrates as saying, "Neither ought one who is injured to return the injury, as the multitude think, since it is on no account right to do injustice. It is not right, therefore, to return an injury, or to do evil to any man, however we may have suffered from him."[5] In later times Cicero teaches a similar lesson. "Let us not listen," he says, "to those who think we ought to be angry with our enemies, and believe this to be great and manly. Nothing is more praiseworthy, nothing more marks a great and noble soul, than clemency and the readiness to forgive."[6] And Valerius Maximus, the Roman

[1] *Prov.* XXV. 21.   [2] Denis I. 14.   [3] *Analects*, XXV. 36.
[4] *Tao-te-king* (translation of Stan. Julien.) II. 73.
[5] *Crito:* Bohn, I. 38.   [6] *De Off.* I. 25.

historian, says still better: "It is more beautiful to overcome injury by the power of kindness, than oppose to it obstinacy and hatred."[1] In Seneca and Epictetus, the like sentiments are found. Marcus Aurelius compares the wise and humane soul to a spring of pure and sweet water, which, though the passer-by may curse it, continues to offer him a draught to assuage his thirst; and, even if he cast into it mire and filth, hastens to reject it, and flows on pure and undisturbed.[2] This recalls the equally beautiful image in the Oriental scripture of the sandal tree, which, in the moment when it falls before the woodman's stroke, gives its fragrance to the axe which smites it with death.

I cannot better close this part of my subject than by quoting that fine passage from Epictetus, where he draws the picture of the true "Cynic," he calls him, as men now say the true "Christian." "The Cynic must fence himself with virtuous shame.... He must purify his soul.... He must know that he is a messenger sent from Zeus to men to teach them of good and evil.... He must tell them the truth, without fear.... He must consult the Divinity, and attempt nothing without God.... He will needs be smitten, yet he must love those who smite him, as being the father, the brother, of all.... When he rebukes he will do it as a father, as a brother, as the minister

---

[1] IV. 2. [2] VIII. 51.

of the Father of all. . . . He must have such patience as to seem insensible and like a stone to the vulgar. . . . Instead of arms and guards, conscience will be his strength. For he knows that he has watched and toiled for mankind, that he has slept pure and waked purer, and that he has regulated all his thoughts as the minister of Heaven." [1]

I am tempted to add as a companion picture that which Marcus Aurelius draws of the good man. "He is as a priest and minister of the gods; devoted to that divinity which hath its dwelling within him; by virtue of which the man is uncontaminable by any pleasure, invulnerable to every grief, inviolable to every injury, insensible to every malice; a fighter in the noblest fight, dyed deep with justice, accepting with all his soul that which the Providence of the Universe appoints him. . . . He remembers also that every rational being is his kinsman, and that to care for all men is in accordance with the nature of man." [2]

IV.

The last great Religious Idea which I named is that of Immortality, or the continued life of the soul after the body's death.

It may surprise those who have been brought up in a different view, but I believe it to be the simple fact, that no truth of Religion has been

---

[1] *Disc.* III. 22.   [2] III. 4.

more universal than this. In all ages of which any history has come to us, in nearly all nations of which we have any trustworthy account, we find this faith: not a hope merely, not "one guess among many," but a confidence, a practical assurance, a *faith* to live by and to die by. Hardly a people so savage but some traces of it are discoverable; none so civilized that they have outgrown it; an essential element in all religions. Superstitions and foolish fancies about it, in plenty, no doubt; but revealed through them all the central idea, the inner belief. From the wisest and best in different ages and nations the clearest statements of faith in it. No doubt, rude nations have had rude conceptions of it; no doubt, as nations grew more advanced the old mythologies about it lost their hold, and were discarded even with ridicule as unworthy the belief of thinking men; and some men, with the going of the fables, lost their faith also in the idea. But in these very times, some of the wisest and best men sought to rescue the faith and establish it on a deeper basis. The idea survived the form which it had cast off.

Cæsar tells us of the ancient Gauls, that, "to arouse their courage, by taking away the fear of death, the Druids preach that souls do not die."[1] And Pomponius Mela says that they believe "that souls are eternal, and that there is another life."[2] And Valerius Maximus confirms the statement:

---

[1] *De Bello Gall.* VI. 14. [2] *De Situ Orbis*, III. 2.

"They are persuaded that the souls of men are immortal." [1]

In later times Spanish conquerors go to Mexico and Peru, and find the faith in immortality, as in God, already there.[2] Roman Catholic missionaries visit India, China, Thibet, and find it there; go among the North American Indians, and find it there. Dr. Livingstone, the English missionary, penetrates into the interior of Africa, and brings home this report: "There is no necessity for beginning to tell even the most degraded of these people of the existence of God, or of a future state, these facts being universally admitted. . . . On questioning intelligent men among the Bakwains as to their former knowledge of good and evil, of God, and of a future state, they have scouted the idea of their ever having been without a tolerably clear conception on all these subjects." . . . "They fully believe in the soul's continued existence apart from the body, and visit the graves of relatives, making offerings."[3] There are travellers, indeed, who report of tribes that have belief neither in immortality nor in God. If it be so, we must regard these as exceptional instances, where the native human faiths are yet undeveloped.

The Jewish Scriptures of the Old Testament contain only faint intimations of a future life. This is the more remarkable since the belief was

[1] II. 6, 10.
[2] Prescott: *Conq. of Mexico*, I. 62.   *Conq. of Peru*, I. 89.
[3] *Missionary Travels in South Africa*, pp. 176, 686.

so strongly held in Egypt at and before the time of Moses. Perhaps the beliefs of their oppressors were hateful to them. Be this as it may, we find the immortality of the soul clearly taught in the "apocryphal" books of Alexandrian-Jewish origin. It seems also to have been brought back by the Jews from their contact with the Persians in the Babylonian captivity. Certainly before the advent of Christianity it was the common belief of the nation, except among the sect of Sadducees. At least the doctrine of the "resurrection from the dead" was so.

Probably the oldest existing record of man's faith in a future life is the ancient Egyptian "Book of the Dead," or "Funeral Ritual." Its chapters are found inscribed on mummy-cases, or written upon rolls of papyrus within them. It is believed to date as far back as two thousand years before the Christian era. It might well be called the Book of Life, for it is full of an intense vitality; and this vivid sense of life shines through all that is obscure, strange, and extravagant in its details. It recounts the experiences of the human soul after death: its passage in the mystic boat through the land of darkness to the blessed fields; its trial in the "Hall of the Two Truths" (or the "twofold judgment") before Thoth, the Lord of Truth, and the forty-two judges, to each of whom it declares its innocence of the offence he specially sits to condemn; the placing its heart in the balance against an image of Righteousness; the declaration of its innocence;

its passage through the initiatory trials to the Blessed Land and the presence of the god Osiris, its Father, in the eternal "dwelling-place of the prepared spirit." I quote some passages from this remarkable book. "The osiris [that is, the soul, taking the name of its father-god] lives after he dies. Every god rejoices with life; the osiris rejoices with life as they rejoice." "Let the osiris go; he passes from the gate, he sees his father, Osiris; he makes a way in the darkness to his father; he is his beloved; he has come to see his father; he has pierced the heart of Set [the Evil Spirit] to do the things of his father, Osiris; he is the son beloved of his father. He has come a prepared spirit. . . . He moves as the never-resting gods in the heavens. . . . The osiris says, 'Hail Creator, self-created, do not turn me away, I am one of thy types on earth. . . . I join myself with the noble spirits of the wise in Hades.' . . . 'O ye lords of truth, I have brought you truth; I have not privily done evil against any man; I have not been idle; I have not made any to weep; I have not murdered; I have not defrauded; I have not committed adultery: I am pure, I am pure.' . . . Let the osiris go; he is without sin, without crime; he lives upon truth; he has made his delight in doing what men say and the gods wish; he has given food to the hungry, drink to the thirsty, clothes to the naked; his mouth is pure, his hands are pure. . . . His heart goes to its place in the balance complete. . . . The Father of the spirit has examined and proved him. He has found that the departed fought on earth the battle of the good gods, as his Father the Lord of the invisible world had commanded him. . . . O God, the protector of him who has brought his cry to thee, he is thine, let him have no harm; let him be as one of thy flying servants. Thou art he, he is thou! Make it well with him in the world of spirits!"[1]

In the Hindu Vedas we find also the faith in immortality. Yama, the god of the dead "waited enthroned in immortal light to welcome the good into his kingdom of joy." There were "the homes he had gone to prepare for them," "where the One Being dwells beyond the stars."[2] "Where there is eternal light, in that immortal, imperishable world place me," sings a Vedic burial hymn. "Where the secret place of heaven is, . . . where life is free, . . . where joy and pleasure abide, where the desires of our desire are attained, there make me immortal."[3] "Let him depart," says another, "to the heroes who have laid down their lives for others, — to those who have bestowed their gifts on the poor." And in the later Brahmanic scripture, the "Vishnu Purana," we read, "He who speaks wisely, moderately, kindly, goes [after death] to those worlds which are the inexhaustible sources of happiness.

---

[1] See Birch's Translation of the "Book of the Dead," in Bunsen's "*Egypt's Place*," &c., Vol. V.

[2] *Rig Veda*, X. See S. Johnson's *Oriental Religions; India*, p. 128.

[3] *R. V.* IX. 113, 7, cited in M. Müller's *Chips*, I. 46.

He who is intelligent, modest, devout, who reverences wisdom and respects his superiors and the aged, goes to the highest heaven." "He who feeds himself, and neglects the poor and friendless stranger, goes to hell."[1] So in the Bhagavad Gita: "There is another invisible eternal existence superior to this visible one, which does not perish when all things perish. Those who attain this never return. This is my supreme abode."[2]

Buddhism teaches the same doctrine. "There is undoubtedly a life after this," says a Buddhist tract, "in which the virtuous may expect the reward of their good deeds. . . . Wicked men, on the contrary, are after death born into hell, as animals. If they have done any good deed in their lifetime, they are after a long time released from punishment, and born into the world again as men. If they abstain from evil, and do good, they may reach the state of felicity, a place full of joy and delight. Judgment takes place immediately after death."[3]

Beyond all the heavens, into which in turn the good are born in their ascending course, Buddhism (as well as Brahmanism) presents a state which is the object of all devout aspiration, — the final reward of the highest devotion and virtue. It is called Nirvana. Some writers have insisted that it means annihilation. But others, equally learned, interpret

---

[1] Wilson's Transl. III. 121, 144.
[2] Thompson's Transl. p. 60.
[3] Upham's *Sacred Books of Ceylon*, III. 158.

it, with far more probability as it appears to me, to be merely the end of the soul's transmigrations, the cessation of re-births into the pain and trouble of this world; not annihilation, but perfect rest, absolute peace.[1]

The religion of Zoroaster taught to the Persians the same great truth. It promised to all who should faithfully keep the law of God, in purity of thought, speech, and act, " when body and soul have separated, the attainment of paradise in the next world;" while the disobedient "after death will have no part in paradise, but will occupy the place of darkness destined for the wicked."[2]

In Greece, where there were no sacred books, no "holy scriptures" as such, but where the poets and the philosophers were the religious teachers of the people, we find no less the doctrine, and the popular belief, of Immortality. This popular belief, founded on the pictures which the poets' fancy had painted, is familiar to all. Hades, the world of spirits; the Judges, Minos, Æacus, and Rhadamanthus; Tartarus, the abode of darkness and punishment; the Elysian fields, blooming with asphodel, radiant with perpetual sunshine, where parted friends meet again, " where life is ever sweet, and sorrow is not, nor winter, nor any rain or storm." Sophocles puts into the mouth of

---

[1] See S. Johnson's *Oriental Religions*, p. 619; and M. Müller's Introduction to his translation of the *Dhammapada*.

[2] *Avesta:* Spiegel, I. 171; cited by Alger, *Doctrine of Future Life*, p. 136.

the dying Antigone the strongly cherished hope that she should be welcomed by her father, her mother, her brother, in that other world.[1] In Pindar we read, "An honorable and virtuous man may rest assured as to his future fate. The souls of the lawless departing this life suffer punishment. But the good lead a life without a tear, among those honored by the gods for having always delighted in virtue."[2] One of the golden verses of Pythagoras is this: "When thou shalt have laid aside thy body, thou shalt rise freed from mortality, and become a god of the kindly skies;" as we should say, "an angel." "Those who have lived in justice and piety," says Plutarch, "fear nothing after death. They look for a divine felicity. As they who run a race are not crowned till they have conquered, so good men believe that the reward of virtue is not given them till after death. Eager to flee away from the body and from the world to a glorious and blessed abode, they free their thoughts as much as in them lies from the things that perish." And again: "Not by lamentations and mournful chants ought we to celebrate the funeral of the good man, but by hymns; for, in ceasing to be numbered with mortals, he enters upon the heritage of a diviner life."[3]

For the thoughts of Plato upon this question, we turn of course to his famed book, "Phædon." Under the form of a report of the conversation of

---

[1] *Antigone*, 897.　　[2] *Second Olympia*, cited by Alger.
[3] Cited by Denis, II. 225, 263.

Socrates with his disciples just before his death, he gives his Master's ideas, or his own, upon the immortality and future state of the soul, with the arguments by which the conclusions are reached. These arguments, long, curious, and elaborate, can have little weight with us; but the conclusions are definite and plain. As a thoughtful and conservative writer has well said, "The reasoning of Socrates in favor of immortality is far from clear, but not so his faith in immortality itself."[1] We find accordingly such sentences as these: —

"Can the soul which is invisible, and which goes to a place like itself excellent, pure, invisible, — to the presence of a good and wise God (whither, if God will, my soul also must shortly go) — can this soul of ours, being of such a nature, when separated from the body be immediately dispersed and destroyed, as the many assert? Far from it." "When, therefore, death approaches a man, the mortal part of him, as it appears, dies; but the immortal departs safe and uncorruptible, having withdrawn itself from death." "The soul, therefore, is most certainly immortal and imperishable, and our souls really exist in the world of spirits." "Those who shall have sufficiently purified themselves by philosophy [religion], shall live without their bodies, received into more beautiful mansions." After a long and minute description of the circumstances and scenery of the future state, he adds:

---

[1] I. Nichols: *Hours with Evangelists*, p. 90.

"To affirm positively that these things are exactly as I have described them does not become a man of sense ; that, however, either this or something of the kind takes place with respect to our souls and their habitations, this appears to me to be most fitting to be believed, since the soul is evidently immortal." "For the sake of these things we should use every endeavor to acquire virtue and wisdom in this life; for the reward is noble and the hope is great." "A man ought, then, to have confidence about his soul, if during this life he has made it beautiful with temperance, justice, fortitude, freedom, and truth ; he waits for his entrance into the world of spirits as one who is ready to depart when destiny calls." "I shall not remain, I shall depart. Do not say, then, that *Socrates* is buried ; say that you bury my *body*."

Cicero tells us that the Stoics believed in a continued life after death, but not in an *endless* immortality. His own faith has been thought to have been variable, or at least his expression of it; though I think that with him, as with Plato, the "if" is often of argumentation and not of doubt; and, with Lecky, I find in his writings "a firm and constant reference to the immortality of the soul." "As an eternal God," he says "moves the mortal world, so an immortal soul moves our frail body."[1] And, again, "the origin of souls cannot be found upon this earth, for there is nothing earthly in

[1] *Somnium Scip.*

them. They have faculties which claim to be called divine, and which can never be shown to have come to man from any source but God. That nature in us which thinks, which knows, which lives, is celestial, and for that reason necessarily eternal. God himself can be represented only as a free Spirit, separate from matter, seeing all things, and moving all things, himself ceaselessly working. Of this kind, from this nature, is the human soul." " Although you do not see the soul of man, as you do not see God; yet, as from his works you acknowledge Him, so from memory, from invention, from all the beauty of virtue, do thou acknowledge the divine nature of the soul. It cannot be destroyed."[1] He represents the aged Cato as exclaiming, " O glorious day when I shall remove from this confused crowd to join the divine assembly of souls! For I shall go to meet not only those great men of whom I have spoken, but my own son Cato, for whom I have performed the funeral rites, which he should rather have rendered to me. His spirit has never deserted me; but departed, looking back upon me, to that place whither he knew that I should soon come. If I have borne his loss with courage, it is not that my heart was unfeeling; but I consoled myself with the thought that our separation would not be for long."[2] With these words of undying affection and faith, I bring my quotations to a close.

[1] *Tusc. Quaest.* I.   [2] *Cato Major.*

How beautifully sound these consenting voices from East to West, from century to century, uttering the great Beliefs of the human race. Into what a "large place" they summon us out of all narrow limits of sect and church, even beyond Christianity itself, into that great and universal Church of the race, whose unity is the unity of the spirit, whose fellowship is the brotherhood of great faiths, sacred principles, and spiritual ideas. One Truth, one Right, one Love, one immortal Faith: the Reason, the Conscience, the Heart of man, in all times and under all skies, essentially identical: and over all one God and Father of all, giving to all his inspiration and his revelations as they are able to receive!

The passages that I have gathered into this paper are but a scanty gleaning from a broad and rich field. Of course, a good deal of a less interesting, less elevated, even opposite, character may be gathered from the like sources. But its existence does not invalidate what I have presented. I have made no claim for entire uniformity, but only for virtual universality, in the great ideas. I do not say that every man has believed, but that among all peoples, and in all times of which we have account, these beliefs have existed; that they perpetually recur, indicating a natural gravitation of the human mind toward them; that they are the common property of the human race, and not the exclusive possession of any special people or religion. The soul of man, human nature, bears these ideas and sentiments of God, of Right, of Love, and of Immortality as certainly, as naturally, as generally, as the earth under all climes produces plants and trees. Superficial variations, of place, climate, race, culture, we find: essential unity of idea.

We have been reading some verses from the Scriptures of the Universal Church, — man in his religious relations. This is the Broad Church, which not only stretches beyond barriers of sects, Romanist or Protestant, but reaches as wide as the world of man. It is as ancient as it is broad. It has a Past which far antedates that from which we are so frequently warned or entreated not to sever ourselves. Its antiquity does not stop with Judea eighteen hundred years ago, but reaches centuries beyond. This is the birthright Church of man. It is founded on the rock of man's spiritual nature, " normally and for ever God's Revealer." Its common thought is in that ground-idea of God which lies back of all the various conceptions of God. Its common life is in that mysterious disposition, that native and irrepressible tendency toward the invisible and the infinite, that universal sentiment of reverence and of dependence upon a superior Power, Goodness, and Right, which make man to be, by force of his nature, in all time and place, a religious being. Overarching all, like the universal sky, encompassing and inspiring all, like the universal air, vitalizing and informing all, like the universal electric force, binding and drawing all like the universal attraction and gravitation, this idea of God, of his love and his law, this religious consciousness, unites earth's millions in the humilities and aspirations of prayer; it moves them to deeds of benevolence and justice; it charms them ever with the ideal of a better world, a perfected society, a kingdom of God upon earth, a heaven of immortality beyond. It creates always its prophets and preachers, men of keener conscience, intenser enthusiasm for truth and right; always its saints, men of tenderer piety, deeper inward life, profounder spirituality; always its reformers seeking to awaken men from dead forms to living faith and righteousness; always its martyrs bearing the reproach of truth and the cross of suffering humanity; always its heretics questioning all traditions, demanding light and liberty; always its radicals protesting against superstitions and mythologies, and breaking down idols. "Before these vast facts of God and Providence," says an English writer, "the difference between man and man dwarfs into nothing. These are no discoveries of our own with which we can meddle, but revelations of the Infinite, which, like the sunlight, shed themselves on all people alike, wise and unwise, good or evil; and they claim and permit no other acknowledgment from us than the simple obedience of our lives and the plainest confession of our lips."

Religious is a higher and broader word than *Christian;* and so is *human.* Jewish, Brahman, Buddhist, Parsee, Mohammedan, these, too, are churches of the One Living God, the Father of all. With advancing light, thoughtful men in all of them will come out of what is peculiar and special in each, and so local and temporary, into the broad ground of universal, spiritual religion, which is Piety, Righteousness, Humanity: that belief in God and in man which is the creed of all creeds.

If ever in the isolation of our individualism we are ready to envy the churchman his sense of membership in a great body of brave and consecrated men and women, whose lips have uttered for centuries the same sacramental words, then may the better thought come to us, that we are indeed, if we will, members of this and of a yet grander company, from whom the churchman cuts himself off. For he, after all, is the schismatic. Look beneath names and words, and feel the life of the invisible, spiritual host of *all* righteous, true, heroic, saintly souls, made ours, if we are in sympathy with them, not by any external organization, but by a spiritual law. Its sacramental words are God, Duty, Love, Immortality. These, written in many tongues upon its banner, have given vigor to more hearts and met more eyes lifted unfaltering in death, than any one church or one religion can count within its pale. This is the Eternal Gospel; this the true Church Catholic: the Church not of

Rome, nor of England; the Church not of Buddha, nor of Moses, nor of Christ; but of God and Man.

NOTE.

I have not introduced any quotations from the Jewish or Christian Scriptures, because they are familiar, and in all hands.

For the reader's convenience I append a few dates, as they are given in the books; some of them approximative: —

Before the Christian era: — The Book of the Dead, 2000; The Rig Veda, 1500; Homeric Poems, 900; Thales born, 610; Lao-tze, 604; Zoroaster, 589; Pythagoras, 580; Confucius, 550. Gotama (Buddha) d. 548; Xenophanes b. 540; Pindar, 518; Sophocles, 495; Socrates, 470; Plato, 430; Menander, 342; Zeno, 300; Cicero, 106; Virgil, 70; Horace, 65; Ovid, 43; Philo, 27. *Within the Christian era:* — Seneca, 3; Quintilian, 40; Plutarch, 50; Epictetus, 70; Marcus Aurelius, 121; Maximus Tyrius, 180. The Talmud was composed in its present form in the fifth century, but from ancient materials. The Vishnu Purana was compiled in the tenth century, also out of ancient materials, as its name indicates.

FREEDOM IN RELIGION.

By Samuel Johnson.

IF, as certain modern schools predict, Religion is soon to be wholly supplanted by Science, that fate will have become possible only through its previous conviction upon the charge of suppressing the just liberties of man. By no axe less penetrating than such condemnation can a root so deeply set in human history be severed. The sharp edge of one inquisition no height nor depth can now escape. For all claims, one test and one title are now indispensable: and these we indicate, when, with a thrill, of which the mystery of the ocean wires is but a symbol, we pronounce the word Freedom.

Of the fact, which will not by my present hearers be disputed, is not this the meaning? Man has become mature enough to know that he at least is real, and his experience valid; that his seeing is by his own eyes, and that he is concerned only with what *for him* is true and just and good, and for his powers the natural culture. All waymarks of history point to this emancipation, as his real goal.

Note, for instance, the ever-renewed escape from spiritual swathes woven of Fate and Godhead, into freer play of the living Human Form. It is the rhythm of history. Asiatic devotions issue in the Buddha, or Man throned above the Gods; Christianity in identifying God with a Man; Homer and Hesiod in the human art of Phidias, the human dignity of Socrates. Confucius, summing up the lessons of Chinese experience, learned "to speak of man, not of God," and placed the foundations of virtue in original human nature. Of modern philosophy the doors are Kant and Hegel: analysis of the human faculties as determinative of all knowledge, duty, faith. And modern sentiment has added to the practical maxim of Terence, "Nothing human but is of import to me," the largest ideal reading of Feuerbach's impressive sentence, "God is an unutterable sigh out of the depths of the human heart." Steadily, on every historic line, proceeds that imperial justification of *the thinking faculty*, which is the condition of all respect for *the objects* of thought; the high recognition that man is himself consubstantial with whatever he knows, or loves, or adores.

The profound significance of the word Freedom for our age lies in the full consciousness, by mind, of its own essential validity. For nothing can this postulate of all future knowledge be bartered. To no tradition in the name of God, to no science in the name of Nature, will it be surrendered. Not though the new heavens fall, as the old hells are burning out, will man dispense with faith in his personality and its freedom.

The new heavens of science are Evolution, and not likely to fall by any such alternative. An inherent law of development, reaching up through all grades of existence, to receive its highest form in man, — so fully certifies growth and progress, that Evolution may well be recognized as the scientific equivalent to the principle of Spiritual Freedom. But this recognition is not founded on the mere fact that evolution is ascension of forms: it depends on the way in which such ascension is interpreted. Pure outgrowth of higher stages from lower ones would imply that the origin of power is found in the crudest forms; which is essential fetichism, and inverts the dignity of mind. That the interests of evolution can be identified with those of freedom is due to the fact that this scientific principle itself involves, as the condition of its ascending line of outgrowths, transcendent resources of universal Mind, by whose constant implication these finite growths are made possible, and whose descent is their inspiration and emancipation.

Neither to the ascent, nor to the influx which conditions it, does the mature demand of freedom in our day admit any ultimate limit. This better shaping of human circumstance, this secular march over the falling redoubts of superstition, this endless invitation to every human need to stand forth and be heard, this growing ideal of social order, quickening the sense of actual depravity and defect, and the absolute confidence of this assault on every form of bondage, — is manifestly an appeal to something of larger meaning than such terms as "evolution" or "emancipation" are wont to suggest. *It proves a constant sense of the Infinite.* The languages of the highest civilizations express their future tense either by the infinitive, or by some combination with it. The very limits within which we find that progress must move, are but the stimulus to an unlimited aspiration, which delights in ascribing to natural law itself every attribute of ideal mind.

Just here is my reason for believing that religion will not die at the hands of science. Freedom, the principle not of science only, but of all culture, rests on man's recognition of infinity as implicated in his own finite conditions. In other words, *Freedom means religion, and Religion means freedom.* If you tell me that religion must last for ever, because it is "revelation," or because it is "supernatural," or because it is "the endless need of sinful man," — your logic is a sieve; my doubts run through it. What *is* supernatural? What is *not* revelation? What proof that sinfulness is endless, or that religion is to stand or fall with that? But I can see that religion is imperishable, if it is essential to development and progress. I can see that this substance of spiritual endeavor cannot be illusory or self-destructive, — if it is the basis and condition of Human Freedom.

Comprehensively to define what I hold to be the meaning of this profound relation, is the task to which I am now invited.

DEFINITIONS.

The question what is to become of religion being now uppermost, restatements of what religion means are the order of the day. Is it not the fine discipline of your platform to learn to construct and apply them? Of spiritual facts, indeed, no definitions can do more than state *relations* with clearness, since the related terms must, by their very nature and their inherence in the infinite, remain ill-defined. Were it not so, they would not permit the very freedom they claim to express. Hence the great number of such definitions now in the field; we are not discouraged to find that no one is quite satisfied with his neighbor's attempt. It is not easy, perhaps it is not possible, so to define, that nothing which belongs to the universality of the idea shall be shut out, nothing ignored, nothing left to loose inference, or to a merely charitable construction. Even if we define religion broadly as "the effort of man for self-perfection, or for endless growth," we may seem to others to exclude, as non-essential to the process defined, the real existence and inspiration of the Perfect itself, without which such effort on man's part, or even the idea of making it, is to most of us inexplicable, and which therefore demands distinct recognition. One of the poles on which the movement turns seems to be wanting to the completeness of the formula.

In the opposite statement, that "religion is the

supernatural action of divine grace in man," — there is, manifestly, wanting what should be allowed as the *natural* pole of the spiritual process, even by those who believe "*the supernatural*" to be real and divine.

Again: two mutually exclusive conceptions have arisen respectively in the East and the West: the one defining religion as " man's sense of his own nothingness before God," — which excludes man from the right to have any sense at all, and even leaves him altogether out of the process; the other as the "worship of humanity," which excludes such a thing as worship *by* humanity, and leaves no term in the process except man. Subject to like mutual criticism are the old mystic absorption in abstract impersonal essence, on the one hand, and our modern idolatry of personal will and definite works, on the other. So, in general, a spontaneity without moral allegiance would seem to be the Celtic onesidedness; moralism without spontaneity, the Teutonic. Even the "Love of God and Man," the "Golden Rule," the Christian Beatitudes, fail of completeness, by not distinctly recognizing the *intellectual* nature: whence in part their degeneracy into the petty sentimentalism of the pulpit, and the unphilosophical narrowness of the creeds. The full idea of Religion is not satisfied by these unipolar elements: they offer no adequate basis for its definition.

Then we have religion represented *organically*, as a supreme sphere, centring in Jesus Christ, with circumference in Bible and Church, and in various limits and monopolies of Christian origin; and again, *personally*, as a sense of absolute self-condemnation, followed by a sense, through Christ's merits alone, of supreme self-gratulation, and by the fullest real security: — of all which the exclusiveness would not be easy to overstate.

On the other hand, we must remember that the purport of terms is open to such latitude, by reason of the mutual involution of ideas in modern thought, that the definer's *intention* must often be read between the lines. Thus the word " Man " may be meant to cover the infinite as well as the finite relations of man; and the word " God " to embrace a divine humanity and a natural order, as manifestations of God. And as by " man's effort to perfect himself " may be intended " man's effort at development, as moved by his relations with the Perfect: " so by " the supernatural " in divine power, may sometimes be indicated, not exclusion of deity from nature, physical or human, but simply that of these, its two spheres, the human, with which religion is concerned, is the higher. Our criticism goes to the form of statements, not to what may be meant by them.

Such margin for interpretation often becomes due, if we would read old or new definitions of religion as they stand in the minds of their advocates. And all the more manifestly is there need of stating, or unmistakably implying, all elements which are essential to the idea of Religion; there being in strict usage of terms no authority for such larger inferential construction as I have ventured to give, for instance, to certain definitions, nor assurance that it would not sometimes be declined as injustice.

Surely this demand for completeness is enhanced by the fact that we are seeking to define Religion so as to express its identity with Freedom.

Shall we then, after these premises, venture to attempt it? Shall I offer the statement that religion is *the natural attraction of mind as finite to mind as infinite?*

Observe that I use this word *mind* in no narrow sense, as of the intellect in distinction from the emotions or the volitions; but in the full sense of intelligence, with whatever of conscious or unconscious, scrutable or inscrutable, can be included therein.

Observe, next, that the statement does not, as is usual to do, speak of God in distinction from Man. Nor does it enter on what seems to me the fatally exclusive analytical process of determining *how far* either of the terms may or may not involve the other. At what point in the growth of any thought, purpose, or desire, at what dividing line, or *suture*, of the living personality of man, one may say that God's work begins or man's work ends, — is to me past all conceiving, or even attempting to conceive. I have no diagnosis on that matter, initial as it is for the creeds. Mind shows me no such suture. Mind is one essence: call it divine or human, it cannot be cut off from itself; what it knows is but that which itself *is*. I do not therefore find religion definable by any distinction of Man from God, but call it the natural attraction of mind in its finiteness to mind in its infinitude. It is such attraction, whether as sentiment, conviction, or conduct, whether as aspiration or inspiration, whether as struggle, or solace, or heavenly peace, or mastering faith, — that we really mean, when we speak of religion. It is a sense of inmost identity with that absolute adequacy and boundless resource to which our actual limits are drawn. This is no arbitrary interpretation. We worship Wisdom, Justice, Love, — not as mere outwardness, but as *our* best and highest; as *our* liberty, *our* infinity: *neither within us, nor without;* but as somewhat eternally real, belonging to us, as we do to it, more than to our actual or provisional selves. The very dread of an outside God, and the agonizing sense of separation from him, which has made up so much of what is popularly known as religion, — intimates, however crudely, that a total alienation of finite and infinite would be nothing less than sundering our own spiritual substance. The notion of eternal punishment itself shows with what horror man regards so monstrous an irrationality; his utmost fears having conceived it as the very last consequence of sin, and the maximum of penalty. On the other hand, our advancing ideals of truth and virtue are announcements of the Infinite; and in our aspiration we simply follow *its* full assurance of freedom to the assumption of our higher selves.

Prayer, indeed, clothes itself in the form of outward appeal, of personal ascription; but the spiritual sense clearly perceives this dress to be simply a form of mythology, required by the inadequacy of human speech and by the natural play of the imagination. As form of public worship, it is sustained only by the sense of a common understanding of those two justifying facts, as by *an atmosphere of consent*, and ceases when the critical faculty is felt to be analyzing and dissolving this. At the same time, it is so far from implying essential distinction of the soul from deity, that its very confidence in that adequacy which the terms do not express, can mean only the precise contrary.

That finiteness in man is thus invincibly attracted to the clear open heavens of the ideal in all real progress, — is its confession that the Infinite is not its mere negation, but the very motive force of its own proper growth. The Infinite is not the less real, because inconceivable: being known to us not at all as a definite object, — any more than space is so to the open eye or to the free wing that traverses it, — but in and through the sense of an open path, and an unprescribed scope; of *spiritual space*, not barred nor walled in, nor anywhere to fail us at last: — a sense, the condition whereof in us is the pursuit of ideal good. This is the secret whispered to us by principle, loyalty, pure devotion and faith, in whatever sphere; and the practicalism that treats it as mere phrase is about as practical as the insect's heady rush by twilight against the window or into the flame.

The Infinite then is the motive power of our personal growth. Not that there is always consciousness of this oneness or this freedom. Your service of your ideal is a battle, sore defeat and hard recovery : bitter sense of impotence to do what it would be more sad or cruel still to have failed of doing. But fast beside all brave and true hearts stands the mystic prompter, with secret touches that *mean* all the prophecy one may not for the moment hear.

As now defined, Religion is in three ways the principle of Freedom.

First, It includes *both elements in the process of personal growth, as pursuit of ideal aims.* It is the relation of finite to infinite, as real poles of spiritual movement, implied and involved in each other.

Second, It is inclusive of *every faculty of actual mind :* all of these alike being called "finite," not in view of their limitations merely, but also of their law of *growth* by an endless upward attraction; in other words, they inhere in the Infinite.

Third, It is the *natural* movement of these faculties : the attraction implies identity of essence in its terms, since we can aspire only to that of which we have guarantee and foretype in our own nature.

Here, then, are three facts in the attraction we have called Religion: unity in the elements of it; universality in the scope; gravitation by inherent affinity.

Now of these three, observe, that to make use of religion as a means of shutting off the infinite from the finite by a great gulf, is to *deny the first;* to confine religion to a special sphere or to certain functions, is *to reject the second;* to divorce religion from nature and spontaneity, by fetching it into man by importation, by graft, by compulsion through miracle, proceeding from a nature alien to its own essence, is *to make void the third.* And are not these three perversions of religion the very causes which have despoiled it of freedom? Shall we then believe religion to be at heart other than radical freedom, or freedom other than radical religion?

PRACTICAL CONDITIONS OF FREE PERSONALITY.

Let us advance another step into the meaning of our definition. Religion is Freedom, because, as service of the ideal, it is attraction by infinity. It is the pure principle of development; as reconciling the elements of spiritual being in their own proper movement. It is thus our personality itself as a freely active force.

What, then, are its *practical conditions?*

The poles of Freedom are positive Rights and Duties; neither valid without the other; both inherent in the personality, whose movement is religion.

So that religious freedom will claim for every power and sphere the right of complete culture, and for all on the same ground; namely, as alike forces of that personality through which alone the infinite is recognized as real, and its attractions followed in ideal aims. This is one side of our freedom.

But the other is allegiance of all these powers and spheres to that which is at once the inmost fact of the personality and its practically unattained object; namely, *Moral Order*. It is the sentiment of reverence for eternal morality; the conviction of duty to obey it; the yearning to be absorbed in it, and to lose what we now are in its grand attraction to what it is nobler for us to be! Not without this side shall come the other, in any way. Religious freedom is spontaneity; but it is not lawless will. If we drop the conscious sense of our actual finite, we lose with it our attraction to the infinite. With the impulse to yearn, to aspire, to revere, passes out of us the power to grow. Heaven save our age from idolatry of self and deification of sense under the name of " free " religion, or " free " — any thing else!

Whatever, then, excludes any gift or function from that open attraction to perfection on which growth depends; or whatever lays on the conscience burdens of allegiance beyond the claims of the Moral Order and the upward aim, — is at once a denial of religion and an offence to rational freedom.

THE WAYS OF OFFENCE TO RELIGIOUS FREEDOM.

And now to apply these principles of criticism. In what ways is religious freedom thus offended?

I. By vain distinctions and exclusions, that supplant its universality. These may be theoretical or practical. To the theoretic class belongs *the separation of Religion from Philosophy, as " realms respectively of authority and freedom."* More than one modern school would subscribe to the statement that " religious faith and philosophical thought cannot coexist ; when one enters, the other withdraws ! " But can any one tell us why religion should be unphilosophical, or philosophy nonreligious ? What " authority " that can be which belongs to affirmations of religion, but not to those of philosophy ; or what " philosophy " that can be which does not rest on ultimates and postulates of pure faith, — it is not for me easy to imagine. But I am sure that a " religion " that puts faith in place of reason, and a " philosophy " that pretends to be reason, after it has excluded all claims of the ideal as attractions of the infinite, because the infinite is a " mere phrase," — are both of them mutilations of mind, and incompatible with its freedom. What is " faith," but that assurance of a better solution of circumstances than we can find specific grounds for predicting,— one which our ideal, a constructive infinite, guarantees to our aspirations ? Is not that the same thing in philosophy and in theology ; in the study of the soul and in the conduct of life? How can you tether, as to a stake, this constant element of your spiritual motion? Its sphere is universal as mind; wherever aspiration is, there is faith, and the freedom that goes with it. What, again, is "authority for belief," but some adequate cause for believing? Oppose it to reason and right, you abolish it. Everywhere its credentials are the same: a stamp of truthfulness, an appeal to your sense of fitness, of probability, of the claims of the ideal on the actual. Does this belong to the sphere of theology any more than to the sphere of philosophy, to the conduct of life any more than to the study of the soul? "Religious authority," in any other sense than this, is simply spiritual despotism, which religion, as essential freedom, outgrows and leaves behind.

Again, we hear it said that Religion is "*the realm of sentiment or emotion as opposed to that of science.*" In the outset, I do not admit that religion is exclusively emotional. Are there no such things as religious convictions, principles, disciplines, persistent cultures? But how, furthermore, can sentiment and science be considered as distinct and opposite? Science is recognition of invariable law; sentiment is feeling for the true, the beautiful, the good, of which law is the symbol. Is there no recognition in such feeling? Is there no feeling in such recognition? Is there to be no sentiment in scientific study, making it unselfish, faithful, ardent, intuitive? Can science dispense with the enthusiasm that makes discoverers, the devotion that cannot despair; with such love of the fair Cosmos for its own sake, as means serenity, gladness, praise? The one form of sentiment inadmissible by the scientific mind is that which clings to a belief as true because we desire or enjoy it, or feel traditionally bound to believe it; and this sentimental-*ism* is no element of religious freedom, any more than of scientific mind. And, on the other part, will you call any worship " free," which does not recognize law as supreme, universal, divine? If religion can properly introduce miracle, then there can be no science : the very possibility of science lies in the postulate that law is universal, a harmony that cannot anywhere admit the slightest break. Freedom, then, can no more permit Religion to be separated from science as sentiment, than from philosophy as faith.

Human practice is always the result of theoretic principles. And so, out of this limitation of religion, as a special sphere, with faculties of its own, comes manifold actual suppression of other spheres and faculties, in the name of religion. It is the constant demoralization of all culture that there should be a prescriptive body of words, phrases, experiences, books, traditions, personages, rites, times and seasons, called " religious," for which special reverence is exacted ; a perpetual assumption that they have a higher function, a more positive moral and spiritual claim, than the powers and pursuits defined as secular and human. Robbed of the saving conviction that wherever he is, there he should be at his best, spoiled of that respect for his real task which is his saviour and his educator, civilized man may well stand in his practical functions, crude, unconsecrated, a palterer with right, a profaner of uses, blinded to their ideal relations and claims. And this while his religion pretends to absolute perfection in creative and redeeming powers! That his "divine religion" may fly on its vicarious wings, his human behavior shall grovel and snarl and snatch and rend! What is this "salvation" that with such absolute complacency generates oceans of phraseology in tracts, commands hosts of functionaries, and spreads itself in endless evangelism of alliances and missions, conferences, camp-meetings, revivals, — while the surrounding world of politics, traffic, and manners is mocking at the possibility of a free personality or an ideal aim? It is surely but little to say of such a master that he is not adequate to the age he claims authority to rule and power to save. Is not this the plain question for us after all? — Shall we have a religion competent to turn the license by which all practical powers are imperilled, into the liberty of upward attractions, and the self-assurance of democracy into the self-respect of becoming disciplines, — or shall we have *no* religion? Can an age of infinite ambition dispense with loyalty to infinite justice, truth, good? Which then shall represent this infinite, — a court of special jurisdiction, with its Christ, Bible, and Church, its elect partnership of piety, its peculiar phraseology excluded by general consent from conversation on practical concerns; or an ideal of duty and desire coextensive with life, invoking freedom and culture for every power and sphere, and moving them all with the sense of endless attraction to boundless resource? This, or a superstition of times and themes and ruts of thought; of "special providences" to discredit the laws of nature, and "Lord's days" to disparage week-days; playing the policeman to constrain free, popular education, and forbid labor or relaxation,— upon an old-time warrant our civil laws cannot in honor respect?

I do not underrate the devotion, culture, humanity contained within that special institution which is called the Christian Church; but I should be glad if it were possible to learn how much the idea that religion, in its free substance, *can* be instituted or organized, and set apart with a machinery of its own, has done to make other human spheres irreligious, by the false standard and prestige it sets up. Organization assumes to be the last and highest form a principle can take, its endowment with authoritative powers; and always claims supremacy, and exacts conformity, on these grounds, in exact proportion to its numbers, its directness and definiteness of aim, and the energy of its working machinery. Of religious organization, Catholic or Protestant, this is eminently true. Now it is simply certain that what is best in any one cannot be outwardly organized, nor mechanized in any way, nor even manipulated to that end by himself, without loss: his self-communion, his aspiration, his openness to ideal suggestion; his personal self-discipline; his mental freedom; his power of suspending judgment; his hospitality to new thoughts and persons; his conscience, not subject to vote or director, nor committed to policies and conformities; his sense of the value of his function, and his aim to fulfil it in the best way; in a word, what goes with one wherever he is and whatever he does, and makes the constant level of his highest qualities. All these vitalities are unorganizable; they keep their essential freedom and claims above all specific combinations to which men may commit what they can of them; and it is these which the pretension of ecclesiastical organism to represent religion deprives of their true educational prestige, as the claim of the ideal and infinite. I think these vitalities are what you specially mean, and would rescue, by your call to "Free Religion." You may well beware of even unintentionally lending its name and example to the side of forces more naturally organizable, but which depress its culture, and which would like nothing better than infecting this free spirit with their own dependence on the strategy of managers, turning it over to political partisanship, and making its adherents eager for roll-call and drill. How real and refreshing to all of us are such reports of the laws of character and the forms of noble conduct as are free of phraseology associated with religious or political machinery! Give us, for once, a brave summer of full reliance on such forces. Do not forget their power, nor the naturalness of their growth in America to-day.

II. A second great class of offences to Freedom in Religion I should refer to the theory that objective validity, essential to all rational conceptions, is to be denied to religious ones: in other words, that God is but a process of human thought. "The sensible object," says Feuerbach, " is out of man, the religious is in him. Religion is the indirect, or imperfect consciousness man has of himself, and the goodness, justice, wisdom he worships exist only as his own attributes."

Now this is, of course, rank heresy. Yet what if I should point it out as plainly visible in certain commonplaces of Christian belief? The Christian actually believes this lack of objective validity to be true of all religious conceptions but his own. His God is a real person; but Jehovah, Brahma, Zeus, he holds purely unreal, existing only in the blindness of the heathen mind, or in the just criticism thereof in his own. He forgets that if, in its attempts at affirming the infinite, religion has been dealing only with phantasm, or mere mental process, for four-fifths of human history, it can only be by a new self-delusion that the continued process of the same faculties is regarded as pointing to a real object at last. Remember, it is not a question of hunting for new planets with a calculus, but of the essential force and constant action of spiritual laws. The Christian cannot apply Feuerbach to judge the heathen, without convicting his own judging faculty of the Feuerbachian defect, — to find no hold on positive truth in its dealing with spiritual beliefs.

The theory that man's ideal attractions imply no correspondent reality enslaves religion, by *treating it as a mere reflex movement within the individual mind.* It is but putting this theory in practice, when one refuses all validity to the beliefs of others but what they have for himself, as conceived within his own limits. This is the pith of theological contempt. From this come assumptions of absolutism turning on the poles of a shallow experience; interpretations of the movement of history as a mere preface to some special religion or sect, narrowing great systems of the elder world to petty meanings; imprisonment in prejudice so total as to forbid the perception of any thing *but* prejudice in other men's endeavors for impartiality and candor.

If you will allow a personal allusion, simply in illustration of this point, I would mark it as worth recording, that a recent literary and historical effort to put religious faiths on their own merits, should have been charged by all the denominational organs with " prejudice and prepossession," for the reason that it did *not* assume for Christianity those exceptional claims which have had the field of tradition and teaching, with all of us, to themselves!

8

To escape prejudices, it would seem, one must hold fast to his Christian education! What shall we say of the eyesight that can see nothing but foregone conclusions in the very effort to escape them? But I offer an instance of higher moment. A grand metaphysical and spiritual philosophy was gradually developed by the Orientals and the Greeks. Christendom found and absorbed it. Observe how it has fared; how it has been stunted within the special phase it assumed for a transitional age of reconstruction, — in a historical person, a book, a church of exclusive claims. Its Trinity, for example, — Infinite Mind conceived at once as essence, as creative power, as energizing life, — how universal and all-productive a conception it was! Is such a truth of ideal being and progress to be crystallized in the prejudices of a Church, and have no validity outside certain endlessly revolving routines of belief?

We are not apt to note what manifold practical tyranny comes of the habit of regarding one's own mental processes about others as comprehending the whole reality, not of one's self only as thinking subject, but of *them* also, *the objects thought.* Is not this the rationale of intolerance? And yet it is but the practical side of a kind of *orthodox-Feuerbachian* assumption, that the Infinite itself exists only as a process of the thinker's own mind.

The noblest movement of modern speculative philosophy is a reaction against this denial of independent validity to centres of thought beyond self. It appears in Hegel's affirmation of the absolute as real, and in his principle, — by him very imperfectly, I think, carried out, — that the aim of religion is to represent under historical, that is, *actual* forms, the positive purport of human consciousness. It is still more observable in the fact that Kant and Fichte save themselves from egoism by bathing in the great waters of Spinoza's religious realism: his One Divine Substance, neither within nor without us, but infinite and real.

III. The third great class of offences to Religious Freedom is referable to the theory that religion is the pure " sense of dependence." As one offence consisted in treating the Infinite as merely incident to the mind of the worshipper, so another consists in worship of a God altogether *outside* him. Now communion between men being possible only through a common nature, and *free* communion only between souls capable of mutual access and interfusion, — the relation of finite with infinite, considered as a mere relation of dependence, can surely be neither productive nor free. This external God creates his world-machine, and man to operate it: plans, stipulates, or works on the pliant or stubborn stuff as a moulder on his clay. The tenderness, gratitude, and trust allowed by the relation as commonly conceived, is counterbalanced by the obligation and subservience implied in it. Not in prayers only, but in sermons, hymns, and private meditation on trial and suffering it has generated a weak and sentimental tone of appeal from realities, which greatly needs infusion of the Stoic faith in nature and fate. Tempered by childlike instincts in its early stages, the theory discloses a deeper evil as it unfolds. Hebrew Jehovah, creating the world from naught, sending his angels to make men prophets, and his wrath to trample them as worms; covenanting with them on good terms to-day, and hardening them for their ruin to-morrow, — embodied many crude forms of this separation of finite and infinite. It has widened, in the Christian theory of "sin," into the "great gulf" which supplies Calvinism with its bottomless pit, crossed by its ineffectual air-bridges of authority, and its arrow-flights of miracle and grace through the void. Its array of infinities includes the remoteness of God and the impotence of man. The idea of the infinite thus becomes the slavery of the finite: the spiritual world is rent to its centre by self-contradiction. Such entire outwardness of relation cannot indeed be effected: God without man and man without God are both impossible. But though so far an illusion, the theory of separateness is none the less capable of imposing base terms of acquiescence on the soul. None the less does it breed offspring after its kind: such as theological "miracle," which means that natural law is external to God; "efficacy of prayer," as appeal to a foreign Will that needs changing and allows it; anthropomorphic creeds, whose eye is to some actual throned Personage, issuing decrees of judgment, and prescribing formal conditions of salvation; enforced rejection of natural doubt and free inquiry; the notion of revelation as a specific infusion instead of a natural development; and, finally, the notion of allegiance due from man to a Power external to his own moral sentiment and rational faculty. Were it possible to carry out this last notion in practice, personality itself would perish. But the theory of pure dependence on a purely distinct and separate Ruler is refuted by the necessities of belief and conduct.

How, for instance, could you reconcile the omnipotence of such a ruler with the amount of suffering in this world, as far beyond desert as beyond relief, on any principle that is not at war with the love and justice which humanity prescribes? The descent of a reconciling Christ into human life does not help the difficulty; since the miseries of Christian civilization are doubtless, like its joys, much greater than those of barbarism. It is only by the insight of spiritual imagination, which makes no pretence of satisfying such outside Deity, but sees infinity as mysteriously involved in the human ideal itself, — in upward attractions self-justified, in a sense of the best and fittest, undismayed by experience, — that life becomes tolerable amidst woes we cannot help to cure, nor yet endure to see. To make paths for such spiritual imagination and faith, such full trust in the very service of ideal good, is, I conceive, the highest function of our liberal thought.

RESUMÉ.

When we use this term, " Freedom in Religion," do we not mean to imply that the Infinite is involved in our ideal attractions, as at once within and without us, but as neither of these exclusive of the other? Religion is the soul's absorption in an infinite essence, since intelligence is that; but only through interfusion thereof with finite processes of culture, — a divinely human growth. The light by which we see principles, the love by which we are moved to humanities, is true spiritual substance. What we know, that we *are:* what we worship, that we become. A truth that is older than Orphic Mysteries, than Plato or the Veda; later also than the last credo of the scientists or the come-outers. Yet I hear it scoffed at as behind the age, because it is so ancient, by smart sectaries who do not know what it means; or, if they did, would not dare to teach it, so revolutionary is it to their childish traditions.

This then is the sum: Our ideal of the right and true is no sense of outwardness, therefore no constriction of freedom; nor is there any place for conceit of special ownership, or of messianic commission, in the grand relations of law and love that reach through all the worlds.

NEGATION AND AFFIRMATION.

Now the substitution of such a Religion of Freedom for Christian beliefs and institutions that are inconsistent with it, will seem to their advocates pure destructiveness. This implication of the Infinite with the upward attractions of the natural and finite mind, will be pronounced " barren negation." Let us see. Plainly the human ideal has a very searching "No" to pronounce in our age. Its dreams of art, science, philosophy, social justice, have to grow, like the infant Hercules, by strangling hydras and eating the sinew of bears. Every reform is at best a plowshare that must cut its way through drifts of prejudice to the world's quick, thus brightening its own edge for the better service of coming husbandry. Do you fear negation? Progress is negation: every step denies a past, disclaims a future. Life and Birth are negation of previous life. God is negation, the *Not* Finite, or Infinite. 'Tis but the *emphasis* on negation, *the destructive spirit*, that harms.

But he who talks of pure destructiveness, of absolute negation, imagines the impossible. No people ever worshipped pure destruction. In the old beliefs, world-lapse into fire or flood was but part of a cycle in which the waste elements were always full of seed, and immortality was the lesson of death. Science, at its slower gait, comes in at last to echo that eternal resurrection-song of the infinite in the finite, with its burden of universal laws, indestructible forces, interchangeableness of motion, heat, light. In vain does theological dogma itself pretend to put pure negation towards the Human into Infinite Mind. " Whosoever shall speak a word against the Holy Ghost it shall not be forgiven him, either in this life or that which is to come." That would seem almost a satanic threat of utter rejection, against the offender. But even Calvinism cannot unfold it into any thing more negative than this; that, with all God's hate of sin, He takes care to make it last; his will to destroy it getting no nearer to doing so than to a love of punishing it which lasts for ever. Sin, instead of being never in his all-perfect mind, is never out of it, — a confession that even "total depravity" is not absolute evil, nor utterly rejected of good, but maintains endless, however perverted, relations with it. So indispensable is it for man to see the infinite as involved in the finite: the sign of this being manifest in his own ideal, redeeming its harsher and gloomier features.

However imperfect human conduct may be, *human nature* involves the perfection of law. So long as he respects himself man believes the shaping force of his own nature to be Moral Order: so interpreting its laws of reward and penalty, compensation, discipline, growth. Here is its inner mould, for ever unbroken, unmarred. No sin touches it, no weakness invalidates. The worst conceivable character or conduct is in some way the inconceivable mingling of this perfect law with finite circumstance and will.

If history is providential, then, to speak in mythic types, God for ever idealizes man. What eternal truths, sown broadcast in time from the first, cleave fast, and grow in spite of failure and abuse! Did He recognize in us no more than the mere wit or virtue we actually put into trade, politics, or even religion, judging our value by our attainment, what growth were possible? Just as the bud is not treated in horticulture as a mere bud, but as promise of a flower, so the spirit-culture we call history is — speaking in symbols, as we must — God's recognition of man as germ of deity: in other words, man's constant upward attractions are implications of the Infinite in his movement and growth.

This is what offsets our "negations;" which we are quite ready to compare with the fierce swoop of dogmatic systems, not only upon the fair humanities and spiritual intuitions of other faiths, but upon human nature itself. Out of these systems the time hastens, as we turn from ages of plesiosaurs and buried footprints to the living world. The mediæval maps put Jerusalem in the centre of the earth, ranged lands and tribes in a circle round it, walled them in with a forbidden sea, with heathen Gog and Magog on its desert rim, and a "Gate of Iron" to keep them off. What a negation of all this when Columbus opened America, when De Gama doubled the Cape, when Marco Polo came back from far Cathay! But what *affirmations* swept then into the hope and faith of man! Such is the religious revolution of our day.

This freedom destroys religion only in so far as

religion is made a threefold bondage: an exclusive sphere and special prerogative; a worship of self; a pure dependence on an outside God. Compared with this faith in humanity, the intensest confidence in Christian dogma is sheer unbelief. It is fed not by prescriptive name, person, or church, but by the constancy of law and life. It sees in common people not the possible pictures and statues seen by Raphael and Michael Angelo in rough marble and on white walls, but minds made for loving right because it is right, for recognizing the Infinite in all ages and creeds. Are they unbelievers who trust in the natural powers by which we come at all we know, and to whose honor all we can be redounds, and of which all founders of faiths are but children and pupils? He is the "unbeliever" whose religion requires him to denounce these; who holds it unsafe to use them honestly, and abide their issues. The "destructive" is he who would suppress or disfranchise them in man or woman. The "infidel" is he who deliberately declines to speak what he thinks, or to trust humanity with what helpful truth has been intrusted to himself. I could not but smile to hear it gravely said the other day, "One assumes an awful responsibility to teach a doctrine not sanctioned by the church." What is that, I thought, to the audacity of refusing your own honest doubt?— Judged by these definitions, it is the church of functionaries that denies; it is free personal force, in or out of it, that affirms, believes, worships, creates. They who speak in this name speak in the highest name. This is he who created Bibles: shall he not rend his own books, when he would supplant them by his own higher light? Shall not the maker *re*-make? How shall he grow but by *out*-growing, or live but by *out*-living, his own work? Dearer the thirst for truth than any waters of opinion or belief it ever yet struck from rocks along its way. Where are the pure destructives our defenders of the faith warn you to avoid? I do not find them. Pure negation is chimera, motiveless purpose: nature never made it. That many should confidently assert it of the old Eastern Nirvana, that refuge of the far-off times and millions, is not strange, since there are so many more who can imagine that honest men, close beside them, criticising a Greek and Hebrew book, can be seeing nothing beyond what they reject.

Believe me, the mere image breaker, who could *only* break images, would never take hold of men's hearts. He would be heard of after his day only to be despised. Not one crumb of the bread by which a reformer's working-force is positively nourished, comes of mere confutation of other men's beliefs as such. There are thirsty winds that descend the western slope of the Andes, sucked dry by intervening heights of barren cold; but even these are not mere wasteful devourers of herb and tree: they pass out beyond into the Pacific, and draw their cisterns full again, then bear them over the opposing trades, and pour supplies into the fountains of Oregon, Missouri, and the Great Lakes. Far more shall our Free Reformer be a child of that grand law of nature, which, while allowing destruction, bids us *live* by creating, affirming, building. I must suspect the breadth of that freedom which scorns history. Our prophecy is no break with the past; but the resumption of all true historic powers: it recognizes history as continuous. Every step is locked with the last and the next: every epoch saves, transmutes, transmits, as well as destroys. Every step presses the whole past, and has that long, grand push for its fulcrum. Men and ages that seem to abolish most, work from grounds, and to ends, beyond themselves. Buddha, Pythagoras, Jesus, Luther, and the rest, are children of their times: out of Greece and Judea came Christianity; out of Christianity and Brahminism and Parseeism and Judaism and Islam, and all the grand currents of this century's civilization, flows the vaster tidal wave of Universal Religion.

All destruction is but a little dust on the wind. Does not humanity itself abide? What truth it ever had is lost? Who are these that stand with arms flung round the old creed or name, or cherished "Body of Christ," trembling lest the universe crack, if that go down? 'Twere a strange universe to be alarmed because things must go down when their time has come!

History is a seamless woof, wherein no thread is broken, nor track lost. What will death do, the rankest of destructives? Shall I keep the special details of my present life beyond that change? I know not. I ask not. If it be best, I shall know them *only in their issues*. But what is of value in them is in the hands of shaping laws that know not waste, nor fraud, nor enmity to man. Our freedom affirms all when it claims that whatever is found to be the law of human nature will be found good for human nature. Do you ask, what if Immortality, Duty, God, shall be proved baseless? I reply that the special meanings we give these terms are of course subject to the same test of value as all other beliefs, — namely, are they true or false? But I must add that it does not express *any fact of actual experience* to say, as is often done, of what is so full of opportunity as immortality, or of what is so essential to the sense of source and resource as the Infinite, or of what is so vital to virtue as duty, — that we really feel we can do just as well without them, should they be proved illusory. The best of us feels nothing of the kind, since he probably knows well what he would lose in losing them; and even while one speaks thus of their disproval, one is in some sense holding fast the substance of them. The ungracious tone of the language is quite uncalled for. Can we hold so lightly what the ages have been teaching, of the conditions of character, the freedom of ideal aims, or of that relation to the permanence of truth through whatever changes of consciousness, which is what we properly mean by " immortality "?

Might I not as well say, that if freedom itself prove false, or truth no better than falsehood, I shall be just as well off? That were true in a verbal sense; but in every practical or vital sense, a mere empty boast or fling. I know that the right to follow truth is more indispensable than any opinion. But if all questions are still open, — even the reality of duty and the possibility of growth, — then, practically, all the centuries have taught us is the *hypothesis*, nothing else, *that there can be no basis for truth in man*. Our Religious Freedom does not believe this: it trusts itself. Duty trusts itself: and the sense of the Infinite in our ideal is a promise that invites to confident work.

FREEDOM AND RELIGION APPLIED AS SCIENCE.

It affirms *for the sciences*, authority to unfold nature, and claims to interpret their results. It demands the guarantee of invariable law for every fact of matter and mind: since this alone admits the absolute confidence which is essential to its upward attractions. To Science it will say, The Infinite is not outside your laws, but implicated in their mystery, in their strength, in their scope. Not without this interpreter may you read their outflow of stars and layers, past count of numbers or term of time: their chain of forms, their foretypes in plant and creature, pointing on to man. Even the mythic cataclysms, the six days' miracle of creation, the gods that dispense with time and growth, the nativities and transfigurations, do not lie; for they come of the poetic faculty which creates its own world, having laws of its own: and the sympathetic heavens and earth of mythology, once rescued from literal historic dogmatists, speak to a finer sense, which the children share with the seers.

Again, it is now the day of physical observation and experience: and these are liable to forget that it is forever Mind by which they see; that mind is the medium and solvent of all knowledge, and so the framer and the postulate of all their facts and laws. I believe our religious freedom will look to this danger also. Nor have we escaped a Biblical sky-firmament to be shut down under a scientific rule that nothing is real which is not definable in terms clear to the understanding. Neither God nor Man, law nor life, freedom nor faith, duty nor immortality, could abide that test: they are no subjects for such handling. Even the practical hope of science to make nature subserve human uses, the harmony of true social relations, and the education of the race, depends on such purely undefinable, illimitable conceptions as unity, liberty, love.

AS ART AND LABOR.

It is but fair to credit our new spiritual freedom with the renewed resort of *Art* to the study and representation of Nature: for this is the healthy reaction from creeds that have contemned the visible world, or confined art to ecclesiastical and mythical cycles : and it indicates the demand for a more ideal truth and purity than social themes as yet afford ; for what is simple, direct, unmortgaged to traditions, impartial, universal. So of practical arts. The appeal to constructive natural disciplines in new schools of all grades, from Kindergarten to Technological Institute ; the effort to make each craft a faculty of finer craft ; and the perfected machinery to which labor is being adapted, — are all signs of higher estimates accorded to æsthetic values, as elements of economy and use. But against all materialistic and selfish elements in this tendency, religion will enter protest. Art is not saved from degeneracy, — from sordidness, sham, or waste, — so long as it obeys no higher principle than force of machinery or pursuit of gain. Its law is not material, but ideal, — freedom to follow beauty for its own sake, to love right and fair doing for the rightness and fairness of it. The labor that turns out faithful, handsome work obeys precisely the same attractions that make the fine art of behavior, the beauty of personal conduct. We shall not escape the fact by calling the demand transcendental and visionary, nor by neglecting this condition because others are unfulfilled. The present selfish strifes of labor and capital are barbarizing, and lack the first elements of constructive power. Nothing can make labor remunerative, harmonious, and free, but positive reverence for the best and fittest way of doing what we personally have to do. For work of head or hand, imagination or skill, the one indispensable redemption is this simple loyalty to the infinite in our ideal. We shall begin solving the great "labor question" only when we take this path for our religion, and have a public sense of its practical necessity. To this end intelligent labor reformers will direct all their outward practical methods, co-operative or personal. Best of educators to it are great works of noble art: they are as yet in the future, because this moral ideal has not yet provided the social atmosphere for their creation. They await a justice that leaves to all faculty the freedom of its best conception and performance. There lies *our* "Italy," doubtless

"Beyond the Alpine summits of great pain."

Let religion hasten to teach what the growth of man at last allows and demands; the identity of the Fine Arts with spiritual experience; of Poetry and Music with the rhythm of noble desires; of the Novel and the Drama with expansion out of the stiff veils we call our "selves" into the manifold forms of human experience, towards that universal sympathy which is man's largest sense of the Infinite.

AS THE STATE.

It will treat the *State* as an ideal. Not as a mere right of majorities or parties to make laws for their opponents, or to substitute pushing legislation and worked-up force for the earnestness of a public sentiment; not as everybody's chance to put his will in act, which is the French madness; or to work springs of patronage, which is the American; or, worse than all, to decide his dues as an officeholder with his own fingers in the public chest. The religious ideal of the State is the fulfilment of functions by the fittest, as the one condition of just culture for all. One absolute allegiance at least is due from every citizen: it is to the personal disciplines and self-restraints that shall secure this end. Worse than kingcraft or oligarchy is the republican politician's pretence of a full right to hold any office he is able to secure. This false show of freedom makes the reality of slavery. A nation rests on loyalty, not on greed; and it is only the idealism of the citizen that can hold it to this law.

When the freedom of religion claimed for humanity a sphere given over to Fugitive Slave Laws and the suppression of personal liberty, it was bidden with sneers to keep its gospel out of politics. Now, *un*-forbidden, it will apply a more penetrative criticism still. An exacting morality, by no organized powers to be over-ridden or escaped, begins to ransack all functions for signs of corruption, and musters its indictments to prove the startling increase of crime. This is, I believe, an evidence of growing standards, moved by freer sense of the infinite, more than a sign of actual degeneracy in public or private virtue. The subtle soul of personal aspiration to freedom, which will not be shut *into* a special sphere, as " religious," cannot be shut *out* of any as *un*-religious. It goes where men do not carry prescriptive church or creed, leavening the practical secular life of a free community. It is this that has abolished union of Church and State; not only that religion may be free, but *that the State may be free to essential religion*. Depend upon it, no propagandist Christism will be suffered to make the Constitution its tool, and qualify voters by a creed; nor are political rights, at last, to be made into an Esau-pottage, fed out by Christian Associations to such as are willing to sell their freedom of thought; nor yet into spiritual constabularies under the old seals of King and Priest and Lord. Our spiritual liberties are protected from bigoted legislation by a growing ideality in the unconscious, as well as the conscious, faith (if not yet in the conduct) of our age and country, — too broad to be labelled or classified, too personal to be specifically organized, too much in the line of social tendency to fail of furtherance from the very effort to suppress it. The *real* dangers to personality, to the life of citizenship, are a selfish individualism and a tyrannous consolidation — working together, a hydra of materialism, in the name of practical rights and interests; and from this we must be preserved by the advancing Religion of Freedom.

AS CULTURE.

So in Culture. The defect of our popular education is in its mechanical tendencies. Drill of children in large schools to uniformity and even concert, in all mental processes; immense details of prescribed knowledge infused by short rules and methods, with severe competition and one field of reward and penalty for all forms of mind, make even our cherished common-school system a kind of social absolutism. It hardly recognizes differences of taste and faculty; leaves no margin for the free self-determination of the ideal; inspires no earnest desire to learn one's own real limits or powers. It does not discipline the dangerous democratic notion of a natural, unconditional right to manage all spheres, public and private; but indoctrinates it with subservience to masses, organization, and mutual supervision. Mechanism and manufacture, applied to mind and morals, is naturally the first essay of republican equality at the great task of self-culture. There is need of certain uniform methods to secure equal opportunity; but uniformity become absolutism is as much the peril of a free State as it is the power of a despotic one. It may make smart human apes and effective parrots; but we must educate our youth to free thought and noble aims. This needed stand for the personal ideal, and its claims in every child, must be made by our religion. It must bring to bear upon our school system the culture of moral loyalty; an appreciation, in political and social life, of real gifts and patient disciplines; an infinite interest, ready to spend and be spent, in adapting its methods to discover special faculty and need, to stimulate self-respect, and to thwart the public rage for uniformity with a noble universality. The mutual influence of the sexes in common cultures and disciplines is conspicuously needed for all these purposes. More vital still is the protection of the school system from theological pretensions. I do not say from *religion*. You cannot exclude that without producing worse caricatures of culture than Mr. Gladstone's proposal for a university which shall teach neither philosophy nor history, because of possible bearings on sectarian questions! Pure " secularism " is no such easy matter as its advocates suppose. The reason why the Bible should not be read in the schools is not that religion and morality are out of place there, but simply because the Bible represents the principle of authority over mental and spiritual freedom; because it would not be read as other books are, for purely educational purposes, but would introduce the denial of that freedom to judge and reject, which is the basis of education. This is not disrespect to its merits. Its immortal best sentences ought to be read in the schools, just as soon as they shall be put *on the same level, in every respect*, with other great sayings of similar purport, in Plutarch and Plato, in Avesta and Veda: such universality being the only possible evidence that no Bibliocracy is intended. Put an ideal desire of free personal conviction and broadest growth into the school system, and the vexing question of religious teaching is solved. One and the same spirit shall secularize and spiritualize our whole public culture; shall quicken free, original mind, and bend it to patient, loyal disciplines, and lift it into the courage to follow simple aims, and homely virtues, and hospitable hopes. No better definition of Culture was ever given than Matthew Arnold's "sweetness and light." Not the less does it define the geniality and insight of Natural Religion. With the new honor to Nature enter all brave faiths and sympathies; with boundless tasks of joy, whose rewards are in *this* life, in the believing and the doing: the world opens its infinite resource like a Father's Heart; and love and duty shall be everywhere at home.

RELIGION AND SCIENCE.

By John Weiss.

A THOROUGH treatment of this interesting subject, which is beginning to attract the attention of all minds that are more or less competent to deal with it, involves more time and more respect for details, more personal and experimental observation, than any morning platform can furnish. I lately heard of a saying of Professor Agassiz to this effect, that the amateur reader of scientific discoveries never actually possessed the facts that are described: they belong only to the observer, who feels them developing and dawning into his knowledge with a rapture of possession that seems to share the process of creation. To that just remark I add my conviction that the practised observer does not always thoroughly apprehend and calculate the drift of the facts which he procures. Still, a mere reader of science, however receptive his intellect may be, or inclined to scientific methods, is not in a position to speak with authority upon various points which emerge from the controversy that now prevails between the two parties of Natural Evolution of Forces and Natural Development of Divine Ideas; for thus I propose to state the matter in hand.

One party may be said to derive all the physical and mental phenomena of the world from germs of matter which collect forces, combine to build structures and increase their complexity, establish each different order of creatures by their own instinctive impulse, and climb at length through the animal kingdom into the human brain, where they deposit thought, expression, and emotion. At no point of this process of immense duration need there be a divine co-operation, because the process is supposed to have been originally delegated to a great ocean of germs: they went into action furnished for every possible contingency, gifted in advance with the whole sequence from the amœba, or the merest speck of germinal matter, to a Shakspearian moment of Hamlet, or a Christian moment of the Golden Rule. Consequently, ideas are only the impacts of accumulating sensations upon developing brains; an intellectual method is only the coherence of natural phenomena; and the moral sense is nothing but a carefully hoarded human experience of actions that are best to be repeated for the comfort of the whole. The imagination itself is but the success of the most sensitive brains in bringing the totality of their ideas into a balanced harmony that corresponds to the Nature that furnished them. The poet's eye, glancing from earth to heaven, is only the earth and sky condensing themselves into the analogies of all their facts, in native interplay and combination, wearing the terrestrial hues of midnight, morn, and eve. The epithet *divine*, applied to a possible Creator, can bear no other meaning than *unknown;* and the word *spiritual* is equivalent to *cerebral. Spirit* is the germinal matter arranged at length, after a deal of trouble, into chains of nerve-cells, which conspire to deposit all they have picked up on their long journey from chaos to man. So that when their living matter becomes dead matter, their deposit drops through into nonentity; and the word Immortality remains only to denote facts of terrestrial duration, such as the life of nations, and the fame of men with the heaviest and finest brains. If the brain-cells discontinue their function, existence cannot continue.

The other party, which inclines to a theory that creation is a development of divine ideas, is very distinctly divided into those who believe that this development took a gradual method, and used natural forces that are everywhere upon the spot, and those who prefer to claim a supernatural incoming of fresh ideas at the beginnings of genera and epochs. The former believe that the Divine Mind accompanies the whole development, and secures its gradualism; or, that the universe is a single, unbroken expression of an ever-present Unity. The latter believe that the expression can be enhanced, broken in upon by special acts that do not flow from previous acts, but are only involved in the ideas which the previous acts contained; so that there is a sequence of idea, but not of actual creative evolution out of one form into another.

The former think that they find in the marks of slow gradation from simple to complex forms, both of physical and mental life, the proof that a Creator elaborates all forms out of their predecessors, by using immense duration of time, but never for a moment deserting any one of them, as if it were competent to do it alone; so that the difference of species, men, and historical epochs, is only one of accumulation of ideas, and not of their interpolation. The latter think that the missing links of the geological record, the marked peculiarities of races and periods, the transcendent traits of leading men, are proofs that the Creator does not work by natural evolution, but by deliberate insertion of fresh ideas to start fresh creatures. One party recognizes the supernatural in the whole of Nature, because the whole embodies a divine ideal. The other party is not reluctant to affirm the same, but thinks it essential to the existence of Nature to import special efforts of the ideal, which are equivalent to special creations: so that the naturalist gets on with nothing but unity and gradation; the supernaturalist cannot take a step without plurality and interference.

What are the opinions entertained by Naturalism upon the origin of ideas, the moral sense, the spiritual nature?

Naturalism itself here splits. One side borrows the method of natural evolution of forces so far as to derive all the contents of the mind from the experiences of mankind as they accumulated to systematize themselves in brains; and when further questions are put as to whether there be an independent origin for a soul, and a permanent continuance for it; whether there be an original moral sense that appropriates social experiences, and gives a stamp of its own latent method to them, the answers are deferred, because it is alleged that Science has not yet put enough facts into the case to support a judicial decision.

But another camp is forming upon the field of Naturalism. Its followers incline to believe that all human and social experience started from a latent finite mind which is distinct from the structure that may surround it; and that the movement of evolution was twofold, one side of it being structural and the other mental, both strictly parallel, moving simultaneously in consequence of a divine impulse that resides at the same moment in the physical and mental nature, — an impulse that accumulated into a latent finite mind as soon as a structure appropriate to express it accumulated; that the history of mankind has been a mutual interplay of improving circumstances and developing intelligence, but that the first step was taken by the latent mind, just as the first step in creating any thing must have been taken by a divine mind; and that the last steps of perfected intelligence reproduce the original method and purposes of a Creator who imparted to man this tendency to reproduce them. In this latent tendency all mental phenomena lay packed, or nebulous if you please; or it was germinal mentality, if you prefer the term; or inchoate soul-substance. The term is of little consequence, provided we notice the possibility of something to begin human life with beside the physical structure that was elaborated out of previous creatures.

We know that the human brain repeats, during the period of its fœtal existence, some of the forms of the vertebrata that preceded it. We also know that when any organ of man's body is diseased, a degeneration takes place that repeats the state of the same organ in the lower animals. The secretion is no longer normal, but recurs to a less perfect kind. So we notice that in degeneration of the brain some idiotic conditions occur that repeat with great exactness the habits and temper of monkeys and other animals. The descending scale of degeneration, no less than the ascending effort of development, touches at animal stages, and incorporates them in the human structure. It would require a uniformity of degenerating conditions, sustained through an immense duration of time, to degrade a human structure into any actual animal form, if, indeed, such a retrogradation be not forbidden by the mental and moral superiority to which any human structure must have attained. Still, the physical and mental diseases of mankind are significant allusions: they mimic, as it were, some stages of structural development.

When Dr. Howe visited the isolated cottages for the insane at Gheel, in Belgium, he noticed that the noisy ones (*les crieurs,* the howlers) could be heard in the dusk crying like animals, but clearly human animals; and he says, " Is it only fancy, or were men once mere animals, shouting and crying aloud to each other; and is this habit of shattered maniacs another proof that all organized beings tend to revert to the original type, like that reversion of neglected fruit towards the wild crab ? "

The popular language notices this tendency to deterioration in the tricks of over-sensual men: we say a man is a hog, a goat, a monkey. Some cunning facial traits remind us irresistibly of the fox, others of the rat. These resemblances were the unconscious elements in the Egyptian theory of metempsychosis, or the retrogression of evil men into the animals whose special tricks were like their own.

We cannot help seeing that Nature slowly felt her way towards us, built her clay models, reframed her secret thought, committed it to brains of increasing complexity, till man closed the composing period, and began to blab of his origin.

But how did he begin to do that? Was his social life a physical result of the sympathies of gregarious animals, who defend and feed each other, protect and rear their young, dig burrows, spread lairs, and weave a nest? That, it is replied, was only the structural and physical side of something that had been preparing to step farther. It could not have furnished the germinal conditions of speech, thought, and conscience. Was it because the fox was cunning, that man learned to circumvent his enemies; because the elephant was sagacious, that he undertook to ponder; because the monkey was curious, that he began to pry into cause and effect; because the bee built her compact cell, that he grew geometrical? The answer made is, that these structural felicities lay on the road between a Creator who geometrized, and a creature who learned to see that it was so, and called it Geometry. At the end of that road is a mind that undertakes to interpret whence the road started, and how it was laid out. If you prefer to derive that latent mind from these previous states of animal intelligence, it does not damage the presumption in favor of independent mind. Estimate the animals to be as sagacious as you please, until they barely escape stepping over into the domain which our reflective words have appropriated,— such as memory, perception, adaptation, causality, also a rudiment of conscience. Even be surprised by traces of self-devotion, like that in the "heroic little monkey, who braved his dreaded enemy in order to save the life of his keeper; or in the old baboon, who, descending from the mountains, carried away in triumph his young comrade from a crowd of astonished dogs." Say, if you will, as Rāma said in the Rāmayana, when a vulture died in defending his mistress: " Of a certainty there are amongst the animals many good and generous beings, and even many heroes. For my part, I do not doubt that this compassionate bird, who gave his life for my sake, will be admitted into Paradise." Believe, if you are a dog-fancier, that in "that equal sky" your faithful dog will bear you company. It would infringe upon my sense of personality no more than to have him trotting by my side in this world. Here he is altogether unconscious how my moral sense sets store by and idealizes his instinctive service, and how I flatter him with imputations of my own self. He licks the hand that extends to him a mood of a Creator's appreciation of fidelity.

But grant that a Creator derived the latent human mind by gradualism out of all kinds of animal anticipations. The mind thus derived reaches to a distinction from physical structure, and to a subordination of it to ideal purposes, at that point of development where the man can say, *I am;* that phrase is an echo against the walls of creation of the first creative fiat of Him who is I AM. When man finds language to express his sense of personal consciousness, God overhears the secret of his own condition told into all the ears he has created by all the tongues of his own spiritual essence. The mouse cannot squeak it, nor the elephant trumpet it; the sparrow cannot cheep and twitter it, nor can the ape chatter his anticipation that he is about to be liberated into speech and personal identity. All the herds of the animals furnish the physical structure of man with the devices of their strength and instinct, but they have no personal freedom to contribute. A school of whales will yield so many barrels of oil to feed the midnight lamps of thinkers who chase the absent sun with surmises concerning a light that never sets.

Certainly it must be true that the physical and chemical forces which are involved in acts of creation cannot suggest to any parts of creation the previous laws of a Creator. We say these forces reach the felicity of making a man: if this be so, they have made something that is different from their own nature. Man himself betrays this difference as soon as he begins to establish science upon universal laws: it is a proof that he is not only a part of creation, in the natural order, but also the member of a spiritual order, by virtue of which he attains slowly to conceptions of the laws that made him, including the chemical functions of his various organs. Which of all our secretions could explain themselves? After they have discharged all their duty of nutriment and defecation they have reached the end of their tether. Could the pancreatic juice, by going into partnership with the liver, kidneys, and stomach, succeed in explaining the manner of its secretion, and how it pours into the duodenum? Can the blood, which is the expression to which these lower functions reach, lift to the brain a report of the way it grew to be red, and of the use of the white corpuscles? Do the countless nerve-cells that weave their telegraphic circuits through the brain — to which every organ sends its message, and receives thence its reply — convert these sensations into something that is not nerve-cell, that is not gray or fibrous matter; do they lose their identity and become deduction, wit, imagination, and synthetic thought? When you can prove that germinal matter made itself, you will be in a condition to show that matter interprets itself. For that is what man does: he interprets not only the matter of his own private structure, but of all organic and inorganic forms. Does matter arm the eyes it makes with the telescope and microscope to overcome its own extension and density? What is it that calculates the weights of the planets, and records the relative ratios of their movements, and announces new planets before they have been seen? Something kindred with the intellect that preconceived the existence of that universe of germs which becomes function, substance, form, and force. When we see daily how all created things hasten to fall in with the logic of the best thinkers, and to crystallize along the lines which they draw, we suspect that such lines are drawn parallel with divine ideas, and that science is made in the image of a Creator.

This position of theistic Naturalism entitles it not to be afraid of all the scientific facts that can be produced. If Mr. Darwin could prove to-morrow that we have descended from an anthropoid ape that tenanted the boundless waste of forest branches, we should as cheerfully accept our structure created out of dust in that form as in any other. There is dignity in dust that reaches any form, because it eventually betrays a forming power, and ceases to be dust by sharing it. I am willing to have it shown that I travel with a whole menagerie in my cerebellum: your act of showing it to me shows that neither you nor I are members of that menagerie. We are its feeders, trainers, and interpreters. We act God's part towards it, as he does upon the scale of zones and continents. In us, in fact, he improves upon his natural action by bringing all his dumb creatures under one roof, where he enjoys the benefit of knowing that his motive in creating them is understood and delighted in; so that though saurians are out of date, and he no longer has the joy of making the mammoth and aurochs, we rehearse the ancient raptures for him, and preserve them in our structures.

> " Thus He dwells in all,
> From life's minute beginnings, up at last
> To man,— the consummation of this scheme
> Of being, the completion of this sphere
> Of life; whose attributes had here and there
> Been scattered o'er the visible world before,
> Asking to be combined, — dim fragments meant
> To be united in some wondrous whole, —
> Imperfect qualities throughout creation,
> Suggesting some one creature yet to make, —
> Some point where all those scattered rays should meet
> Convergent in the faculties of man."

> "Man, once descried, imprints for ever
> His presence on all lifeless things: the winds
> Are henceforth voices, in a wail or shout,
> A querulous mutter, or a quick, gay laugh, —
> Never a senseless gust now man is born."

> "So in man's self arise
> August anticipations, symbols, types
> Of a dim splendor ever on before,
> In that eternal circle run by life."

I submit to you the doubt whether germinal matter, long cradled in the earth's evolving periods, and then baptized as the individual, Robert Browning, could have composed those lines which contain prevision of the whole drift of modern science. Could nerve-cells, nourished by roast meat, revel in those "august anticipations" of a state and attainment that depend upon a continuance of our life?

We need be afraid of nothing in heaven or earth, whether dreamt of or not in our philosophy. It is a wonder to me that scholars and clergymen are so skittish about scientific facts. I delight, for instance, in the modern argument which reproduces and systematizes the ancient fire-worship of the Persian, by showing that the sun's atmosphere contains all the stuffs of the solar system, and is its God whose vibrating emanations wake all things to a morning of living. The more possibilities you attribute to the sun, the more exhaustive you allege its creative power to be, to the extent, if you please, of sending the fine ether which courses through the brain-cells; the more correspondent to the solar nature you show that all life-action may be, the more you help me to my belief in a latent mind as the first term of human existence. You have made that fluent and wallowing sun a solid stepping-stone in the great river of phenomena, and it takes me across dry-shod, with not the smell of its fire upon my garments,— takes me directly to a Cause for something so glorious, for such a mobile and flaming minister to all things. On the way toward that Cause, if I choose, I can step to suns more distant, each of which is the life-centre of its system and the distributor of germs; but though this pathway may stretch to the crack of doom expected by the theologian, I shall find at the end of it something that sands the floor of heaven thick with suns. Something; not another sun, but sun's Father. I started with an idea of Cause, and now I find the reason why I did, because nothing is uncaused. I get justification for using the term; for it appears to be the language used at length by One who can no longer be content that his heavens should have no sound, and that their voice should not be heard. Latent mind first betrayed its presence on the earth by beginning to grope from effects to causes, to account for things. Thus the mind, like a weak party of soldiers, separated from its base by formidable streams, has slowly pontooned its way back to the main Cause, by successive discoveries of causes. It is recognized afar off, it is welcomed, and rushes with the hunger of long absence into the arms of comradeship.

It does not disturb me to be told that the mind has no innate ideas; that, in fact, the entity called mind is a result of the impressions which the senses gather from Nature, a body of sifted perceptions; that all our emotions started in the vague sympathy that the first men had for each other when they found themselves in company; that a sense of justice is not native to the mind, but only a consequence of the efforts of men to get along comfortably in crowds, with the least amount of jostling; that the feeling of chastity has no spiritual derivation, but was slowly formed in remote ages by observation of the pernicious effects of promiscuous living; that, in short, all the mental states which we call intuitions, should be called digestions from experience. For, supposing this theory to be the one that will eventually account for all mental phenomena, why need one care how he grew into a being who throbs with the instantaneous purpose of salutary ideas, with the devotion of his thought and conscience to the service of mankind, with a ravishing sense of harmony and proportion that breaks into his symphony and song? When a man reaches the point of being all alive, thrilling to his finger-tips with all the nerves a world can contribute, shall he distress himself because, upon examining his genealogy, he discovers no aristocrat, but a plebeian, for his ancestor? If, in fact, he should discover something that had fallen to the conventionality of being an aristocrat, it would, as the world goes, breed a suspicion that something previous had maintained the dignity of being a plebeian. Manhood ennobles all ancestors, and they enjoy princely revenues in its vitality. Must

I make myself miserable because I am told that for nine months of my existence I was successively a fish, a frog, a bird, a rabbit, a monkey, and that my infancy presented strong Mongolian characteristics? This, then, was the path to the human mind, that outswims all fishes in a sea where no fish can live, that leaps with wit and analogy more agile than frogs or kangaroos, that travels by aerial routes to spaces where no bird's wing could winnow. So be it, if it be so. I do not care for the path when I come in sight of the mansion of love and beauty that has been prepared for me. Its windows are all aglow with " an awful rose of dawn." What delicacy of sentiment or imagination can be desecrated because barbarian ancestors felt like brutes or fancied like lunatics? Can the mind's majestic conception of a divine plan of orderly and intelligent development be unsphered and brutalized because the first men felt the cravings of causality more faintly than the pangs of hunger? Causality has reached its coronation-day: its garment of a universe is powdered with galaxies and nebulæ, suns glitter on its brow, the earth is its footstool, its sceptre is controlling Law. You cannot mortify or attaint this king by reminding it of days spent in hovels and squalor, when it hid from the treason of circumstances, and was sheltered and fed precariously by savages. Would you unseat it? Then annihilate a universe.

This latent tendency to discover cause rescues the first beginnings of the human soul from any materialism that would deny its independent existence. It provides the human structure with a tenant, who improves it as his circumstances become more flattering, until both together frame one complete convenience. We do not require a theory of innate ideas to establish this soul upon earth and set it going. All we require is the theory of innate tendency, of latent directions, of inchoate ideas, that pervade this germinal soul-substance just as the divine ideas pervaded primitive matter. I conceive that our mental method and our moral sense were possibilities of soul-germs, but that experience stimulated them into improving action and expression, till at length our idea of sequence and origin, and our sense of right and wrong, have become normal conditions of intelligence. Why not say, then, that they are at last intuitive? But it is chiefly important to accept them as essential elements of a human person, without regard to the method of their derivation. For derivation is not in itself fatal to the independence of the thing derived. It is not among genera and species: why should it be among personal ideas?

People do not like to have their conscience derived from gradual discoveries of acts that turned out to be the most useful or the most sympathetic, nor to feel that they have no inner guide but this inherited succession of selfish experiences. And, indeed, the theory does not account for all the facts. It is unable to give any satisfactory explanation of the moral condition of such men as Woolman and John Brown; of any brakeman or engineer who coolly puts himself to death to save a train; of Arnold of Winkelried who "gathered in his breast a sheaf of Austrian spears," and felt Swiss liberty trample over him and through the gap.

This theory, that the moral sense was slowly deposited by innumerable successions of selfish experiences, could make nothing of the story lately told of the way a little girl was rescued, who had " wandered on to the track of the Delaware Railroad as a freight train of nineteen cars was approaching. As it turned the sharp top of the grade, opposite St. Georges, the engineer saw the child for the first time, blew 'Down brakes,' and reversed the engine. But it was too late to slacken its speed in time; and the poor baby got up, and, laughing, ran to meet it. 'I told the conductor,' says the engineer, 'if he could jump off the engine, and, running ahead, pick the child up before the engine reached her, he might save her life, though it would risk his own; which he did. The engine was within one foot of the child when he secured it, and they were both saved. I would not run the same risk of saving a child again by way of experiment for all Newcastle County, for nine out of ten might not escape. He took the child to the lane, and she walked to the house, and a little girl was coming after it when we left.' The honest engineer, having finished his day's run, sits down the next morning and writes this homely letter to the father of the child, 'in order that it may be more carefully watched in future,' and thanking God 'that himself and the baby's mother slept tranquilly last night, and were spared the life-long pangs of remorse.' It does not occur to him to even mention the conductor's name, who, he seems to think, did no uncommon thing in risking his own life, unseen and unnoticed on the solitary road, for a child whom he would never probably see again."

The feeling of utility would confine men strictly within the limits of the average utility of any age. Each generation would come to a mutual understanding of the things that would be safe to perform. The instinct of self-preservation would be a continual check to the heroism that dies framing its indictment against tyrannies and wrongs. The great men who fling themselves against the scorn and menace of their age could never be born out of general considerations of utility or sympathy; for each man would say that a wrong, though not salutary to its victim, would not be salutary to one who should try to redress it. Sympathy that was spawned by the physical circumstances of remote ages could never reach the temper of consideration for the few against the custom of the many. You could no more extract heroism from such a beginning of the moral sense than sunbeams from cucumbers. We owe a debt to the scientific man who can show how many moral customs result from local and ethnic experiences, and how the conscience is everywhere capable of inheritance and education. He cannot bring us too many facts of this description, because we have one fact too much for him; namely, a latent tendency of conscience to repudiate inheritance and every experience of utility, to fly in its face with a forecast of a transcendental utility that supplies the world with its redeemers, and continually drags it out of the snug and accurate adjustment of selfishness to which it arrives. The first act of such devoted self-surrender might have been imitated, no doubt; and a few men in every age, having learned by this means that a higher utility resulted from doing an apparently useless thing, might be developed by a mixture of reason and sympathy into resisting their fellows. But how are you going to account for the first act? How for a sentiment of violated justice, if justice be only the precipitate of average utility? How for a tender love for remote and invisible suffering, for wrongs that are a nuisance at too great a distance to be felt or observed, if sympathy is nothing but an understanding among people who are forced to live together? I should as soon pretend that my nostrils were afflicted by a bad smell that was transpiring in Siam.

This reminds me to ask how any particular odor was first discovered to be nauseous. If the reply be offered, that olfactory discrimination must have resulted from experiences of the effect of odors, gradually acquired, and slowly modifying the organ, I say that the process must have begun in a capacity to perceive, no matter how imperfectly, that a scent is disagreeable. What is that previous capacity? It must have been something that was not created by the scent. It is no objection to this that people differ in sensibility for odors, so that a flower may be disagreeable to one and pleasant to another. If odors create the organ that corresponds to and discriminates them, they ought to appear the same to everybody. But there is a latent perception that varies among individuals, and decides their favorite perfumes; and it is curious to notice how they correspond to mental characters, and seem to have a faint analogy with the condition of the moral sense. Discrimination in smelling could not have been originated by the things that were smelt, any more than a man's trail or blood-drip must have preceded and created the blood-hound's tracking.

The moral sense to which we have attained by stages must have started from an original tendency to become sensitive to moral acts. We cannot say that the results have established the tendency, any more than we can say that marks of design have originated a designer; that an eye, for instance, developed light, or that light created a light-maker.

The phrases, *I ought, I ought not,* are not merely functional, as when a blood-hound tracks, a pointer points, a watch-dog listens through the house. We detect even in the animals a sense of duty in carrying out their instincts, and a deferring to man, as if to a source of the instincts, or at least to a power that holds them responsible for good behavior. So we instinctively refer our moral attitude to a source of moral law.

It is possible we have reached a moral sense from the anticipatory types of conscience in some animals, by drifting along with them through Mr. Spencer's experiences of utility and Mr. Darwin's social instincts. But a latent mental tendency must have fallen in with that structural drift at some point, else man would never agonize to say, *I ought, I ought not.* Is it any the less divine because it has consorted with animals and savages, and found their company no hinderance to this elaborating of a sense of right and wrong? It is all the more divine, because it betrays conformity with the great order of development, at the same time that it has been forereaching through it to perfect moral actions.

What was the nature of John Woolman's secret satisfaction when he insisted upon non-compliance with the habits and allowances of his time? If conscience be the result of discovering what turns out badly for a person who is living on the scale of other persons, why should he, a tailor, have discouraged the making and wearing of fine clothes; have refused to touch, to his own serious privation, one of the products of slave labor; have protested, to the loss of sympathy and gain of contempt, against ownership in men? Was he an abnormal variety, a deteriorated specimen, a man whom advantage hurt? Where do Mr. Darwin's social instincts come in? Woolman withstood all these for distant and abstract incentives, and originated, without social and intellectual material, a fresh epoch of moral feeling. The latent tendency attained to liberation from all its previous experiences.

One of the bases of conscience is said to be the intellectual capacity to recall past impressions, to compare them with present temptations, and to decide upon the most advantageous action. Possibly; but it cannot be a *sine qua non*, as we see in the cases of those uncultivated souls who have a new scruple or a sudden heroism. And some of the best intelligences are dull and uncertain in the moral sense. Is it because they are at the same time weak in the social instincts? Some very acute and long-headed pirates of society are fond family-men, love to gather children around their knees, have sympathetic impulses; and, when they are not on a plundering excursion among widows and orphans, as directors of mills, railroads, and trust companies, would be selected to found a society of correct men in consequence of immaculate dicky and domesticity.

The lower senses, by repeated experiment and observation, acquire an unconscious, automatic movement. When the higher senses have passed out of their experimental stages, they acquire a spontaneous movement. In the region of intellectual and moral ideas this becomes intuitive; that is, they attain to a power of looking into themselves, of comparing and deducing, and also of anticipating other ideas, or at least evolutions from existing ideas, which sometimes lead to the fore-feeling of a law of nature in advance of its confirmation by experiment, — as when Lucretius anticipated moderns with a theory of evolution, of the magnet, and of the constitution of the sun; and Swedenborg divined fresh planets before Leverrier was furnished with the calculus which might have led him experimentally to the fact; or when Kepler saw dimly in his mental firmament the law to which at length the sky responded. This was latent correspondence with the law: it was stimulated by all his scientific knowledge; but when it stepped upon planetary ratios into a new secret of creation, it announced its independence of experience, and betrayed a similarity in essence with the Creator.

Let us now consider if this latent mentality, which reaches thus to independent action, has any chance of surviving the dissolution of the cerebral structure, by means of some force, called Vitality, distinct in kind from all the physical and chemical forces that build our frame. Naturalism denies a special vitality, because it is so engrossed with showing how functions develop by the instrumentality of human forces: it affirms that the whole drift of experimental analogy sets against the conception of another force, unless it be one that shall differ only in degree, and not in kind, — not in essential independence, not in permanent continuance, — from the rest. Observation has lifted these forces to the level of so many functions, till at length it has detected them conspiring in the action of the brain, that scientific men are cautious about predicating the existence of a finer force that comes to use the deposits of the brain-cells, or that is exhaled from them into an independent essence. This modesty is not mistimed, for its singleness of purpose supplies marvellous facts and hints about the human organization which no religion can afford to do without. It is childish to be afraid of their tendency, and weak to declare that they yet decide the question.

What is Vitality? I notice, in the first place, that our common contrast of *animate* and *inanimate* — which means, when we make it, that we believe that the former could not have been developed from the latter — is really only a contrast derived from a general optical impression. We think we see that one object is alive and that another is not, and our sight applies the tests which experience has preconceived as being correspondent to life and to death. But it does not follow that the *origins* of life, which are removed from us by immense duration, and thus far, if they are still going on, by inadequate means of observation, must be distinct acts of germs that exist in a plane apart from the inanimate. They may have been, and may still be, evolutions through forces out of inanimate matter. *Inanimate* may be only latent animate.

But I think we ought to discard this old-fashioned contrast, and substitute the terms *organic* and *inorganic;* for a bit of wood or stone will show, beneath the most powerful microscope, a gathering and shifting of granules, a confused intermingling, that is enough to betray motion at least, and to put us on the track of the suggestion that a primitive ocean of germs was set on its creative way by motion. Nothing, then, can be called inanimate that contains the first quality or essential towards vitality. But it may be called *inorganic* if its structure admits of passing to no other function. An organism is something that announces vital force or function; that gathers the universal cells, granules, cytods — or whatever you may please to call protoplastic stuff — into some definite gesture, however faint, and begins to use the inorganic to nourish and sustain its organs.

Mr. Beale, an eminent advocate for a special and indestructible vitality in man, says: " If a particle of living matter, not more than $\frac{1}{100,000}$ of an inch in diameter, were made in the laboratory out of non-living matter, — if it lived and moved, and grew and multiplied, — I confess my belief in the spiritual nature of my faculties would be severely shaken."

Why should it be shaken any more than if it should turn out to be true that living matter *originated* the spiritual nature? It is certain that living matter is instrumental in *expressing* our faculties, whatever their origin may have been. Then of what consequence is it whence the living matter is derived? We are not appalled at the possibility that organic matter may be made out of non-living — or, more properly, inorganic — matter. We are nerved for such a result, whether it occur in the laboratory or in nature, by the conviction that the spiritual functions are no more imperilled by using matter originated in any way, than the Creator hazarded his existence by originating matter in some way to be used by himself and by us. His vitality resides in the whole of matter; so that, even if the inorganic be convertible into the organic, or the organic into the inorganic, he has to no extent fallen dead. Then there can be no danger to our mind that may result from either process, to the mind that may receive its material instrument from either.

There is nothing really inanimate in all creation; for the Infinite Life has gone into representation by each of its epochs, from the primordial germinal matter through all its evolutions: no form or result of it can be dead. There is no such thing as death, but an incessant shifting into and out of all forms. The stone arrests for the present the shifting, but it must have a certain kind of life in itself in order to do that, — something that tends to be not long or constantly arrested, that is all the time vaguely tumultuous with its imprisoned particles. If any thing could be really dead, God would, to that thing's extent, cease to be alive.

I have sometimes indulged the speculation that the molecular activity observable in inorganic substances is a degeneration of the germinal activity which is observable in the amœba and other vital stuff. That is, I suppose that the germinal has preceded the molecular activity; and that all stones, minerals, and gems were held positively vital in the original nebulosity, — in that ocean of creative germs, which was not inorganic, though it was undetermined. What we call dead matter is the excrement of a germinal universe; but it may still go into fertilizing, and is doing it, perhaps, all the time. It once shared the life of all germs, though it now seems to have become inert and solid merely to build continents for the support of vital forms. The word *inert* cannot represent an absolute fact of death, but only a relative condition of vitality.

But what is vitality in a human structure? It may be only a part of the universal vitality, raised to very high conditions, or it may be a special mode of it; but in either case I do not see why it does not share the universal advantage of being indestructible. "Yes," says the scientific man; "but it also must share the universal tendency of forces to shift into force again when the structure that contains them is destroyed. The man's vitality may still exist, but only in some mode of impersonal force, as motion shifts into heat. When all the known forces are discovered constantly at this interplay, we cannot assume that another force, yet undiscovered, will be differently endowed." What have we got to say to that?

The only attempt which I have noticed, of purely scientific pretension, at an answer, is contained in a paper on Vitality, read by the Rev. H. H. Higgins, M.A., before the Literary and Philosophical Society of Liverpool. He says: " The most delicate tests for indicating minute changes in electrical, thermal, and other conditions, have been applied at the moment of death, and have shown no sign. Now it is certain of the forces of heat, light, motion, &c., that they are absolutely indestructible: they may be converted one into the other, but they cannot cease to exist. If the vital principle was analogous to these agencies, it might escape in any one of them; but of this no well-ascertained trace has been observed in any investigation of the phenomena of death."

But this statement proves too much. If the tests applied at the moment of death discover *no force at all* in the act of escaping, it only shows that no force at all is discoverable under the conditions of a dying moment. But we know that thermal and electrical conditions exist in the functions of a living body: they ought, then, to be intercepted as they pass away. Where, for instance, does the thermal condition go, and why should it not be seen in going? For it certainly existed just before the moment of dying, and for some time after. This, then, is not a decisive test of the undetectable presence of a special vitality.

This is the question. If there be specific vitality, does it escape from death with the mental contents of the person whose body died, to prolong his identity, or is it only another physical force, though a specific one, with character distinct from heat, light, &c., but still a force that joins after death the unconscious equilibrium out of which it first allied itself to a human organization?

To call vitality specific, and to claim that it is prior to organization, does not answer the above question.

All the steps of modern investigation seem to disprove the theory of personal continuance. Functions of the body which were long supposed to depend upon a specific vitality are now referred to known chemical forces, and are repeated in the laboratory. The theory is pushed from post to post, till it seems to have only a base of moral probability to fall back upon.

Far from undervaluing that, — finding, on the contrary, in the manifestations of personal character a hint of immortality that is superior to, at least, the resurrection of any dead body, — I still claim that science is not so neutral on this question as it thinks to be. I am quite content to wait for some special investigation of the point, while the co-ordination of all phenomena by mental laws that explain creative acts, and refer us back to a pre-existing mind, shows me, with the emphasis of a universe, that the minds which can interpret and spiritually reconstruct the plan of creation must share the nature of a Creator. It is his nature to have pre-existed distinct from his germinal material. It must be the nature of corresponding mind to be distinct from its germinal material, to have been allied to human structures in a state of latent mentality.

I own I find it difficult to conceive how this latent mind was gradually developed out of the structures that passed through animal into human conditions. It seems at first as if the mental quality must have been homogeneous through all its gradations. In what manner could it have begun to be different in kind from itself as it was in its previous animal expressions? At first, in trying to meet that question, we appear to be driven to put up with one of two alternatives: either that the animals have shared independent vitality, if we have; or that we started from germinal soul-monads that were outside of, and previous to, physical structure, but were in some way attracted to all the points of human development.

But I suggest whether there can be any germinal soul-substance except the mysterious force which we call vitality wherever we see it in the human state. It went into creation allied with all the germs which have subsequently taken form. It carried everywhere a latent sensibility for the creative law out of which it came. It swept along with a dim drift of the Personality that first conceived it and then put it on the way to self-expression. It mounted thus by the ascending scale of animals, and its improvements in structure were preparations to reach and repeat Personality, to report the original sense of the Creator that he was independent of structure. At length it became detached from the walls of the womb of creation, held only for nourishment by the cord of structure, till it could have a birth into individualism. Then the interplay of mind and organism began, with an inherited advantage in favor of vitality. Now vitality, thus developed and crystallized into personality, tends constantly back towards its origin. The centrifugal movement through all the animals is rectified by the centripetal movement in man. The whole series of effects recurs to an effecting cause.

At any rate, it is quite as difficult to conceive that there were pre-existent soul-germs which could be attracted from without to human embryos, to become their vital and characteristic forces, as it is to frame a clear statement of the way in which independent minds became developed out of all the previous animal and semi-human conditions. How or when could a soul-monad become buried in a fœtal form? If such an act could take place, it would break up the inherited transmission of characters; for it is not credible that every door of descent is waylaid and watched by just the style of soul-germs that can straightway be at home and carry on the business at the old stand. It is plain that the whole process of evolution of vitality into personal consciousness must take place within the limits of human structure, and that the child is father of the man.

Could the unconscious form of the embryo select its appropriate soul-germ, and detach it from the world-cluster to absorb and incorporate it through the mother? By what nicety of instinct or affinity, could the moment of fertilization, or a subsequent moment of the fœtal throb, pick out of some great ether of vital monads just the proper soul-germ, so that each human family might propagate its traits and accumulate its ancestors? It is impossible to conceive of any descent or amplification of vitality except in the direct line of fructification, conception, and birth.

It is not absurd, then, to suppose that each human being started from a finite beginning. He pre-existed only in the impulse of vitality. It is objected that, if he was not an actual essence or monad that pre-existed before his finite structure was brought up to the felicity of receiving it, he could not continue after the physical structure had disappeared. Why not? Personal continuance need not be supposed to depend upon any special moment of eternal creativeness from which the person may have started. It might be early or late: in Judæa, Greece, or California. When a person starts, he need not be imagined to stop until the infinite Personality out of which he started declines to project the vitality that propagates persons. If there be such a fact as personal continuance, it must depend only upon the impulse of vitality.

It does not trouble me that I cannot put my finger on the period of human development when man began to have independent personality. Who can tell when a child begins to have a consciousness of self, and to say *I*, with a distinct feeling of what his speech involves? Yet at length he is found to be saying it, and to be converting the identity of consciousness into personal character. Ages of semi-human conditions may have preceded, as years of characterless infancy precede, the assertion of personal identity. The men of those developing ages may have perished like ants that swarm in the pathway of feet. What of that, if a day comes that speaks an imperishable word?

That word is, I know Unity, I share Unity, I pass into consciousness of Creative Laws, I touch the Mind from whom my mental method started, and I thus become that circle's infrangibility. My law of perceiving is so complete an expression of the law of creating, that I perceive, as the Creator once perceived, that matter alone could not start with it nor end in it. I know the laws which matter did not make. Then matter does not make my knowledge.

Science grants me this inestimable benefit of providing a universe to support my personal identity, my moral sense, and my feeling that these two functions of mind cannot be killed. Its denials, no less than its affirmations, set free all the facts I need to make my body an expression of mental independence. Hand in hand with Science I go, by the steps of development, back to the dawn of creation; and, when there, we review all the forces and their combinations which have helped us to arrive, and both of us together break into a confession of a Force of forces.

Science has performed a mighty work against theology, in freeing us from its superstitions. We have picked ourselves up from Adam's fall, and are busy shaking that dust from our garments; geological cemeteries, full of dead creatures, speak to exonerate us from the unhandsome trick of having brought death and sin into the world; we shake the tree of knowledge, and woman helps us to shake it and devour the invigorating fruit; there's nothing edible which we do not perceive to be a divine invitation to eat, with a conviction that the great Landlord is not plotting murder to pillage our persons. We feel perfectly safe in every part of the house, and are learning how to promote the interests of the Builder, by clearing out corners that grow infectious, and correcting our own carelessness; so that there is not a slur left to cast upon God. Death is discovered to be a process of correlation and recombination of force; and we detect Heaven's wonderful footprint, that can never be mistaken, in the paths of evil. Only let us know enough, re-enforce every gift with the beneficial facts, irrigate the whole surface of the mind with law, that our structures may more happily repeat the health that mantles on the face of a universe.

Scientific men find themselves in opposition to

almost every form of theology, because the world is: they have no personal motive, and indulge in pique no more than the great system whose movements and causes they express. But theology has so systematically libelled the Creator and misled the creature; so deliberately substituted trains of arbitrary thinking for the law of Evolution; so depraved God by pretending the depravity of man, to make a jailer of one and a felon of the other; so placarded the spotless plan with whimsical schemes of redemption; and so represented the universal love, as if it were confectionery to stop the whimper of returning sinners, — that Science might well transfix it with the contempt of a gaze that is level with the horizon, and as brimful hot with the noonday sun.

When the great observers are accused of disrespect towards religion, it would be well to remember how long, and to a period how late, men have understood religion to be something that is brought down by modified systems of theology, and to be dependent upon an act of faith in them. Science takes men at their word; they point to a number of articles that embody mental propositions; they extol emotional and mystic states, and exclaim, Behold, here is something better than good behavior, better than health, superior to scientific interpretation, — behold Religion! Science, armed with all its glasses, curiously investigates this portent that assumes to be divinely accredited, and cannot discover a single germinal dot, not a bit of plasma, that might make one honest animalcule of a spiritual man.

In the mean time, real religion is busy with moral sense, right mental method, true social feeling, ecstatic vision of the divine order, to appropriate every genuine fact and put it to service in its scheme of humanity. However violently science may pretend to be hostile to religion, there is nothing in the world so religious as its method and industry. For religion, instead of being, according to the old definitions, a restoration of rebellious human nature to divine favor, attained by theological beliefs and emotional practices, by prayer and praise, by pietistic exaltations and homiletic absorption, is simply *the recurrence of human nature to the facts of the universe.*

At first, this definition seems to be a dry, pragmatic one, fit only to express that old function of theology which was imperfectly exercised by it in metaphysical notions about the divine plan and nature. Theology always presumed that its statements represented facts. But religion, recovering of late from mediatorial emotions, enlists intelligence, arms itself with a mental method that is the counterpart of the divine plan, and casts loose forever from the speculations of theology. Then it assumes the function of indicating realities; and every fact it gathers is a proclamation of God's law, or will, or wisdom, and an invitation to man to be on healthy terms with these attributes. In recurring to the facts of a universe, man recurs most sensibly to God. But this gesture can be made only with the help of intelligence. Facts must be taught and known, not metaphysical contrivances or scriptural formulas. The brain must learn to act upon its own facts, in order to present the world with a body in normal condition to perform a normal work. The relation between the finite and infinite must be found upon lines of forces and stepping-stones of laws, not upon phrases and ceremonies. These weave no features of the infinite into our life. As well might a woman expect by knitting to embroider the zodiacal light upon her stocking. If she croons a favorite hymn of Watts or Toplady over her work, the sky is still too cunning to descend, being content to overlook her patient labor and to light the daily steps of the little feet she covers. Her automatic action is superior, for religion, to all her darling sentiment.

I close by noticing that science benefits religion with hints at a more practical treatment for the objects of moral and spiritual culture. The technical results of scientific observation now begin to enrich every department of life, as they flow into the kitchen and workshop, and down all the streets; so that a man may draw at his door health and mental nourishment, and find an alarm-box in every ward that will report whatever threatens sanity and comfort. All the kingdoms of nature contribute their economical facts, which slowly find their way into social science, into the methods of domestic life, into education and amusement. Man was never so sumptuously served before with things to depend upon. He learns what to eat, drink, and wear, how to ventilate his dwellings and to build his fire. The most inventive minds teach him labor-saving processes, which aspire even to regulate and economize religion. This prompt and convenient way of life begets a desire for facts: we want nothing encumbering the house that we cannot use; theories go into the waste-basket, with a good many superfine emotions that were once thought to be essential to a spiritual life. Sometimes, by picking over the basket, we discover that gifts very dear to the household, legacies of eternity, have been hastily thrown there, in the greed for clearing out all the corners and ambushes for rubbish, to have nothing around that is not portable and ready for immediate use.

This tendency to bring the art of living down to its practical minimum has gone so far that some sources of spiritual culture have fallen into discredit. The newspaper, the lecture-room, the scientific cabinet, the technological school, the special platform, is commended: men crave exactness and the current intelligence. They long to live creditably in the present, because they have discovered it is the master of the future. And American pulpits have certainly earned the distrust, if not contempt, of the more robust portion of the people, by approaching all the critical moments of the private or public life with their pill, their plaster, or buchu, as they sound the trumpet of the quack before them in the market-place, to call their livelihood together.

There is something which may be called the vestry-sentiment, that acts like choke-damp upon all natural ideas; it will breathe an artificial compound, or prefer to be asphyxiated. A badly ventilated Scripture is responsible for these moods, which cower over their little pile of smouldering texts, and shudder and protest at leaving all the doors ajar. It is nourished upon phrases in books of mediatorial piety, and drops theatre-tears over its futile feeling of dependence, its consciousness of sin, or faded appreciation of good behavior. Its disciples are the victims of fatty degeneration when it is their boast that they are nothing but heart. To some of the churches of this want of faith, intelligence has penetrated far enough to excite suspicions that the old phraseology has been outgrown; they are almost ready to espouse the new Bibles of human information and enthusiasm, not quite ready to cast off the damaged phraseology of the clerical believers in miracles and grace: so that they remind one of the garret of the eminent but rather penurious lawyer, which was found, after his decease, filled with suits of clothes, each labelled, "Too old to wear, but too good to give away."

Verbal statements of imaginary relations between man and God, set off with appeals to a kind of average religiosity, compose the sanitary method of such churches. It lets more blood than it makes:

precious life-drops of the common people, squandered in artificial excitements, in political compromises, and in the awful campaigns that restore natural religion to mankind.

A better method will set in whenever the pulpit prefers confirmed realities, and looks for them in every province that the wit of man visits, — when the only question it asks relative to any subject is, What are the facts? Let us know the conclusion of the best minds and the most devoted hearts, let us preach the salvation that intelligence reveals. Open wide the door of the meeting-house, so that the six days can wheel up to it, and deposit what the earth and sky manufacture, all the certainties of all the arts, and every emotion that bears the stamp of sincerity.

Nothing can come amiss, if it comes from a quarter where honest handwork or head-work has been engaged. The whole universe is let down to the level of the preacher's desk, creeping things as well as winged. The voice says: "Slay and eat them, for there is nothing common or unclean that God has made." Nature has sometimes furnished the pulpit with illustrations: she is ready now to provide the texts and substance also, and to occupy the whole discourse.

But the treatment must be ideal. All the facts, after passing through the technical treatment of the platform, the lecture-room, and scientific session, to receive their diplomas of utility, must come into the pulpit bringing mankind with them, as into a place where separate localities can be seen to melt into one broad horizon, stretching so far that eternity is overtaken and included, and the souls of the spectators are greatly ennobled to perceive that all their little functions build the endless view.

What is ideal treatment? A kind that is neither metaphysical nor traditional. It is not the investiture of subjects with a poetical form, nor the speculative infirmity that broods upon an empty nest. There must be a real egg beneath, for warmth and devoted patience to quicken. The ideal treatment is that deference to the natural law which puts the breath of life into every thing and person; for laws are congenial to the imagination, having indeed been often suckled in her open air, and thence adopted by the family of man. They can never quarrel with her genuine emotions. It would be strange, indeed, if one function of our intelligence should contradict or disable another. In fact, the test of the sacredness of any feeling will be that Law can comfortably dwell with it; and the test of the genuineness of Law will be that it discriminates the truly sacred feelings from moods which counterfeit, and proffers to the former the alliance of a universe. Religion's work is so sweet and awe-inspiring that it resents the waste of time in manipulating the sentimental preference of people who want their whims to be protected against laws. It perceives that the sacramental attitude is less adorable than its own worship of

Truth and Beauty, whose elements it distributes to all communicants, pronouncing them to be the body and the blood of every soul.

Science and religion may together undertake the task of showing that the earth, the air, the water, swarm with vital germs; that no substance is too solid to resist their penetration, none too thin to support them; that man himself is a compendium of them, and in his soul they find a tongue to express how religious they are, how implicated with the life and love of the Creator. Ideal treatment sets forth the ideas that correspond to every fact and circumstance. It is bent upon proving that they arise in the soul, and are not transitory views, or impressions depending upon the position of the spectator, or digested from his food; that they have a continuity in the laws of nature and in the persons of men and women, and are thus connected with the moral order, are self-sustaining, and derive no authority from any source save Nature herself; and that the only religious certitude we can enjoy is provided by the harmony between things, necessities, organizations, and the laws of things.

CHRISTIANITY AND ITS DEFINITIONS.

By William J. Potter.

It is a most significant gauge of the distance which Christendom has travelled away from the primitive conditions of the Christian faith, that the question is now everywhere earnestly discussed within the limits of Christendom itself, what Christianity is. In the early days, unbelievers from the outside are reported to have pressed around the apostles to ask what the new doctrine was whereof they spoke. But we can hardly imagine that there was any inquiry of this kind among those who had caught the holy contagion of the new religion, and with whom it was an enthusiasm of the heart rather than a conviction of the understanding. There was a warm dispute, indeed, between Paul and some of the leading apostles of the original twelve; a dispute which, we can now see, indirectly involved very vital issues bearing on the development of Christianity. And we may easily find, too, in the New Testament, the germs, perhaps, of all the different interpretations of Christianity that have been made; for it is apparent that the new faith presented, even in the earliest days, somewhat different aspects to different classes of believers, according to the angle of mental or moral condition from which it was met and accepted. Still, those primitive believers all gathered at the same rallying-cry, and saw at the centre of Christianity essentially the same thing; and in the dispute between Paul and the other apostles the only question actually raised was with reference to the amount of ceremony to be required of Gentile converts: there seems to have been no division as to the substance of Christianity.

But now the question debated is, What is Christianity itself? What is that which has given it its peculiar character and power? What the vital elements that define it as a specific religion? And to this question, What is Christianity? nearly as many answers will be given as there are Christian sects; for each of the sects has originated in something which its members have regarded as essential to Christianity, and which they have not found in the other sects. Leaving aside, however, minor differences of belief, and all differences in regard to ecclesiastical administration merely, we may group the various definitions of Christianity in some three or four divisions around a few prominent, distinguishing points; though the separate groups will shade into each other by imperceptible gradations of denominational and individual belief.

First, we have what may be called the Orthodox-evangelical definition, — the definition which has prevailed most largely in Christendom, and which is still maintained by the vast majority of the adherents of the Christian church. This definition is that Christianity is a system of religion which rests on the recognition of Jesus of Nazareth as the supernaturally commissioned and therefore authoritative and infallible revealer of spiritual truth, as the Messiah of the world and the Saviour of mankind. There is room for wide latitude of difference in respect both to dogma and ecclesiastical forms among those who set out with this definition. One may accept the trinity or reject it; may believe in vicarious atonement and salvation through Jesus' death on the cross, or only in simple mediatorship through his character and life; may be a Catholic or a Protestant, — receiving the Bible only or the Bible and tradition, as the depository of spiritual truth, — and yet make this definition of Christianity. The essential point of the definition is covered by what is well enough understood under the common theological phrase, "the confession of Christ."

And this definition is based on what was really the beginning of Christianity as an historical religion, the confession of Jesus of Nazareth as *the Christ;* that is, as the expected Messiah of Jewish vision and prophecy. The New Testament makes this sufficiently plain. The demand made on the first disciples, the covenant of the primitive Christian church, was this, and only this: " Believe on the Lord Jesus Christ, and be saved ; believe in him as the Messiah, though crucified ; for he is risen from the grave, and will yet appear as the redeemer of his people." That belief—saying nothing now of what was meant by the Messiahship, nor of the early transformation of the idea; nothing of the strength or weakness of the alleged evidences for the resurrection; nothing of the dogma of sacrificial atonement which was connected very early with the fact of crucifixion and made the ground of salvation — that simple confession of Jesus as the Messiah was what, and all that, defined a Christian when Christianity first began its development as an organized religion. This was the burden of the apostolic preaching; and this too, if we may trust the record of the Gospels, was considered by Jesus himself as a good definition of a disciple. Certainly, if he said what the record puts into his mouth, " Whosoever shall confess me before men, him will I confess also before my Father who is in heaven; but whosoever shall deny me before men, him will I also deny before my Father who is in heaven," — if he said that, then he drew the lines of his communion pretty strictly between those who accepted him as Messiah and those who did not. The record, however, on this point is to be taken with some precaution. But whether Jesus uttered this and other kindred sayings in just the form reported, or whether the reporter and biographer warped what he did say into a narrower and more polemic purpose than he ever intended, it is certain that he did lay claim to the Messiahship in some sense, and that it was on the recognition of this claim and of the spiritual authority with which the Messianic office was believed to invest him, that the discipleship which he attracted eventually developed into the Christian church. Those, therefore, who define Christianity as the confession of Jesus as the Messiah, and as consequently an authoritative Lord and Saviour for mankind, have a strong ground of argument in the earliest records and usage of Christendom. The word "Christianity" itself is standing evidence in favor of their definition. And there can be no reasonable doubt that Christianity historically, as an organized religion, did begin with this confession as defining itself.

But in the course of eighteen centuries it has come to pass that this confession, though continued accurately in terms, means practically something very different from what it did to those primitive followers of Jesus. The confession of Christ has drifted away from its primitive moral and spiritual significance, to be little more than an act of the understanding, or even an act of mere ecclesiastical or social conformity. The moral life has gone out of it, and left it little more than an empty shell. What a vast difference between the actual significance of the confession of Christ to the great majority of Christendom in modern times, — the majority even of those who take an active interest in religious institutions and are church-members, — and what it meant to Peter and Matthew and Paul and Stephen! To those primitive disciples, and for several centuries, to confess Christ to-day meant to go to prison or to the cross to-morrow. To declare one's self a Christian was to declare one's self an outcast from reputable society; it was to take up the most unpopular cause of the time; it was to be ready for any contumely, for any suffering, for any death. To confess Christ then meant mockings and scourgings and bonds; it meant perils by land and sea; it meant cold and hunger and loneliness; it meant living in caves of the earth and in tombs with the dead; it meant being stoned to death by furious mobs, and being thrown for the sport of a jeering populace to contend for life with wild beasts; it meant all that man can do and bear, for the sake of a conviction of truth, against the united opposition of the established government and religion and society, and against the cruelest forms of persecution which the depraved ingenuity of man can devise. All this did it mean practically in those early days to confess Christ, and to call one's self a Christian. And more or less of this was meant by the Christian confession, until Christianity conquered the Roman Empire, or unfortunately was adopted by it, and became itself the established religion. This confession, therefore, in the origin of Christianity was not merely a test of intellectual belief; it was hardly that at all; it was a criterion of character. It was something that tested the inherent manliness in man. It was a touchstone of moral rather than of mental soundness. It was an appeal to what was deepest in the faith of the human heart, and summoned all the forces of human bravery and moral pertinacity and fidelity into the arena of public conflict, to fight for spiritual liberty and for truth oppressed and scourged.

But what does it mean practically to confess Jesus to be the Christ now? Is there any test of character in the act? That is, does the bare confession of belief in Christ compel character to any such test as it did then? Does it necessarily bring any popular reproach? Does it cost the sacrifice of one's good name? One can but smile, indeed, at the contrast between the Christian of to-day and the Christian of that early time. In all the leading nations of the world, the Christian to-day is in the majority; he is on the popular side; the sword is in *his* hands; wealth and worldly opportunity are with him; respectability and fashion give him their indorsement. It is not the man who confesses himself a Christian, but the man who confesses that he is an infidel to Christian belief, who to-day is likely to lose position and honor and to fall under the social ban, and has to bear the cross of popular odium for his confession. Even the mobs are Christian to-day, and in their frenzied profanity swear by the name of the holy Nazarene; which no man in a mob of Paul's time could have done without challenging the violence of his fellow-mobocrats as being himself traitorously a Christian. Of course it is not asserted that all these people who are counted as Christians — the mobs, the foolish players with fashion, the worldly and the powerful — are regarded as really Christian in their hearts and lives: that touches a sense of the word which we have not yet considered. But so far as to confess Jesus of Nazareth to be the Christ, and to accept him as an infallible religious authority, makes and defines a Christian, which was the original definition, they are so; for they give an intellectual or a traditional assent to that confession, and are accordingly counted in the world's census as Christians.

Let me not be misunderstood. The point now made is simply this, — that, owing to the changed outward conditions of Christianity, to acknowledge Jesus as an authoritative messenger from God does not in modern times, as it did in the early centuries, necessarily require moral heroism. The confession has become a part of the common stock of hereditary opinion in Christendom. And even to the majority of those who take pains to assume the name Christian, and who connect themselves with religious institutions, and become the active partisans of Christianity, the confession costs little more than a walk or drive to a comfortable, perhaps luxuriously appointed church, on Sunday, and an annual ecclesiastical tax. And even this much of cost is often expected to be paid back in improved social and business position, the *sacrifice* being very shrewdly invested where it will realize most rapidly in these expectations of social or business success. It is an open fact that men going to new places to set up in business — young lawyers, physicians, merchants, teachers — often seek an eligible church relationship in order to secure a good business constituency, just as shop-keepers seek a good stand for their trade. A young lawyer goes to New York to begin his professional career. Ambitious, determined to win position, not very scrupulous concerning the means, after he has hung out his sign in Wall Street, he hires a seat in one of the fashionable up-town churches, and takes a class in its Sunday school. He does it, as he does not hesitate to say, not because he has any faith in the religion there taught, or in any religion; but to advertise himself, and get the *entrée* of New-York society. And so long as he has need of the advertisement he keeps his interest in the church and the Sunday school; though his life through the week may give the lie to all that he says and does in church on Sunday. And this is no imaginary case. Who does not know that much of the church-going in modern days, and much of the support that is given to religious institutions, is of this character? It is largely an act of religious conformity for the sake of social or business success, without the slightest basis in religious sentiment or principle. It must have been one of this class of modern confessors of Christ whose principles seem to follow their interests, who, having been driven out of his Unitarian pew into an Episcopal church by the disagreeable politics of his old minister, and being rallied one Sunday morning by one of his Unitarian neighbors on the Service Book under his arm, replied with dignified piety, " This is my *Lethargy*." What an exquisite satire — all the more for being an unconscious Mrs. Partingtonism — on the objects and methods of very much that calls itself Christian worship in modern times? An æsthetic device for lulling reason and conscience to sleep! I suppose it may be quite safely asserted that half of the stock-manipulators and gold-gamblers in New York are regular attendants of churches, and would make a perfectly orthodox confession of faith. Some of them are noted for their zealous piety, for their efficiency in prayer-meetings, and for their generosity, too, in handing over to Jesus what they have cheated out of their own confederates in financial wickedness. What wonder, seeing that such men can be accounted Christians, that speculation and the gambling spirit have got into the church itself, and that many ecclesiastical corporations are conducted upon the same principles upon which the great stock companies are managed! The same skill that successfully " waters " railroad stocks is invited and welcomed to try its hand at " watering " the gospel.

We hear much said in recent days about the irreligious tendencies of people as manifested in the multitudes who do not go to any church; and the prospect is in some respects bad. Yet, to my mind, there is a thousand-fold more ground for solicitude concerning the moral and spiritual welfare of society, in the fact that there are so many habitual church-goers who are no more religious in their characters and lives than if they had no contact whatever with religious institutions, and to whom religious habits have only become a convenient cloak, not only to cover the want of real moral and spiritual earnestness, but to conceal decently from the public eye positive moral deformity and rottenness. To such an extent does the insincerity prevail, that it is a wonder the maskers, as they meet in their Sunday pilgrimages to their respective churches, do not peep out from under their masks to laugh at each other's attempt at pious deceit. The deceit, however, has a sort of conventional success. At least the mask answers its purpose of advertising where the wearer is, and in what social circle he may be found. As to character, it cannot be said to vouch for, nor perhaps to impeach that. For, to the shame of Christendom, it must be confessed that no sagacious man trusts another any sooner for being an attendant or member of a church, or for calling himself a Christian. If one wants testimonials of character that are of mercantile value, he knows he must have something more than a certificate of church-membership. So little does a mere confession of belief in Christ remain in any way as a test of character!

And so patent has this fact become, that many people in Christendom — some of them attached to the church, but more, probably, outside of the church — have refused to define Christianity any longer by this old phrase, "the confession of Christ." Even those Orthodox sects that assert intellectual belief in Christ to be essential will say that there must be something more than a mere lip-confession: the confession, they add, must be experimental and of the heart. The most enlightened teachers of Orthodoxy, while they assert that the moral life of society can have no security without a belief in Christianity, will reject the idea that there can be any real Christianity in those people who do not connect their confession of belief in it with purity of morals. And full justice must be done to this distinction. It is an attempt to restore to the act of confessing Christ something of its old moral significance; and there are, as all must most gladly acknowledge, very many noble men and women who sincerely believe that the confession of Christ requires of them to-day something of the same practical, self-denying life of simplicity and charity which was assumed by Jesus himself, and something of the same struggle against the power of fashion and popular applause which was forced upon the primitive disciples. But that it is exceedingly difficult, if not impossible, to maintain this distinction in an entire Christian community, the confessedly worldly condition of the Christian church itself bears conclusive evidence. The idea of confessing Christ by some technical mental experience has become ingrained in the very organization of Orthodoxy. Ministers of Calvinistic belief have admitted that the most discouraging fact in their professional experience has been, that the people under their charge have been accustomed to make so little connection between a confession of Christian faith and the practice of Christian morality; that it had so frequently happened that those who were foremost in their professions of religion, and zealous talkers for Christ in conference-meetings, and who were reputed to be Christian men and women, were not only not distinguished above others in respect to moral practice, but were positively wanting in the common virtues of truthfulness, integrity, and charity: so that it could hardly be claimed that church-members were, as a rule, better men and women than those attendants of churches who had never made any confession of Christian belief.

But many other people have gone still further in the attempt to rectify the old definition of Christianity. Seeing what delusion and hypocrisy are possible so long as a confession of belief in Christ is made the essential thing in Christianity, they deny that such confession is in any form the essential thing. They look into the New Testament, and they say, that, though Jesus claimed to be the Messiah, and seems also to have taught the importance of being accepted as such, yet this was not the main thing in his teaching or his work. What he did teach as essential to vital religion, they claim, was love to God and love to man; the fatherhood of God, the brotherhood of man. It is said, for instance, that the essence of

Christianity is contained in the sentence, "Bear ye one another's burdens;" and that that man is a Christian, no matter what he believes or does not believe, whose life and ethics grow out of this central root of Christianity. Others say, meaning substantially the same thing, that Christianity is synonymous with goodness; that the man who is just, generous, loving, reverent, humane, whatever his belief, is the Christian man. What are the dispositions and affections of the heart, what the grand aim of the character, what fruit is borne in the life, — these, they allege, are the test questions in the gospels. And hence another definition of Christianity has arisen, which may be called the Liberal-evangelical definition; not, however, that it is coincident entirely with the so-called liberal Christian sects, and not found in any others. It may be found to some extent in all the sects. There are ministers in Evangelical sects who preach it more than some of the prominent clergymen of the Unitarian and Universalist denominations. According to this definition, Christianity is the substance of what Jesus himself taught, — that is, God's love to man and man's love to God and to his fellow-men, — and does not consist in any doctrine about Jesus; and the Christian is one who lives habitually in the same attitude towards God and man as did Jesus. The definition is to be called *evangelical* as well as *liberal*, since it professes to find its authority in the Gospels.

Now abundant argument can be found for this

definition of Christianity in the New Testament, and especially in the reputed words of Jesus himself. For even if he said, "Whosoever shall confess me before men, him will I confess also before my Father who is in heaven; but whosoever shall deny me before men, him will I also deny before my Father who is in heaven,"—he may have been thinking of such people as Nicodemus, who had not the moral courage to come to him by daylight, and so did not really belong to his communion: for he said, too, "Not every one that saith unto me, Lord, Lord, shall enter into the kingdom of heaven, but he that doeth the will of my Father," where he clearly puts the doing of the divine will before any personal homage to himself. If we are to take the Sermon on the Mount, and the larger and more important of the parables, as embodying the substance of Jesus' teachings, it does seem as if we might very accurately sum them up in the formula, "Love of God and man." The Sermon on the Mount, though probably never uttered by Jesus as it stands, yet, in its relation to the biography of him in the first Gospel, appears in the character of an inaugural discourse, setting forth the main principles of his public teaching. And they are certainly such as would not be regarded as a sufficient qualification for admitting him to membership in any of the so-called evangelical churches which make him their head. In the parable of the Good Samaritan, under the characters of the priest and the levite, he clearly rebukes the orthodox and ceremonial religion of the time, and selects the heretical, despised, and outcast Samaritan as the example of the kind of piety in which he believed.

But a stronger argument for that definition of Christianity which we are now considering than any reputed discourses or words of Jesus, is his general attitude towards his nation and its beliefs and institutions; and concerning his general attitude there can be no doubt. However fragmentary and uncertain may be the biographical accounts of his career, we instinctively feel that Jesus was the great Radical of his age. He was the moral and religious reformer; the dangerous innovator; the pestilent agitator; the believer in an ideal; the champion of humanity against the tyranny of institutions; the ecclesiastical and social revolutionist; the determined, merciless foe of cant and hypocrisy and a mere traditional piety; the Hebrew Protestant, who fought, almost single-handed, against the whole organized power of the Mosaic religion, though it was backed by the Roman Empire, and who, so fighting, was hunted down at last by a conspiracy between the synagogue and the state, and died a martyr to his faith and his fidelity. The heroic heart of the world does not easily give over such a character to a few sonorous phrases bandied between pulpit and pew, in the exclusive service of the very kind of conservative and traditional piety against which it was once a living protest. The character of Jesus, and the movement in which Christianity began, are instinctively felt to be in the interest of human progress and freedom, — in the interests of the rights of man as against the power of superstition and the authority of ecclesiasticism; and hence they have always furnished argument and stimulus to social and religious reformers, to the Savonarolas and Luthers and Garrisons and Theodore Parkers, to the outcast, persecuted, and martyred minorities, in all the centuries since the Christian era. Against Christianity as it is, both in the church and in society, some of the mightiest weapons that have been hurled have been easily found in its own original armory.

This definition, therefore, that identifies Christianity with the main substance of Jesus' teachings, — with the general drift and emphasis of his work, — is doubtless correct so far as it attempts to define the essential principles which lay underneath his specific teaching and mission. And it establishes a very broad basis of fellowship, — broader than has ever been realized in any Christian church or sect. By it those may really be Christians who are not called so, and who do not even call themselves so, or who have never even heard of Jesus. By this definition, as has been well said, "There are men called infidels who really are Christians, as also there are men calling themselves Christians who really are infidels." Those Jews in Baltimore who, though no circular was sent to them when the Northern appeal for educating the freedmen was forwarded to the churches of that city, were yet among the first to respond to it, were by this definition more Christian than the Christian churches that let the appeal go unread and unanswered.

But, though this definition of Christianity which keeps in sight only the spiritual and ethical substance of Jesus' teachings, is a very natural one, and will do, and has already done, excellent service as a reaction against the moral inadequacy of the more Orthodox definition previously spoken of, yet it may be questioned whether historically it is strictly true, and whether it really meets and explains all the facts in the case. It is not meant to explain and cover all the events and facts in Christian history. It throws many of them aside as corruptions. But the deeper question comes, — does it adequately explain the origin of Christianity? does it account for the phenomena attending that wonderful renewal of religious life and thought which made the Christian epoch? Would the simple preaching of the doctrine of the Love of God and Man, even by the greatest of Jewish prophets, have brought at that time a new religion? The doctrine in itself is not new, not distinctively Christian: it belongs to Judaism; and Jesus himself, in his most explicit statement of it, simply quoted from the law of Moses, "Thou shalt love the Lord thy God with all thy heart and soul and strength, and thy neighbor as thyself." This was the essence of the Hebrew religion. It may be said to be the essence, the seed-germ, the important and permanent thing, in all religions. But the question is, Is it an adequate statement of what Christianity actually is as a specific religious system? It may be more important than that statement; but is it that statement? It certainly does not distinguish Christianity from other forms of religion. The liberal Jew will make precisely the same claim for his religion; the reformed Hindu and the Parsee, the same for theirs. If Christianity means simply natural reverence and goodness, if its whole significance is covered by the phrase, "love to God and man," why a new word to represent that old thing? How did the new word arise? Let it be that Christianity is only a new phase of an old sentiment. Have we then truly defined Christianity when we have defined the old sentiment, and left aside just that which marks a new phase? To define Christianity as love to God and man, is to make it independent of any specific form or phase or teacher; independent of Jesus himself. Is it therefore a correct definition of Christianity?

The inadequacy of the definition, certainly, from an historical point of view, has long been felt even by the liberal portion of Christendom; and hence there has come up in these later years a supplement to it in what we may call the Sentimental-historical definition; using the word *sentimental*, not with any intention of casting slight on the view of Christianity thus characterized, but because this representation is an attempt to explain Christianity by allowing more than does the preceding definition to the action of the emotional side of religion, and because it lays special emphasis on the reverence and love excited by the personal character of Jesus, and brings into central prominence the influence of his personality itself. And it is to be called *historical*, because it emphasizes the actual facts of Jesus' career. According to this view, Christianity arose in an unbounded enthusiasm for the person of Jesus, and, through the personal magnetism of his character, for the ideas which he preached; an enthusiasm for the kingdom of God as coming through him, its earthly head and representative. He, from this point of view, is the hero of this great religious revolution; the central figure of the whole world's history, summing up in himself all that was past, and prophetic and typical of all that was future: and so he still remains, the ideal, representative man, holding, by virtue of his consummate spiritual intelligence, and the historic results of his character and life, the place of headship to the human race. And Christianity from this point of view may be defined as the fellowship of those who recognize Jesus in this historic position, and acknowledge in any way their personal allegiance to him. This view is represented by such books as the English "Ecce Homo," by Schenkel in Germany, by Renan in France, and by our own beloved Dr. Furness in America. All these authors, and the school to which they belong, though differing widely on many points among themselves, yet agree in this, — that to write truly the biography of Jesus is to define Christianity both in its origin and its continued inspiration, and that the new spirit coming into the world through the personal power of his life is the bond of the Christian fellowship and the source and strength of Christian faith.

Now this class of writers deserve high honor for the real service they have done in rescuing Christian history from narrow dogmatists, who have heretofore done most of the historical writing in its interest, and in restoring to the character of Jesus and his times the vividness of human reality and personal life, — features greatly wanting in the representation of those who would make Christianity nothing more than a new proclamation of old spiritual and ethical truths. They have attempted to write Christian history, and to describe the character of Jesus, as if both were human; and so have succeeded in giving a picture of both that has touched the hearts of all readers, and drawn them back into living sympathy with the experiences of those early times. And to this extent they have made a real contribution to the true history of Christianity.

Yet their statement of Christianity is defective, for the reason that to dissolve history into biography must always give unsound history. It is to commit the same error that Carlyle makes, when he selects a few heroes and writes their lives for the life of mankind during their times. The method gives us no true philosophy of events, nor of character. It misses the great forces that lie back of events, — the great providential forces of race, of country, of climate, of ideas, of institutions and temperaments, — that help to mould events and to make character. And hence this method of defining Christianity does not sufficiently take into account the antecedent elements in other religions which came by natural descent into Christianity at its origin, nor the popular ideas which went into it while it was in process of organization, nor the contributions that came to it from contact with other modes of thought and from emigration to other lands and peoples after the time of Jesus. It gives us a picturesque drama of Christianity, but not its philosophy, and therefore not its true history nor definition.

The attempt, too, to resuscitate at this day the old feeling of attachment and fealty to the person of Jesus, which animated the hearts of the first disciples, and to make that the fountain and inspiration of religion to this age, must be futile. We cannot, indeed, study his life without constant admiration of his wisdom, and without learning to love and reverence the rare beauty of his character; we may even adopt him as our spiritual example and authoritative religious teacher; or, as many do, come to worship him as Deity: but it is impossible to revive in our hearts the active personal enthusiasm for him as a living, human being, which was felt towards him by those who heard the words from his own lips, who touched the warm brotherly blood in his hand, and to whom his face and character were familiar by daily intercourse. The communion that gathers about him now must be held by the force of ideas, and not by the ties of personal magnetism.

And it is remarkable how soon the influence of Jesus as a person seems to have passed away after his death, and how quickly his official character as Messiah, and the dogmas which were woven about him as filling that position, came in to take the place of personal recollections. One of the most striking features of Paul's epistles is the absence from them of allusions to the personal career of Jesus. There is in them all hardly a reference to any thing that Jesus said or did; and yet some of them are the earliest extant records of Christianity. Though Paul had had no personal acquaintance with Jesus, it is yet strange that he should not have been the medium of preserving some of the multitudinous personal traditions about him which, one would suppose, must have come to his knowledge. And this fact can only be explained by the hypothesis that it was not so much the personal character of Jesus which made its impress upon Paul's mind as his official character, — a supposition which is abundantly supported by evidence which fills his epistles. He seems even to have taken pride in not knowing Jesus after the flesh; and shows throughout his writings that it was his own ideal conception of Jesus' position in a providential plan of salvation that was the animating impulse of his enthusiastic faith and labors. And this was clearly the case, too, with others among the earliest Christian believers and laborers. And to-day, when it is claimed that Jesus is felt as a personal friend, especially by the poor and wronged and suffering, we may find the ground of the claim in the fragrant memory of his human life of devotion to all forms of disease and distress, which tenderly mingles with the dogmatic idea of him as the continued administrator of the divine mercy by virtue of his place in the Godhead or in a special providential scheme of human redemption.

And so we must seek another statement of Christianity still, — something more comprehensive and more scientific than either of the definitions we have considered. Each of these marks an important part of Christianity, but not the whole; and none of them is consistent with any philosophy of Christian history. What we want is a statement which we may call the Scientific-historical definition of Christianity. The great modern civil historians attempt not only to gather up and set forth in order the events of communities and nations and the doings and influence of leading persons, — they attempt not simply to tell what happened, but to trace back events to ideas and principles, and to show the relations that exist between persons and the impersonal laws and forces with which persons deal. And we shall not have Christianity set in its true position in the world's history until we have its history written from this point of view, — until we come to see it, not as a piece by itself, interjected into the general course of history through the power of any person, however eminent in wisdom or character, but as a fluent, social force, the momentum and resultant of many confluent religious and moral ideas, and of many generations of thought and sentiment and action, — not beginning with Jesus, nor confined to Hebrew history alone, yet coming to specific organization and activity through the instrumentality of the Hebrew Messianic idea, and through the spiritual genius and power of the Hebrew prophet, Jesus of Nazareth, as the accepted representative of the Messianic office; not leaping, however, as a completely organized system even from his brain and heart, but enlarging and essentially transforming the Messianic conception, its own instrument, in order to meet the religious demands of the age; and, as it proceeded in its work of organization, assimilating to itself various other ideas and modes of thought foreign to the Hebrew faith and to the views of Jesus; receiving in its course contributions from different climes and nations and persons and philosophies, and modifying its nature as well as its volume by these fresh increments to its constituent elements, until it has grown from a small, despised, persecuted, and, to our modern ideas, a somewhat ascetical and fanatical Jewish sect, into the gigantic religious and social power, interpenetrating almost all modern life with its influence and modern civilization with its machinery, which we see Christianity to be to-day.

And when we have the history of Christianity written from this stand-point of scientific philosophy, we shall see that it is indeed true that its most vital and durable elements are not specifically and exclusively its own, but are universal, — such as the doctrines of the divine fatherhood and human brotherhood, — and that in a very important sense, therefore, Christianity did not begin with the Christian era. We shall find its roots far back of that epoch, far older and deeper than the popular estimate would reckon them. It was the appearing above the soil of society, in new and more powerful combinations, of elements that had long been active beneath. It was the natural ripening of religious ideas and aspirations, which had long been living and growing in the human mind, into a definite form of organization and activity. Its coming was inevitable. It would have come in some form, or some new religion would have appeared corresponding to it, though Jesus had never lived ; yet in the unfolding of the infinite plan of human history he was the leader whose large and strong personality helped to concentrate the stirring religious elements of the time, and to shape them to a definite purpose and end. But he did not make the religious crisis ; that was prepared for him. He did not introduce the ideas which made the constituent elements of Christianity; they were before him, and helped to make him what he was; and he sought and could have no higher office than to be their faithful interpreter, their devoted instrument. The old religions fell away, because pushed off by the growing life of the religious aspirations and ideas that were astir in the popular heart, and Christianity came as the natural result and expression of those aspirations and ideas, — just as in political progress the growing conviction of national freedom and justice and power in the heart of a people is finally able to push off a despotic and outgrown monarchy, and put a freer and higher form of government in its place.

But such political revolutions sometimes fail for the want of a fit leader, — for the lack of some one representative man of strong personal characteristics who harmoniously combines in his own nature the progressive but still somewhat uncertain aspirations, convictions, and will of the people. America had such a man in Washington. The great political reformation in France in the eighth and ninth centuries was specially embodied in Charlemagne. And the religious revolution that brought Christianity had its leader in Jesus. A philosophic statement of Christianity, therefore, will not trace every thing to universal principles and impersonal ideas working in the minds of men in mass. It will take due account of the increased power of ideas when embodied in such a life-giving and commanding personality as was possessed by Jesus. It will show that it was the force of his religious genius which persuaded people into accepting him as the Messiah, although he came with none of the expected royal insignia of the Messianic office ; that it was the inherent authority of the truth he saw and proclaimed, and the tender humanity animating his heart, which drew the multitudes to follow after his steps, and to hang upon the gracious words that proceeded out of his mouth. A true philosophy of the origin of Christianity will detect the inner spiritual fact, that the people who accepted him were convinced that he must be the Messiah, not so much because he so announced himself and gave outward proof of the office, as because their own yearning, aching hearts instinctively felt in his virtue the secret of their own healing and blessedness. A peasant by birth and training, inheriting neither noble blood nor culture nor social rank and opportunity, with aid from neither synagogue nor state, it was the power of his personal genius as a religious teacher and reformer that elevated him to the Messianic office.

But after all, great and pure as he was, it was not Jesus the man, but Jesus the Messiah, who was the recognized founder of the new religion. And hence a scientific statement of Christianity must take account not only of its universal elements, and of the personal power of Jesus, but also of his Messianic office. For the medium through which these universal elements were concentrated into such specific concrete shape as to make a new religious era, and the instrument with which Jesus worked as the prophet of the era, was the Hebrew Messianic idea. The service of this idea in the first organization of the primitive elements of Christianity can hardly be overestimated. In that childlike age, among a childlike people, something more was needed than a bare proclamation of moral and spiritual truth, with whatever power of personal genius. And this need was supplied by the old Hebrew conception of the speedy coming of the Messianic kingdom, — a conception that appealed with all the vividness of a drama to the spiritual imagination and hopes and fears of men. This idea is the one thread of unity that runs through all the varieties of writings in the New Testament from Matthew to Revelation. It was this that gradually lifted Jesus himself out of all human and historic proportions into the colossal magnitude in which he has been seen by Christendom for eighteen centuries. It was the belief, after his crucifixion, in his second Messianic advent — an event which his followers looked for in their lifetime — that gave the immediate animating impulse to their cause, and attracted such numbers of people to confess him as the expected Christ; for this advent was to solve all life's trials and perplexities; it was to bring redemption to the sinful, rest to the weary, wealth to the destitute, and comfort to the sorrowing. And around this simple, childish hope, which was yet full to bursting with the deep life of spiritual aspirations and yearnings, the first Christian church was gathered, — a sect of Judaism accepting Jesus as the Messiah, and looking for his second coming to complete and establish his sovereignty.

But Christianity was early moulded by external influences, as well as by its internal idea; and of these its scientific history must also take note. This process began even in the apostolic days. Paul and Apollos and others, bred in the Grecian school of culture, soon appeared on the stage by the side of the original apostles; and from them the Christian movement received a new tone of thought, and took a new direction and a broader way.

Paul, the most important of this new class of apostles, and the greatest intellect of the primitive Christian period, emphasized, as has already been intimated, still more than did the original apostles, the official character of Jesus; and, what is of more moment, he attached new ideas to the Messianic office. With him began that interpretation of the crucifixion which made it a sacrificial atonement, breaking the power of the Mosaic law, and introducing a new dispensation of faith and love, — a dogma which has played a very influential part in Christian history. He opened Christianity too — another most momentous change — to the Gentile world, and sought to bring Gentile and Jew into one fellowship through the uniting bond of faith in the Christ. And we may find perhaps in him, certainly in the author of the Epistle to the Hebrews which proceeded from his apostolic circle, the germ of the idea that the Christ was pre-existent, the first-born Son of God and the Creator of the world; and that in his earthly Messianic character he was a miraculous incarnation of Divinity, and redeemed the world by sharing its infirmities and bearing its sins in his own divine person. This dogma, which we find developed to some extent at least in the Epistle to the Hebrews and in the fourth Gospel, and which is a great transformation of the Hebrew Messianic idea, was largely instrumental in making Christianity acceptable after it had passed westward beyond the limits of Palestine, and into countries where the Hebrew conception in its original form could have little power.

Christianity, indeed, under Paul effected, as has been well said, "a change of base." Jesus came to be represented, not only as the Messiah of the Jew, but as the Messiah and Saviour of the world; and Christianity was enlarged by new ideas and aspirations, and its power increased by the adoption of a more logical method of thought. From being a small Jewish sect, it advanced to the hope of becoming a universal religion.

That was the first great change; the precursor of all changes, some of them for good and some for evil, that have followed in Christian history. Christianity then began the process, we might almost say the policy, of adapting itself to the varied conditions, as to intelligence and temperament, of the people it was to serve. As it was open to Gentile believers, it became conformed quite as much to the traditions of their ancient faith as to the Hebrew. It was through the power of pagan philosophical and religious ideas that Jesus was gradually idealized from the Jewish Messiah into a demigod, and then to a place in the Godhead itself. It was through the power of pagan traditions that the doctrine of the Trinity was developed, that the saints were elevated into the niches of the ancient gods and goddesses to be worshipped, and that the magnificent ceremonies of symbolic sacrifice, such as we see now in the Roman Catholic Church, were established. Nor would any philosophical statement of Christianity be complete which should not especially show how much it owed its progress, at a very early period, to the practical organizing and aggressive power which it learned from the Roman Empire, even before the Empire came under its nominal sway; and how the Papal ecclesiastical system which finally resulted — with its supreme monarch at Rome, with its combination of spiritual and temporal sovereignty, with its royal pomp and wide-spread dominion and marvellous vigor of organization even to the minutest details — was the legitimate issue of the marriage of the religion of the Christ to the empire of the Cæsars.

In the old half-ruined castle at Heidelberg, on the beautiful façade of Otto Heinrich's building, are to be seen images of Old-Testament heroes, mingled promiscuously with figures from Greek mythology, and busts of Roman emperors of pagan days, and allegorical representations of Christian graces; while above the whole stand colossal statues of Jupiter and Pluto, which no shocks of war nor ravages of weather have been able to shake from their solid pedestals. So do pagan ideas still reign over large portions of Christendom; and this well-preserved wall, commemorating so many ideas and times, finally illustrates how the united contributions of Hebrew, Greek, and Roman nationalities have gone into the construction of the religion which holds the memory of the gracious virtues of Jesus.

Christianity, however, has been open not only to the reception of old tradition, but to the forces of advancing civilization, of progressive thought and reason. It has taken shape according to the taste and temperament and mental and moral vigor of the people accepting it, — among the passional, warm-blooded nations of the South, or among an excitable and æsthetic people in any climate, developing into gorgeousness of form, into ritual and architecture and symbolism. Among a people more thoughtful, critical, individual, and cold-blooded, it has been more fruitful in logical systems of theology and practical righteousness. In Germany and England, it yielded after a stormy conflict to the Saxon spirit of free inquiry and the demands of individual reason, and gave shel-

CHRISTIANITY AND ITS DEFINITIONS. 211

ter to the Reformation and Protestantism. The claim often made by Christian writers that all the distinguishing and beneficent characteristics of modern civilization in Christendom — its science, literature, diffusion of knowledge, free thought, mental and material enterprise, progress in government and in useful discoveries and arts — are to be referred back for their source to primitive Christianity, is most futile in the light of actual history. The same forces that may be said to have brought the Protestant Revolution in Christendom, were the productive causes of these special features of modern civilization; and Christianity did not carry these germinal forces in its bosom from the time of its own birth, but found them in the mental temperament of the nations of Northern Europe and in the atmosphere of a new mental era which had set in without much of its aid. The most that can be justly claimed for Christianity is that a large section of the Christian church yielded to the influence of these forces, and honestly attempted to assimilate the new ideas and spirit of the age to its old faith. And so in the history of Protestantism, the Christian faith has again and again given way before the rights of private judgment, and recognized the formation of sect after sect to embody some new theological thought, or some new interpretation of an old thought, till it covers almost every phase of religious opinion that is found in the world, and almost every form of worship, from the practice of Fetichism to the silent communion of the soul with the Infinite. In fine, Christianity in its historical development, since it became the recognized religion of the modern civilized world, while it has been tethered fast on one side by the immovable organization of the Roman Catholic Church, has been free on the other to follow the advance of public opinion, though always halting behind the most progressive pioneers of opinion. Never leading public opinion, never taking the initiative in any forward step, it yet has yielded and given voice to beliefs that have been accepted by any considerable number of minds, and conformed in progress to the average intelligence and moral convictions of the people adopting it.

Whether Christianity shall make still further advance in order to receive the new thought and science of this age, and stand ready to respond to all the demands of reason and reform, and be able to become the permanent religion of the world, is the question which now confronts us. The question is twofold, — First, what are the probabilities in respect to the future progress of Christianity? And, second, is Christianity likely to become the permanent and universal religion of mankind? Through our answer to the first question we shall reach the answer to the second.

There is surely no ground for asserting that there is to be no further progress in Christian history. On the contrary, Christendom is most certainly tending by direct steps to the adoption of this rational view of its own history which I have here attempted to indicate, far from it as the majority of the Christian church may now appear to be. The signs of the times point thither; the movement is in this direction. The later books about Jesus and his times that have excited the most interest are all attempts to set the career of Jesus in natural relations with the world. Rationalism appears in the very citadels of Orthodoxy. Half of the Church of England is converted to rationalistic views. Germany, Switzerland, Italy, are fast ripening for a new Protestantism freer than the old. The old dogmas of Calvinism are passing away in churches nominally Calvinistic, or are appearing under rationalistic forms of interpretation. Even the popular missionaries of the Roman Catholic Church make their appeals for converts on the ground that Catholicism harmonizes with the freest reason; and a large section of the Church of Rome seems ready to revolt in the interest of reason against further reactionary attempts to centralize power in the Pope. Meantime, science and literature outside of the church, though in the territorial limits of Christendom, are working everywhere in the interest of spiritual liberty and a rationalistic interpretation of Christianity. Science makes constant war on the very idea of miracle, — of miracle in the procedure of history, no less than in the mechanics of the universe. Rarely now by any scholarly writer of any sect do we find the old idea of miracle advocated. Instead of being regarded as a direct abrogation of natural law by supernatural will, miracle is now pretty generally interpreted as the temporary action of some higher law, just as natural, though rarer in its operations; and some theological writers even go so far as to affirm that reason may yet explain miracles, — a concession that substantially abandons the miracle-idea; as does also the use by many modern theologians of the word *supernatural* in the sense of *spiritual*. Such reasoning only indicates the path by which Christendom is to pass from the common view of its religion, which makes it a supernatural and mysterious interpolation into the general course of events, to the rational and scientific view, which puts it into natural relations with all history. That this passage is to be made, and that this latter is to be the ultimate and generally accepted view of Christianity, we may feel just as sure as we are that reason will finally dispel superstition, and that the light of to-morrow's sun will scatter the darkness of this coming night.

Not very soon will this step be made by the great majority of the Christian church; but at some day in the future it must be made, unless we are to have the singular spectacle of a cessation of progress in religious ideas, while people shall be advancing in all other directions of thought. But this will not be. Christianity will be forced to conform to the fresh thought of the age; it must be moulded by advancing science and reason; it must follow in the current of modern civilization.

And all of it that does not so follow must be left behind to perish as an effete institution. Already there are signs that Christianity in its dogmatic and instituted forms is disintegrating. The tendency to identify it with its universal elements of truth and love is strong in all the sects. Already its freest thinkers and most rationalistic sects are at the very limit of the way down which it is possible to carry the banner of a supernatural religion. They have developed Christianity to the utmost verge it will bear as a supernatural system. One step further, and the thin wall of supernaturalism which has hitherto served to protect Christianity as a specific religious system is broken through, and they stand over the line on the ground of natural religion. Some of them are already over, and are calling back to those lingering on the line that the ground is solid, that the imagined pitfalls are not there, and that the way is clear and bright, and stretches before them into the illimitable truth.

And now we reach the answer to the second question, — Is Christianity to be the permanent religion for man, destined to convert and absorb all other faiths? And we may answer this question by putting another in this form: As soon as Christianity comes thus to be recognized, in Christendom generally, as a natural phase in the progress of natural religious ideas and forces, and Jesus is put in the line of our natural humanity, will it not follow that Christianity will then lose just those things which have made it a specific religion, and hence, as such, cease to exist? The belief in the Messianic character of Jesus, or in his having been more than a naturally endowed man, will then have passed away. He will stand by the side of other great religious teachers and prophets, with no authority different from theirs; and the New Testament will take its place among other religious books of the past, of precious value, but to be submitted in all its parts to the rational judgment of mankind. The Christian-born man will then stand, not as having found a finality in religious truth in some past authoritative revelation, but as a *truth-seeker*, — gratefully recognizing and using all that the past has to give him, but keeping his face towards the future, and looking for revelations to come out of the infinite word of truth that shall eclipse in glory all revelations that have preceded. He will stand with no infallibly authorized religion behind him; with no exceptionally inspired teacher, no exceptionally written books, as his standards; with no Lord less than the Infinite for his spiritual Sovereign. His own mind, through which pulses the vital energy of the universal life, must supply his authority, and cultured reason furnish him the standard by which all books and teachers and revelations are to be judged. He will see that Christianity, like Judaism before it, is provisional, preparatory, educational; containing, alongside of the most valuable truth, much that is only human error and bigotry and superstitious imagination; and that it will only have truly accomplished its providential

CHRISTIANITY AND ITS DEFINITIONS. 217

mission when it shall have opened into a form of faith that shall adhere to natural law, and not to miraculous interjections of power, as the manifestation of the Divine Mind both in things material and things spiritual.

But though the Christian-born man, taking this view of his religion, will have no specific revelation behind him, no past which he is to take on implicit trust as religious authority, yet the whole of the past — not only Christianity, but the religions before it — will have contributed to the formation of the solid ground on which he will feel his feet to be planted. He will not have narrowed his religious sympathies, but widened them; nor lost religious and moral teachers, but added to them. The number of his saints and heroes will have increased rather than diminished. And beneath him, feeding the very life which he shall live, will be the religious thoughts and experiences, the struggles and triumphs, the wisdom and prophecy and aspiration, the integrity and virtue and beatitude, of all the races and ages and religions that have ever existed. By the growing light of human intelligence, kept burning by continued connection with the eternally vitalizing power of truth, he will select the good and true from all, while the evil and false he will leave aside.

In fact, the "Christian," in the historic and ecclesiastical sense, will then be no more. If the name shall linger, the old meaning will have gone out of it, never to return. But even the name cannot remain, if it shall stand in the way of that large and generous fellowship which the spirit of this epoch is striving to effect. When men shall come even to that point that they say that every man is a Christian who shares his brother's burden, no matter whether as to faith he is Mohammedan or Confucian or Infidel, they will not deem the name Christian a very important one to keep, but, forgetting names, will join hands in the fellowship of fraternal love and good works.

And it is not alone in Christendom that there are indications of this coming broader fellowship. The old Hebrew faith has not been stagnant during these eighteen hundred years since Christianity parted company with it. It, too, especially in these latter years, has been progressing; so that now between the most advanced Jews and the most progressive portion of Christendom there is scarcely a shade of difference in theological belief. Following their present tendencies, these pioneer divisions must inevitably come together. But why should the Jew take the name of the Christian, more than the Christian the name of the Jew? Or, in India, why should that growing and already vigorous sect of native Hindus, who have abandoned the idolatrous faith and practices of the popular religion, and profess a pure theism, adopt the Christian name more than the Christians theirs? They have really passed beyond all that the word Christian means as defining a system of faith; and, if they should assume it, would be going back upon their path. They gratefully acknowledge their obligations to Christianity, which has come to them through British literature and civilization rather than by direct Christian teaching, as they also confess their indebtedness to the spiritual philosophy and inspiration of their own ancient scriptures. But they claim that the human soul has as direct access to truth to-day as it ever had, and that no authoritative final revelation has been given in the past; and hence they stand essentially on the same platform with the rationalistic divisions of the Christians and the Jews. But why should they call themselves by either of these names, or by one of them more than the other?

In China, too, and in Japan, now that they have been opened to the fresh enterprise and thought of the nineteenth century, progress in religious ideas will inevitably come as the accompaniment of advance in other directions. But is this religious progress likely to take the Christian name? The Jesuits, who are already on the ground, may make some converts from the masses of the people; for the reason that the mediæval form of Christianity which the Romish Church represents, and which was to a great extent the product of the pagan contributions which came into the stream of Christian history, is nearly on a level with the old Buddhistic faith of the Oriental masses. But the intelligent and thinking class in those countries will not be so likely even as the Hindus to change their religion for Christianity, for the reasons that they have a more rational religion than the Hindus and are more averse to change. But they will readily accept a religion that shall be developed out of their ancient faith, yet still have that faith beneath it, — a religion that shall keep all that is true in their own scriptures, and welcome all that is truth in all other scriptures, and never close the canon of the continually uttered Word of revelation. They will hardly adopt a religion that degrades Confucius and Buddha into the position of blind heathen guides, unworthy of confidence, and deifies a prophet of another race; but they will receive a religion which shall count Moses and Jesus and Confucius and Buddha, and all the greatly wise and good, in the line of its prophets, giving to each the honor due for the truth he saw and told, and for the good his life achieved.

Am I visionary, — a mere dreamer, — if I seem to see that from all these manifest tendencies will come forth eventually another form of faith and worship, which shall not be Hinduism nor Buddhism nor Judaism nor Christianity nor any system of faith now existing, but a broader religious development of humanity, in which all technical distinctions between these specific forms of religion shall be obliterated, and nations and races shall meet in a spiritual fellowship whose limits shall be commensurate with humanity itself? Nay, not a dreamer. I believe I am but reading the future by the light of past history and of present social and mental forces. This epoch of the nineteenth century repeats to some extent, though with vastly larger and more favoring opportunity, the religious conditions and combinations that existed just prior to the origin of Christianity. As that epoch witnessed a decadence of old religious systems, and brought together in Western Asia the elements of religions and of civilizations that had previously flourished apart, and from their union there was begotten a higher form of faith and life, so now it seems as if the various religions of the world, having served their providential purpose apart, are being brought into contact, in order that they may serve to show each other's defects, and confirm each other's truths, and stimulate to higher thought and a larger charity and a more beneficent activity; and thus ultimately may be created, not by any mechanical eclecticism but by the organic laws of social growth, a purer form of religious belief and practice, under which all nations and races shall be joined as different members in one household, to serve one Parental law of truth and right, and to stand by each other as brothers whose hearts beat with one blood and respond to the pulsations of one love.

THE GENIUS OF CHRISTIANITY AND FREE RELIGION.[1]

By Francis Ellingwood Abbot.

TO say that the age we live in is pre-eminently an era of revolution, is to utter a stale and profitless truism. The fact mirrors itself on every open eye, and voices itself to every unstopped ear. Not merely in the forms of government, the adjustments of society, and other external matters, constant changes occur which are perceptible by all; but the more observing also detect indications of some profound and hidden movement in the depths of the human spirit. The world's heart is ill at ease. Miseries and oppressions and crimes are, it is true, like the poor, ever. with us; but cancel these, and the world's unrest will still remain. Its secret inquietude betrays itself even in the tone of the popular poems and novels of the day; and although the Church, abundantly assiduous with prescription and pill, promises to cure the distemper, she encounters a most alarming symptom in the patient's distrust of the physician. In fact, the patient refuses to be a patient; and what the Church accounts disease turns out to be a new-born hunger for truth and life, — a most excellent

[1] A lecture delivered in the First Course of "Sunday Afternoon Lectures" in Horticultural Hall, Boston, February 14, 1869.

sign of spiritual health. The world needs, not to be doctored, but to be fed; and whoso brings substantial food fairly cooked finds a hearty welcome.

The old faiths, like cotyledons well stored with starch, are perishing as the spring advances, yet only to yield their contents as nourishment for a better faith. Although there are no "new truths" except as the discovery, or riper development in human thought and life, of truths old as God, yet in this sense new truths are creating to-day a new faith in the world before which the elder faiths lose their power. The grounds of human hope, the motives of human action, the objects of human aspiration, are slowly changing; and because change in these respects involves corresponding change in all the relations of public and private life, the great visible movements of the age are but indices of the greater invisible movements in the spiritual consciousness of mankind. Because all questions of immediate interest in the amelioration of society depend ultimately on deeper questions in the soul, there can be no theme of profounder practical importance than that to which I now invite your attention, — the "Genius of Christianity and Free Religion." In the conflict between these two faiths, and in the law of spiritual development by which the one must increase and the other decrease, lies, as I believe, the secret of the religious restlessness of the times. With the seriousness befitting so great a subject, and yet with no shrinking from the plainness of speech which equally befits it,

I wish to express convictions neither hastily formed nor weakly held, for which I ask from you only a calm and candid hearing. Whether right or wrong, they must affect profoundly the well-being of every one who makes them the basis of intelligent and fearless action. Let them, then, be intelligently and fearlessly judged.

A savage coming to the sea-shore at several distant points might perhaps imagine that he had come to several disconnected seas, not knowing that the sea is one. So he who beholds without reflection the great religions of the world might conceive these to be separate and distinct, not knowing that religion is one. It must have been from some such conception as this that men used to class Christianity by itself as wholly true, and all other religions in a group by themselves as wholly false. But this distinction cannot stand. The question of the truth or falsity of different religions is purely a question of degree. They are all expressions of the universal aspiration of humanity, and are so far all based on eternal truth. But each of them has its own special historic form, determined by the personality of its founder, by the spirit of the age in which it arose, and by the character of the historic forces by which it was developed; and so far it must share the error which clings to all things human. The worst religion has its truth, — the best has its error. Thus all religions are *one*, in virtue of their common origin in the aspiring and worshipping spirit of man; while they are *many*, in virtue of the historic form peculiar to each. The universal element in each belongs, not to it, but to universal human nature; while its special element, its historic form, is its own.

Whoever, therefore, would find the oneness of all religions must seek it in the universal spiritual consciousness of the race; while he who would learn the characteristics of any particular religion must seek this in its history and origin. The object of the first seeker is generic unity, — the object of the second is specific difference. Their methods, consequently, must correspond with their objects, and be the converse of each other. The one must neglect peculiarities, and attend to resemblances; the other must neglect resemblances, and attend to peculiarities. To claim as peculiar to one religion what is common to all religions, — a claim often made in behalf of Christianity, — is unreasonable; but it is equally unreasonable to ignore its actual peculiarities. No estimate of a great historical religion can be just, unless formed by the impartial, scientific application of the historical method.

In attempting, therefore, to determine what Christianity actually is, as a great fact in human history, I shall not endeavor to frame a transcendental or mystical formula, and thus, spider-like, evolve a definition of it out of my own consciousness. On the contrary, believing Christianity to be the loftiest of all historical religions, I believe that, like all other historical religions, it can only be understood by the study of its sacred books, its traditions, its institutions, its origin, its history. What were the ideas, purposes, and character of Jesus, and what was the nature of the faith which took its name from him and became Christianity as we see it in the world to-day, must be learned historically or not at all. Abstract speculation can throw no light on these questions of fact. History is the key to the problem of Christianity.

CHRISTIANITY HISTORICALLY DEFINED.

Viewed, then, as one of the world's great historical faiths, Christianity is religion as taught in the New Testament, developed in the history of the Christian Church, and based on faith in Jesus of Nazareth as the Christ of God.

If we attempt to make Christianity independent of its founder and of the only records we possess of his life and teachings (an attempt sometimes made by modern radical thinkers), we simply abandon the historical ground altogether, identify Christianity with Religion, and annihilate the specific difference between Christianity and all other historical faiths. It thereby becomes impossible to distinguish it from them on the same level; we resolve it into "natural religion," and must treat all other religions as merely various modifications of it. I need not say how arbitrary and irrational this seems to me. If Christianity is itself "natural religion," — only love to God and love to man, — how can we escape calling Brahmanism and Buddhism and Confucianism and the rest *different forms of Christianity?* Would there be nothing absurd in that? If, on the other hand, we say that religion is always natural, and that Christianity, Brahmanism, Buddhism, Confucianism, Zoroastrianism, Mahometanism, and so forth, are all diverse historical forms of this one natural religion, I think we take the only sensible ground. We then put all historical faiths on the same level, and can distinguish them one from another by their different historical characters. But to do this is at once to sweep away all the fine-spun metaphysical, transcendental, and purely ethical definitions of Christianity, in order to make room for its only historical definition, namely, religion as taught in the New Testament, developed in the history of the Christian Church, and based on faith in Jesus of Nazareth as the Christ of God.

The ethical and spiritual teachings of the New Testament are not peculiar to it; as is well known, they can all be paralleled in other ancient writings. These, therefore, will not help us to comprehend that which is peculiar to Christianity and makes it a distinct historical religion; they belong to the universal religion of man, appear in the sacred books of all religions, and are the private property of none. In accordance with the true historical method, therefore, I shall pass by these universal truths, which find perhaps their best expression in the New Testament, in order to concentrate our attention on the fundamental characteristic of

Christianity, namely, its faith in the Christ. It is this which separates it from all other religions, constitutes its prime peculiarity, and serves as foundation to the other leading doctrines of Christian theology. Purity, benevolence, mercy, forgiveness, humility, self-sacrifice, love, and so forth, are nowhere more beautifully taught than in the discourses, conversations, and parables of Jesus; but these make the universal, not the special, element in the New Testament, — these make its religion, not its Christianity, — and it is now its Christianity that we seek to comprehend.

So far as our present object is concerned, we need not be embarrassed by the doubts resting over the authorship, the dates, and the historic credibility of the various books of the New Testament. No critical scholar of the present day regards the gospels as wholly mythical. Yet, unless they are wholly mythical, it is impossible to doubt that Jesus did actually claim to be the Christ or Messiah, that is, the founder and sovereign of the "kingdom of heaven." So all-pervading is this claim, that to eliminate it from the gospels is to reduce them at once to unadulterated myth. If misunderstood on this point, there is no reason to suppose that Jesus has been understood on any point; if his reported sayings on this subject are ungenuine, there is no reason to suppose any of his sayings to be genuine. In the words of James Martineau ["National Review," April, 1863]: "Whoever can read the New Testament with a fresh eye must be struck with the prominence everywhere of the Messianic idea. It seems to be the ideal framework of the whole, — of history, parable, dialogue; of Pauline reasoning; of Apocalyptic visions. '*Art thou he that should come?*' This question gives the ideal standard by which, on all hands, — on the part of disciples, relations, enemies, of Saul the persecutor and Paul the apostle, — the person and pretensions of Christ are tried. His birth, his acts, his sufferings, are so disposed as to 'fulfil what was spoken' by the prophets: so that the whole programme of his life would seem to have pre-existed in the national imagination."

That these words of Martineau are true, I am profoundly convinced. The Messianic faith is the soul of the entire New Testament, giving unity to the gospels, epistles, and apocalypse, and making Christianity a vital organism. In vain shall we seek to comprehend the spiritual power of Christianity, and determine its agency in the evolution of modern civilization, until we have first comprehended the Messianic idea, and discovered the sources, the channels, and the limitations of its power. In vain shall we seek to solve the mystery of that spiritual Nile which has fertilized the centuries, until we discover its Lake Nyanza in the Messianic hope of Judaism and its widening Delta in the advent of Free Religion. History, not theology, must reveal the true origin of Christianity; and when we are prepared to accept her calm instructions, we shall learn that the greatest of the world's historical religions is no bastard with the bar-sinister of miracle athwart its scutcheon, but the lawful offspring of Jewish faith and Greek thought. In the New Testament, if we will but read aright, is ample proof of its pedigree. In the first three gospels we find the Jewish Messiahship assumed by Jesus; in the fourth gospel, we find it interpreted by the Logos doctrine, and thus rationalized by Greek philosophy; in the book of Acts and in the Epistles we find it stripped by Peter and Paul of its local and national limitations, and thus fitted to become the basis of a world-wide church. The organizing genius of Rome supplied the element necessary to convert the idea into an institution; and the triumph of Christianity was assured.

THE MESSIANIC IDEA THE GREAT TAP-ROOT OF CHRISTIANITY.

Here, then, in the New Testament itself, the Messianic idea appears as the great tap-root of Christianity; and we see, already fulfilled, all the intrinsic spiritual conditions of its subsequent growth. Given the corresponding extrinsic historical conditions, what need of a miracle to account for its wonderful development? It would have been a miracle indeed, if, in the actual state of the Roman Empire at that time, Christianity had failed to become the State Religion. Into what a melancholy and senile decrepitude had fallen its pagan competitors! The decaying mythologies of Persia, Egypt, Greece, Rome, were the spiritual compost whence the vigorous young plant derived its sap. Universal putrefaction is a powerful fertilizer. To the spread of every religion, however rapid (and Christianity is in this respect no more remarkable than Buddhism or Mahometanism), the same explanation applies, — adaptation to the spirit and circumstances of the times. It is customary among Unitarians to extol the purity of "primitive Christianity," and to bewail what they call its theological and ecclesiastical "corruption" during the first three centuries. This is to praise the blossom at the expense of the fruit, — to indulge in that idealization of childhood which is practical depreciation of manhood. The triumph of Athanasius over Arius, and of Augustine over Pelagius, was not accidental. On the contrary, the gradual formation of the Athanasian and Augustinian theology was the strictly logical and natural development of the claim made by Jesus of being the Saviour of the world; while the gradual erection of the Romish hierarchy was the equally logical and natural result of the attempt to found a universal church upon this claim. How could a *man* be the Saviour of the world? Only by being also *God*. The Romish Church, with its theology of salvation through the God-Man, so far from being a "corruption of primitive Christianity," was its necessary historical evolution; the Messianic idea, freed from its merely Hebrew application, enfolded mediæval Catholicism as the acorn enfolds the oak. As the Jewish theocracy was at last obliged to enthrone an earthly king as the representative of Jehovah, so the Christian Church was obliged at last to enthrone the Pope as the representative of the Christ. It betrays, therefore, a lack of the philosophical, the scientific, the historical spirit, to call that a corruption which was in truth a development.

ROMANISM THE TRUE CHRISTIANITY.

As the history of philosophical systems is the truest exponent of their logical tendencies, so the history of religions is the truest interpreter of their genius and innermost spirit. The Romish Church, whether in its hierarchy, its institutions, its architecture, its painting, its music, its literature, its theology, its spiritual power, its types of spiritual character, or its missionary zeal, is the ripened fruit of the Messianic germ, the supreme culmination of Christianity. Christian poetry and art, no less than Christian character and faith, have reached their zenith in the Catholic Church. The cathedrals, the Madonnas, the anthems, Dante's Divine Comedy (the great poem of Christianity, setting it to eternal music), were born in the souls of Catholics. The Protestant Reformation was simply the first stage in the decay of Christianity. In Wickliffe and Huss, in Luther and Calvin and their compeers, the modern spirit came to self-consciousness. These men were, although unwittingly, the first apostles of Free Religion. Socinus, Priestley, Channing, Parker, and the other reformers of the

Reformation, carried the work of disintegration still farther, and gave voice to the deepening demand of humanity for spiritual freedom. "Liberal Christianity," which means Christianity as liberal as it can be, has reduced the Messianic idea to its minimum dimensions and its minimum power; the next step is outside of Christianity altogether. Gradual in its growth and gradual in its decay, — coming to its prime in the Romish, and lying at Death's door in the Unitarian Church, — Christianity has realized the highest possibilities of the Messianic faith, has accomplished the utmost which that faith can accomplish for man, and is now destined to wane before a faith higher and purer still. Its history, from beginning to end, is the history of men's faith in the Christ; its first and last word is, by the law of its being, — "Come to Jesus!" In proportion as the name of Jesus grows infrequent on its lips, — in proportion as his person fails to attract its supreme homage and worship, — in that proportion it ceases to be Christianity, and becomes merged in that universal religion whose only history is the history of soul. Let me repeat, with emphasis, that, while Christianity is the perishing form, religion is the eternal substance, — that the universal truths, the inspiring hopes, the tender consolations, the quickening impulses, the divinely beautiful spirit, which have made and still make the name of Christianity so dear to the undistinguishing many, belong to the eternal substance and not to the perishing form. Religion must endure; but as Christianity came into history, so it must go out from history. Its inspiration and life have come in and through its faith in the Christ, the one Lord and Master and Saviour of the world; and its church, or visible embodiment in a social and spiritual fellowship, has planted itself from the beginning on this faith as its own eternal rock and corner-stone.

There is no clearer recognition of the fundamental character of the Christian Confession than in the following words of Dr. Hedge, a Unitarian clergyman who perceives how much is involved in the apparent truism that Christianity has a history: —

"I am far from maintaining that Christianity must stand or fall with the belief in miracles; but I do maintain that Christian churches, as organized bodies of believers, must stand or fall with the Christian Confession, — that is, the Confession of Christ as divinely human Master and Head. . . . Things exist in this world by distinction one from another. Enlarge as you will the idea and scope of a church, there must be somewhere, whether stated or not in any formal symbol, a line which defines it, and separates those who are in it from those who are without. The scope of the Liberal Church is large; but every thing and everybody cannot be embraced in it. The Christian Confession is its boundary line, within which alone it can do the work which Providence has given it to do. . . . The distinction involved in the Christian Confession is organic and vital; its abolition would be the dissolution of the ecclesiastical world and the end of Christendom." — ["Reason in Religion," pp. 218, 219.]

This statement of Dr. Hedge is the verdict of history itself. On the Christian Confession, Jesus himself founded his church; on the Christian Confession, Peter, John, Paul, and the rest, built up its walls; on the Christian Confession, Augustine, Athanasius, and their fellow-workers, roofed and completed the great historic edifice. From the vast ecclesiastical hierarchy of Rome to the puny "National Conference of Unitarian and other Christian Churches," all the sects and sub-sects of Christendom, with one consenting voice, confess that Jesus is the Christ, the Saviour of the world, the spiritual King of mankind by the grace of God. In all the endless controversies respecting doctrines, forms, or politics, all parties have accepted the Christian Confession as the universal creed of Christians. Whatever differences of opinion exist or have existed concerning the nature, the official function, or the spiritual mission of the Christ, the Christian Confession has remained the corner-stone of the Christian Church; and a Christian will no more challenge the Christian Confession that "Jesus is the Christ," than a Mahometan will challenge the Mahometan Confession that "there is but one God, and Mahomet is his prophet."

It is in the first gospel, not the fourth, that Jesus

says to Peter, on his confessing him to be "the Christ, the Son of the living God," — "Blessed art thou, Simon Bar-jona; for flesh and blood have not revealed it unto thee, but my Father who is in heaven. And I say also unto thee, That thou art Peter, and upon this rock [*i. e.*, your faith in me as the Christ] I will build my church; and the gates of hell shall not prevail against it." It is in the first gospel, not the fourth, that Jesus replies to the high priest, adjuring him to declare whether he is the Christ, — "I am. Moreover I say to you, Henceforth ye will see the Son of Man sitting on the right hand of Power, and coming on the clouds of heaven" [Noyes' translation]. It is in the first gospel, not in the fourth, that Jesus explicitly makes the Christian Confession the necessary condition of salvation: "Whosoever, therefore, shall confess me before men, him will I also confess before my Father who is in heaven; but whosoever shall deny me before men, him will I also deny before my Father who is in heaven." It would be easy to cite scores of passages to the same effect; but these are amply sufficient.

In the same spirit, Peter declares, in the book of Acts, that "there is no other name given under heaven whereby men can be saved." In the same spirit, Paul declares to the Galatians, "There be some that trouble you and would pervert the gospel of Christ. But though we, or an angel from heaven, preach any other gospel unto you than that which we have preached unto you, let him be accursed;" and to the Romans, "If thou shalt confess with the mouth that Jesus is Lord, and shalt believe in thy heart that God has raised him from the dead, thou shalt be saved; for with the heart man believeth so as to obtain righteousness, and with the mouth confesseth so as to obtain salvation." In the same spirit, John exclaims in his first epistle, "Who is a liar, but he that denieth that Jesus is the Christ? Whosoever denieth the Son, the same has not the Father." And so on. Sayings such as these meet the eye on almost every page of the New Testament; and so far from being accidental or non-essential, they utter the heart-faith, the inmost spirit of Christianity, as a distinct religion.

CHRISTIANITY IS DEVELOPED JUDAISM.

The one grand aim of Jesus was to establish the "kingdom of heaven;" and this, however universalized and spiritualized, was in essence the ancient ideal theocracy, in which the Christ was to be the God-appointed king. From the day when, on the very eve of death, Jesus boldly affirmed before Pilate and the high priest his title to the Messianic throne, the highest and deepest prayer of his disciples has been that his throne may be established for ever in the hearts of all mankind. Was it an *accident* that the new faith took its name, not from the individual Jesus, but from his royal office? Christianity was the faith of the Christians, and the Christians were those who believed in the

Christ. Hence the condition of Christian fellowship has always been fealty to Jesus as common Lord and Master; and in this, the organic bond of union in all branches of the Christian Church, the innermost life of Christianity has, by the very law of its being, only expressed itself outwardly in social form. In short, the history of Christianity is simply the history of the Messianic faith, deepened and widened, developed and spiritualized, in the highest possible degree, — the history of the varying fortunes which have befallen the attempt of Jesus to found a universal spiritual empire in the hearts of men; and he will seek in vain to fathom the depths of Christianity who looks elsewhere than to this Messianic faith for the secret of its peculiar religious power.

Furthermore, unless liberal thinkers cease to philosophize loosely about Christianity and learn to do complete justice to its Messianic or special element, a problem of great importance will remain permanently insoluble. It is only by tracing the course of the Messianic idea back to its fountain-head in the living faith of Judaism, that it becomes possible to discover the *natural origin* of Christianity. If the sources of Christianity reach no further back than to the individual soul of Jesus; if so mighty a power in the world's history was born of one man's single life, and owed nothing to earlier ancestors; if no deep unity can be discovered between Jesus and the spirit of his age, in virtue of which he became the natural representative of humanity in his day and generation, and brought to a living focus the religious forces of his times, — then is Christianity indeed a miracle, and Jesus may well have been God. The naturalistic interpretation of Christianity fails utterly, unless it can reveal an adequate cause for its tremendous influence on the course of history. Once admit that a Jewish peasant lifted the whole world up to a higher spiritual level, not by embodying in himself the best religious life of his era, but by the sheer strength of his own individuality, — and I, for one, must perforce admit him to have been Omnipotence in disguise. The incarnation of God would be a less miracle than the upheaval of the planet by a human arm. But if Jesus was a man, and acted under natural human conditions, then his power must have been the power of humanity; behind him, beneath him, within him, must have been the spirit of his age, concentrating in his word the vitality of his race. Somewhere must he have found a foothold in the profoundest faith of his own nation, or he could not have moved the universal consciousness of man. The secret of success, with every great soul, lies in sympathy with his times, without which his most magnificent utterance perishes on the air. Given, therefore, the humanity of Jesus, it is imperatively necessary to discover the faith which he and his countrymen must have held in common. Where shall we search for this except in that Messianic idea which is the core and heart of his religion?

Here we find established a vital relation between Jesus and the Hebrew people. The moment we accept the clew here offered, the labyrinth ceases to bewilder, — our path is clear. It would be at the same time tedious and pedantic, were I to rehearse in detail the evidence which has convinced my own mind that *Christianity is only a developed Judaism.* From the time of the Babylonish Captivity, the narrow theocracy of earlier ages began to develop in Hebrew thought into the dazzling dream of a universal "kingdom of heaven," designed to succeed the great empires of antiquity and to embrace in its dominions all the nations of the globe. The so-called Jewish Apocalyptic literature, which sprang up as a transformation of the primitive prophetism, and of which the most important writings are the book of Daniel, the Sibylline oracles, the book of Enoch, and the fourth book of Esdras, enables us to distinguish successive stages in the formation of the Messianic faith. At first an aristocracy of the saints rather than the monarchy of the Messiah, the conception of the "kingdom of heaven" incorporated into itself more and more of the personal element, until this at last came to predominate. Long before the birth of Jesus, the chief features of the Messianic idea as contained in the New Testament were strongly marked, both with regard to the "end of the world" and the "coming of the Son of Man." The same place, Jerusalem; the same time, the immediate future; the same symptomatic signs, wars and rumors of wars, and the gathering of Gentile armies against Jerusalem; the same coming of the Messiah with his angels on the clouds of heaven; the same solemn Judgment, with the Son of Man on the throne of his glory and all nations before his tribunal; the same sentences to the wicked and the righteous; the same resurrection of the dead from Hades; the same passing away of the old earth and appearance of the new;—all these, and more, were definite Messianic beliefs in the century before Jesus. Nor this alone. The "kingdom of heaven," as conceived in the later of these Apocalyptic writings, was highly spiritual in its character, bringing at once happiness and holiness to all mankind. The "kingdom of heaven" was to ultimate in a universal brotherhood of man, an era of universal peace and righteousness, introduced through universal submission to the Hebrew Messiah or Christ. Every generous aspiration for spiritual perfection and the welfare of humanity thus found its satisfaction in the vision of Messianic redemption to the chosen people of God.

THE EDUCATION AND CAREER OF JESUS.

Into this circle of ideas and national aspirations Jesus was born; and were they not also his own? They were the very atmosphere he breathed; they filled his soul from the earliest days of childhood. The gospels represent him as not wholly illiterate, being able at least to read. He undoubtedly was ignorant of Greek, which even at Jerusalem was but little known and regarded as dangerous in its tendencies; and there is no trace in the gospel narratives of the influence of the Hellenic culture upon his mind. The study of the Mosaic Law was alone considered reputable and safe by devout Jews. The Rabbi Hillel, however, who fifty years before Jesus anticipated his Golden Rule and others of his finest sayings, in all probability exerted a deep influence upon his development. It is evident from the evangelists that Jesus had earnestly pondered the Old Testament, especially Isaiah and the book of Daniel, — perhaps the book of Enoch also, and other Apocalyptic writings. "The advent of the Messiah," says Renan, "with his glories and his terrors, the nations dashing one against another, the cataclysm of heaven and earth, were the familiar food of his imagination; and as these revolutions were thought to be at hand, so that a multitude of people were seeking to compute their times, the supernatural order of things into which such visions transport us appeared to him from the first perfectly natural." The conception of universal and invariable laws of nature which had been developed to a considerable degree in the Greek mind by the philosophy of Epicurus, and which, nearly a century before the birth of Jesus, had been admirably stated by Lucretius in his great poem on "The Nature of Things," was utterly foreign to the thought of Jesus and his countrymen, who believed in the habitual agency of demons and evil spirits, and had unwavering faith in miracles. The great idea of Jesus, the immediate advent of the "kingdom of heaven," was also the dominant idea of his times; but, various attempts to realize it by political means having ended in utter failure, especially that of Judas the Gaulonite or Galilean, he early perceived the folly of military Messianism, and relied implicitly on the establishment of his Messianic throne by the miraculous display of the divine power. Thus was Jesus educated by his age.

Repelled though he was by the vulgar conception of the Christ as a mere warlike prince, the idea of spiritual supremacy through the religious reformation of his people struck a responsive chord in his soul. His deep nature was thrilled and kindled by his country's hope, and with intense earnestness must he have asked himself, — "Can I fulfil it? Am I the Called, the Anointed of God?" The consciousness of his wonderful religious genius, fertilized and developed by the spirit of his age, fanned the wish into a prayer, and the prayer into a conviction, and the conviction into an enthusiasm, and the enthusiasm into a calm and omnipotent faith, that he was indeed the Messiah, — singled out from all eternity by the will of God, foretold by prophets and kings, and awaited for weary centuries by humanity in tears. Impossible as it is for the cool intellect of the West to comprehend the mystic fervor, the religious intensity of the Semitic race, it is yet evident that

Jesus acquired faith in his Messianic destiny by an inward experience analogous to that which convinced the prophets of their divine missions. Fathom it or analyze it we cannot; but we can yet perceive that the phenomenon of Hebrew prophetism, with its sublime identification of impassioned thought with the direct mandate of God, repeats itself in the history of the young Galilean carpenter. It is a fact to be studied, — not to be denied.

Let no one meet me here with the bigot's worn-out dilemma — "If Jesus was not in reality the Messiah he claimed to be, he was either a madman or an impostor!" Was John Brown a madman or an impostor, when he aspired to be the redeemer of an enslaved race? The moral sublimity of such an aim is not to be measured by the six-inch rule of vulgar souls, but by the astronomic spaces of the heavens above. There is a madness that is more than sanity, — a veritable inspiration to dare the impossible, and by bloody failure to achieve a somewhat greater than "success." The hero is always a fool in the eyes of him who counts the cost. If it be madness to obey the enthusiasm of ideas without stopping to count the cost, God grant us all the wisdom to go mad! Such madness is the glory of humanity. The insane man is he whose thought fatally contradicts his surroundings; but he who comprehends the profoundest, though it may be the unconscious, movement of his age, and carries its underlying ideas into fuller and higher development, — this man, I say, is the sanest of the sane. To his contemporaries, the idealist is always crazy; to posterity, he appears as the only practical man of his times, — the guide of his generation in the pathway of progress. In the soul of Jesus, the great aspiration of the Hebrew race became purified from its alloys, and stamped for ever with the impress of his superior spirit. But, being essentially Hebrew still, it is incapable of expansion into the aspiration of universal humanity; and Jesus, though endowed with that sanity of genius which is madness in the eyes of mediocrity, is no longer in the van.

To him, however, who, in face of sincerity like that of Jesus, ventures to whisper the word *imposture*, I will not do insult to my own reverence for human greatness by addressing any defence of Jesus from such a charge. It should blister the mouth that makes it. Enough for me that in the privacy of his own self-communings Jesus believed he heard the summons to a work of unparalleled sublimity, — that he valued not his blood in comparison with obedience, — that he claimed the Messianic diadem with death for its Koh-i-noor. Surely, the suspicion of duplicity as the root of such vast historic influence betrays in the suspecter a disgraceful faith in the power of knavery.

The transcendent greatness of Jesus appeared in this, that the popular hope of a Priest-King ruling by the sword transformed itself in his musing soul into the sublime idea of a spiritual Christ ruling by love, — that he sought to establish the "kingdom of heaven," not over the bodies, but deep in the hearts, of men. So pure and piercing was his spiritual insight, that, once possessed with the Messianic idea, he entered into the best that was in it, and forgot the rest; seized on the elder and diviner meaning of the prophets, and cast away as rubbish the popular selfishness with which this was overlaid. Believing himself to be the Anointed of God, he aspired to become, not merely king of the Jewish theocracy after its miraculous restoration by God at the great " day of judgment," but also king of the very heart of regenerated humanity. I would fain put upon this ambition the noblest possible construction; for, so far from wishing to make out a case against him, I am only anxious to do him exact justice, and penetrate the spirit of the faith which he bequeathed to mankind. To become the object of human imitation and the quickening ideal of human aspiration, — to be the One Way to purity and love and peace, — to reign in men's souls, as the sun reigns in the solar system, by developing the seeds of all goodness and beauty; — this, and no selfish empire, was the ambition of Jesus. He aimed to be Lord and King by drawing all men to God, and thus to make himself the great centre of the world's divinest life. To reconcile his supreme self-emphasis with his supreme self-sacrifice, is the great perplexing problem of the gospels. The doctrine of his Deity, which is the orthodox solution, is not a possible one to humanitarian thinkers. Where shall we find another?

THE ORIGINALITY OF JESUS.

On the one hand, the claim of Jesus to the Messianic crown did not grow out of a vulgar lust of power, but out of a profound faith that it was God's will that he should wear it. Belief in the "divine right of kings" was universal in the Jewish world, and Jesus fully shared it. How it happened that he first became convinced of his own divine election to the throne of the "kingdom of heaven," will never, I think, be explained; that is a secret, buried with him. But that he did become convinced of it, and that this profound conviction, rather than any desire of personal aggrandizement, was the root of his Messianic claim, seems to me the simple verdict of justice. His self-emphasis, therefore, was the necessary product of his education, his spiritual experience, and his faith in God; and in the necessity of this connection between cause and effect lies his defence against the charge of overweening and selfish egotism. But there was nothing original in this conviction of a special Divine mission; every founder of a religion shares it. The true originality of Jesus lies, I conceive, in the means he adopted to accomplish his end and realize his ambition. Here he stands alone. Strange as it may seem, he aimed to win absolute power by absolutely renouncing it. This is the identification of contradictories, — the very Hegelianism of conscience. With a new conception of what constitutes true royalty of soul, he sought to earn his kingship by the more than regal majesty of his service. The "great Masters" have been rare indeed; yet how much rarer have been the great Servants! It is the grandest and most original trait in Jesus' character, that he sought to realize his supreme Mastership through a supreme Servantship. Here lies the reconciliation of his self-emphasis and self-renunciation. Here also I find the secret of his wonderful success in subduing souls to his sway. He would govern, yet through love; he would secure absolute allegiance, yet bind men to it by the spontaneous outgush of their own gratitude; he would wear a crown, yet bow his head to receive it from the hands of subjects burning with eagerness to place it there. Thus, and thus alone, he aspired to reign, the welcome Sovereign of every human soul.

What astounding, yet sublime, audacity! How mean, compared with this, the ambitions of Alexanders and Cæsars and Napoleons! How brutal is the ambition that relies on force, compared with the ambition that relies on love! Yet, because it involved his own elevation to a throne, albeit a spiritual throne, his ambition was ambition still, the "last infirmity" of a most noble mind. It precluded the possibility of self-forgetfulness in service, — of that supreme modesty which teaches that the value of the grandest soul is not personal, but inheres in the universal humanity it contains and the universal ideas it represents. There is but one ambition sublimer than to REIGN BY SERVING, — and that is, to SERVE WITHOUT REIGNING. I cannot shut my eyes to the nobler purpose; I cannot forget that Socrates both lived and died to make it real.

THE RADICAL DEFECT OF CHRISTIANITY.

In vain is all the modern noise and bustle about a " Liberal " Christianity. Christianity is based on forgetfulness of liberty; the love of perfect freedom is not in it. Spiritual servitude is its corner-stone, — none the less hurtful, if voluntary. Many a slave has loved his chains. Interpret as loosely as you may the Lordship which Jesus claimed, — it is no Lordship at all, if it leaves the soul supreme Lord over itself. Run down the scale from slavish imitation to simple deference, — it avails nought; there is no spiritual freedom but in reverence for the still, small voice within the soul as supreme above all other voices. This made the greatness of Jesus himself; would that he had fostered it in his disciples! Yet no! Even the mistakes of lofty spirits help on the great cause of human development; and, mistaken as was the Messianic ambition of Jesus, the world's debt is immense to this magnificent mistake. Mankind were not yet ripe for self-government in spiritual freedom, — are not wholly ripe for it to-day, — will not be wholly ripe for it this many a long year. The overpowering influence of a spiritual King whose law was love met the world's wants as the freedom of self-government could not then have done; and thus the gospel of authority accomplished a work not yet possible to the modern gospel of spiritual liberty. The grave responsibilities of independence befit only the ripe maturity of the soul.

Whether we consider Christianity with regard to its essence, its origin, or its history, we are thus led to one and the same conclusion, — that its fundamental characteristic as a distinct religion is its faith in Jesus as the Christ. Faith in a Christ or Messiah as "the coming man" had become, long prior to the birth of Jesus, an integral part of Hebrew monotheism; and Christianity, historically considered, is only the complete development of Judaism into its highest possibilities. "In its earliest aspect," says Martineau, "Christianity was no new or universal religion; Judaism had found the person of its Messiah, but else remained the same." All of high truth and spiritual power that are compatible with the Messianic idea, Jesus, I believe, put into it, when he made it the cornerstone of his religion. The Christian Church has expressed outwardly the genuine character of Messianism, and realized, both in their best and in their worst directions, its necessary historical tendencies. Gradually developing until the Papacy reached the zenith of its prosperity, and gradually decaying from that day to this, Christianity becomes daily more and more discordant with modern civilization and modern religion; and those sects that dream of adapting it to modern life are unconsciously officiating at its funeral. Construe it as largely or as loosely as you please, Christianity, as a great historical and spiritual power, will nevertheless remain *religion within the limits of the Messianic idea.* Idealize or transcendentalize the Christ as highly as you may, his practical power is gone the moment you make him aught less than a person. It is the vitality of Jesus that has made, and still makes, the vitality of his religion. Pass beyond the circle of its supreme influence, and, whether you know it or not, you have passed outside of Christianity. Detach Christianity wholly from the person of Jesus, and you destroy all meaning in the Christian name by destroying the historic root from which it sprang. The Christian Confession remains the boundary line which no Christian can overstep.

However some may yearn, having lost all faith in the Messianic idea, to retain nevertheless the Christian name, whether from love for its venerable associations or from reluctance to bear the odium of its distinct rejection, I believe that the proprieties of language and increasing perception of what consistency requires will slowly wean them from this desire. The world at large can never be made to understand what is meant by a Christian who in no sense has faith in the Christ. If Jesus really claimed to be the Christ, — if he made this claim the basis of the Christian religion, —

and if through this claim he still infuses into his Church all its Christian life, — then the world is right, and may well marvel at a Christianity that denies the Lord, yet wears his livery. For myself, I cannot evade the practical consequences of my thought. The central doctrine of Christianity is for me no longer true; its essential spirit and faith are no longer the highest or the best; and with the reality, I resign the name. Far be it from me to do this in levity or mockery or defiance! Far be it from me to turn my back in scorn on my own most hallowed experiences in the past! Once I felt the full power of the Christian faith; now I cleave to a faith diviner still. If I am in fatal error, and rush madly into the woes denounced against the Anti-Christ, even so must it be; but come what may, let me never plunge into the deeper damnation of moral faithlessness, or make my heart the coffin of a murdered truth!

THE HIGHER FAITH.

If, then, there is a higher faith than Christianity, he who shall cherish it is bound to make known what it is, and how it is higher than Christianity. Bear with me while I endeavor to discharge this duty. It is no easy thing to do. Free Religion, the higher faith I hold, has no history, save the history of the human spirit, striving to work out its destiny in freedom. It is spiritual, not historical, — universal, not special, — inward, not outward. It has no list of doctrines to teach, no

Church to extend, no rites to perform, no Bible to expound, no Christ to obey. With none of these things, it is the soul's deep resolve to love the truth, to learn the truth, and to live the truth, uncoerced and free. It is Intellect daring to think, unawed by public opinion. It is Conscience daring to assert a higher law, in face of a corrupted society and a conforming church. It is Will setting at naught the world's tyrannies, and putting into action the private whispers of the still, small voice. It is Heart resting in the universal and changeless Law as eternal and transcendent Love. It is the soul of man asserting its own superiority to all its own creations, burning with deep devotion to the true and just and pure, and identifying its every wish with the perfect order of the universe. It is neither affirmation nor negation of the established, but rather a deep consciousness that all the established is inferior to that which has established it. It is the spirit of self-conscious freedom, aiming evermore at the best, and trusting itself as the architect of character. In fine, it is that sense of spiritual unity with boundless Being which fills the soul with reverence for human nature, and disables it from worshipping aught but the formless, indwelling, and omnipresent One.

But the difference between Christianity and Free Religion will best be made evident by a direct comparison between the two, with respect to their leading characteristics. This will show that by the intrinsic truth or falsity of the Christian Confession, that "Jesus of Nazareth is the Christ of God," Christianity must stand or fall. Let the issue be met fairly and squarely. The heart of the great controversy which is now shaking the world to its profoundest depths can be found nowhere, in the last analysis, but in this question of the truth or falsity of the Christian Confession. Here lies the battle-ground between freedom and authority, the vast Christian Church and the spirit of the nineteenth century, the great historical faith of the Old World and the genius of American liberty, — in one word, between Christianity and Free Religion. The time has come to see and to say that the Christian Confession is not a truth. *Jesus was not the "Christ of God."* The "Christ" prophesied and longed for has never come, and will never come. The office and function is a mythical, an impossible one. No individual man has ever stood, or can ever stand, in the relation of Lord, King, and Saviour to the whole world. It would be an infinite usurpation for any man to occupy that office, either in a temporal or spiritual sense. A comparison between the Christian idea as it has always been and must ever remain, on the one hand, and the ideas which are now asserting eminent domain over the development of humanity, on the other hand, will show that this issue between Christianity and Free Religion is an absolute and irreconcilable one, and that the former is doomed by the very nature of things to fade away and make room for the latter.

THE TWO CORNER-STONES.

The corner-stone of Christianity is the Christ himself, believed to have actually come in the flesh as the Divinely appointed Saviour of the world, the one "Life, Truth, and Way." His mission is unique, not to be accounted for by historical causes, but only by a special miraculous influx of Divine Power into the course of history. However this conception is refined and subtilized by the more thoughtful minds in the Christian Church, Jesus remains still, in the religion it teaches, the one Vine of which all his followers are merely branches.

But the corner-stone of Free Religion is the universal soul of man, the common nature of humanity, as the source and origin of the world's religious life. Out of this have sprung, in accordance with unchanging spiritual laws, all churches, faiths, and religions. Nothing less than the entire history of humanity can reveal all its possibilities; and through its own inherent possibilities alone can the world ever be "saved" from its own miseries and imperfections. The spontaneous energies of human nature, which is the great fountain-head of all history, all civilization, all religion, are the power of God gushing up and revealing in each soul afresh the Infinite Life that fills all space and time. It is faith in these human yet divine spontaneities, wherever and whenever and however manifested, that inspires the free soul to its highest life, and bids it realize its own inborn ideal as the consummation of its noblest possibilities. Faith in the individual Jesus, — faith in universal human nature: these are the two corner-stones.

THE TWO FELLOWSHIPS.

As is the basis of faith, so is the fellowship built upon it. The Christian fellowship is as wide as all Christians, but no wider. Those are Christian brethren who acknowledge the same common Lord, and thus drink at the same general fountain of Christian life. It was their love *for each other* that made the ancients marvel at the early Christians; and they who forget this limitation of their love fail to understand the spirit of the primitive Church as impressed on the New Testament. From that day to this, the same limitation of fellowship has existed; and so long as the Christian Church continues to survive, its organic bond of union must still be the original Christian Confession.

But the fellowship of Free Religion is as wide as humanity itself. All who are born of woman are brothers and peers in virtue of their common nature. There is no right of spiritual primogeniture, no monopoly of inspiration, no precedence of creed; all men are but seekers after truth, and despite all pretensions and delusions they reach it only by using the natural faculties of the mind. The impartial God sends his sunshine and his rain to all. There is no privileged or commissioned interpreter of Divine oracles.

> "Now there bubbled beside them, where they stood,
> A fountain of waters sweet and good;
> The youth to the streamlet's brink drew near,
> Saying, 'Ambrose, thou maker of creeds, look here!'
> Six vases of crystal then he took,
> And set them along the edge of the brook.

> "'As into these vases the water I pour,
> There shall one hold less, another more,
> And the water unchanged in every case
> Shall put on the figure of the vase :
> O thou who wouldst unity make through strife,
> Canst thou fit this sign to the Water of Life?'"

These beautiful lines of our own American poet breathe the true spirit of Free Religion, — a deep humility in the presence of infinite truth which forbids any one to despise another's earnest faith. How all dogmatic arrogance fades away, when reverence for our own souls begets an equal reverence for the souls of others! It is out of this profound sentiment of human equality in respect to all spiritual privileges that a profound regard for all other human equalities is born, nor do I see how it can have any other origin. Yet in the conscious equality of all human rights, whether before God or man, must be found the seed of all universal brotherhood that deserves the name. These, then, are the two contrasted fellowships, — the brotherhood of the Christian Church limited by the Christian Confession, the great brotherhood of man without limit or bound.

THE TWO SOCIAL IDEALS.

A similar contrast meets us in the social ideals held up as the great end of collective human activity. The supreme object of the Christian Church is to *christianize the world*, and thus secure the salvation of all in the world to come. That is, its efforts are all directed to the one aim of bringing all men within its fold, of making its brotherhood universal on the basis of the Christian Confession, of absorbing the world into itself, and thus including all men under the sceptre of its Lord. In the prime of its glory the mediæval Papacy went far towards accomplishing this object; and, although now the Christian Church is shattered into fragments, each separate piece or "sect" endeavors to accomplish it anew. "Church Extension" is the primary aim of all denominations as such, the evidence and measure of all denominational life. To evangelize or christianize the world is the ideal end of all Christian activity of a social kind; and this means to make conterminous with the globe that "kingdom of heaven" in which the Christ is the Divinely appointed king.

But the supreme object of Free Religion is to *humanize the world*. That is, it aims to liberate, to educate, to spiritualize, in one word, to develop the race. To bring out of man the best that is in him, — the best in thought, in feeling and sentiment, in moral action, in social, political, and religious life, — this is the work it proposes.

Whatever inward or outward conditions favor this symmetrical development of human nature, it strives unceasingly to secure; and thus all high philanthropies and all generous reforms and all noble endeavors to ameliorate society grow out of the essential purpose and dominant idea of Free Religion. Man does not need to be christianized: he does need to be humanized. While thus the social ideal of the Christian Church is that of a "kingdom of heaven" on earth with the Christ for its king, the social ideal of Free Religion is that of a Commonwealth of Man, in which there is neither king nor lord, but all are free and equal citizens.

THE TWO SPIRITUAL IDEALS.

A profounder contrast still exists between the two spiritual ideals held up to the private soul. The highest possible exhortation of Christianity is — "Be like Christ;" its highest eulogy is to say — "He is Christlike." By rigid self-examination and laborious imitation to model the character after the pattern set by the "Great Exemplar," is the crowning achievement of the Christian saint. The little work of Thomas à Kempis, called the "Imitation of Christ," which is said to have passed through more editions than any other book except the Bible alone, is chiefly a devoutly passionate outpouring of the Christian aspiration to attain the character of Jesus. Suppression of the stubborn individuality and complete reproduction of the Master's likeness is the spiritual ideal of the

Christian mystic; and the heroes of Christian history are precisely those who, like Fénelon or St. Francis of Assisi, are supposed to have most successfully imitated it.

But the highest exhortation of Free Religion is — "Be thyself;" its highest praise — "He was true to himself, and therefore true to humanity and to God." It recognizes no absolute ideal in Jesus; it perceives that, even were it possible (which it is not), the successful imitation of Jesus by all mankind would extinguish individuality, make original and independent character impossible, and destroy the very roots of all civilization. It proclaims the servility, nay, the utter irreligion, of spiritual imitation. The character of Jesus exhibits but one out of an infinite number of spiritual types, and could be an ideal to no one but himself, even supposing that he had made his own ideal identical with his own real. The law of endless variety in natural temperaments and organizations, and in the relative strength of elementary faculties, involves another law of endless variety in individual ideals. A single absolute ideal for all mankind would be an appalling curse, if it were possible to hold all to it. Each soul must have its own ideal according to the balance of its natural capacities and powers, the nature of its surroundings and conditions in the world, and the quantity and quality of its being; and as the soul grows in attainment, so must its ideal evermore enlarge. It is supremely mischievous to be a copyist in character. Facsimiles of Jesus are impossible; good imitations of him are excessively rare; caricatures of him are plentiful. The ideal of another, like a die stolen from the mint, can at the best make me only a counterfeit. Hence the highest maxim in this matter is simply this: "Be true to yourself." Thus, while the spiritual ideal of Christianity is to sacrifice all individuality in the reproduction of the character of Jesus, the spiritual ideal of Free Religion is to develop the individuality of each soul in the highest, fullest, and most independent manner possible.

THE TWO ESSENTIAL SPIRITS.

But the profoundest contrast of all lies in the fundamental unlikeness of spirit and tone. The spirit of Christianity, as manifested in the chief saints of Christian history, has always been on the one hand that of self-abnegation, self-distrust, self-contempt, and on the other hand that of utter spiritual prostration before Jesus and utter submission to his authoritative will. To be absolutely obedient to the Christ, and to find this obedience made easy by a divine passion of love for his person and his character, has always been and must always be the governing, secret aspiration of every Christian heart. Whether believed to be the incarnate God or simply the one Divinely ordained Way to God, the supreme motive to holy living has always been, in the deeply devout Christian, absorbing love for his Saviour; and this love always tends to produce the suppression of the free self, the paralysis and humiliation of the individual will, in order that the will of the Master may be accomplished in heart and life. Meekness, patience, submission, resignation, passivity, absence of self-will, complete surrender of the whole soul to a will outside of itself, — these are the especial graces and virtues of the Christian character, and determine the type of the " Christian spirit."

But the spirit of Free Religion is fundamentally different. The same self-consecration to God which in the Christian soul produces self-surrender and self-humiliation, produces in the free soul self-reliance and self-respect. God in Christ is God outside of self, and devotion to him must be self-suppression. But God in Humanity is God in every soul; and devotion to him becomes the putting forth of every energy to attain freely the individual ideal. The spirit of Free Religion, as the name imports, is the spirit of freedom, of manly and womanly self-respect, of deep religious trust in human nature; and because its faith in self is at bottom faith in the divineness of universal Nature, it is the perfect blending of sturdy self-reliance with noble humanity and devout repose in God.

THE SUMMARY.

Thus from a thoughtful and independent comparison of the great faith of the past and the greater faith of the present, it becomes clear, I think, that there is a deep spiritual antagonism between them. The one must wane as the other waxes. The one must die that the other may live. *God in Christ* is the spiritual centre of Christianity; hence in Christ himself must Christianity ever have its basis and corner-stone, — in the Christian Confession it must ever have its bond and limit of fellowship, — in the universal extension of the Christian Church it must ever have its social ideal, — in the imitation of Jesus it must ever have its spiritual ideal, — in the suppression of self and utter submission to the will of Jesus it must ever manifest its essential spirit. But *God in Humanity* is the spiritual and central faith of Free Religion; which has thus its corner-stone in universal human nature, its fellowship in the great brotherhood of man, its social ideal in a free republican commonwealth, its spiritual ideal in the highest development of each individual soul, its essential spirit in a self-respect which is at once profound reverence for human nature and profound repose in universal Nature.

Am I not right in calling this the higher and diviner faith, — the faith of manhood as contrasted with that of childhood? I recognize the great services rendered to man by the Christian Church; I appreciate the peculiar beauty of the Christian character; I know the mighty power of the Christian spirit. But I cannot conceal from myself that Christianity is not adapted to the present as it has been to the past, and that a deeper, broader, and higher faith is to-day silently entering the heart of humanity. If, out of all the sayings attributed to Jesus in the New Testament, I were asked to select that one which most profoundly utters the spirit of his religion, I should select these beautiful, gracious, and tender words: —

"Come unto me, all ye that labor and are heavy-laden, and I will give you rest. Take my yoke upon you, and learn of me; for I am meek and lowly of heart; and ye shall find rest unto your souls. For my yoke is easy, and my burden is light."

How many aching hearts and wounded spirits have taken upon them the easy yoke of Jesus, and found the promised rest! And how many more will find repose and peace in the same gentle bondage! If the free spirit could indeed wear a yoke, — if it could indeed purchase rest on such terms without abjuring that spiritual independence which is its very life and breath, — then might it wear the yoke of Jesus. Once I rejoiced to wear it; but I can wear it no longer. The rest I need comes no longer from spiritual servitude, but must be sought and found in the manly exercise of spiritual freedom. It is to those who feel this Anglo-Saxon instinct of liberty stirring in their hearts that my words are addressed, — not to those who feel no galling pressure from the easy yoke. My duty is discharged; my task is done; and, as I have freely spoken, so do you freely judge my words.

THE SOUL OF PROTESTANTISM.

By O. B. Frothingham.

THE subject of this lecture is "The Soul of Protestantism;" by which is meant the essence of Protestantism, its cardinal idea and principle. This is not so simple a thing to get at as people commonly imagine. They who think they have it fast locked up in the phrases, "an open Bible," "freedom of conscience," "liberty of private judgment," "spiritual emancipation," or other popular motto, are gravely mistaken. Such will probably be surprised to learn that some of the deepest scholars and hardest thinkers of Germany, where the Protestant Reformation began, where its genius was native, and its spirit should be most easily caught, have written bulky books to show what the soul of Protestantism was, and so little agree in their descriptions of it that their chief strength is expended in correcting, criticising, and refuting one another. A glance at three or four learned articles by first-rate men, in the "Theologische Jahrbücher," will satisfy the incredulous of the extreme difficulty of saying precisely what Protestantism was or is.

Men protested long before Martin Luther; but Protestantism, as a solid movement in Christendom, began with him. It was no new thing for the Church of Rome to be assailed. Malcontents had had their fling at her for two hundred years and more. Wycliffe in England, Huss and Jerome in Bohemia, Savonarola in Italy, had said their say, — paid dearly for the luxury, to be sure, but spoken, nevertheless, and been heard. Eminent men in Catholic universities had dealt hard blows at the papacy. The Church was used to complaint, fault-finding, and opposition from her children. She felt secure and good-natured, and let the malcontents wrangle on and devour one another. The great popes sat securely on their throne, suspecting no new danger. The patient old world was wonted to their ways. The cavillers had said their worst, and, as for *doing* any thing, the power was not in their hands. The elegant Leo X. accepted from the mighty Julius II. the duty of rebuilding St. Peter's church. Michael Angelo laid before him his plan of hanging the dome of the Pantheon three hundred feet in the air, and filling in the space between the dome and the earth with an architecture that should do justice to the conceptions of his colossal brain. The imagination of Leo was enchanted, but his exchequer was low. Angelo was not a cheap builder. Good architecture was never cheap. He planned for no earthly monarch, but for the Vicar of Christ, who was supposed to have at command the treasures of invisible kingdoms. For such building even the Pope was poor; the Roman State was poor. The rights to the Church in France had been sold to Francis I., but the price paid by a king for a national church left but a scanty allowance for the celestial design. Thirty new cardinals were created, each at a handsome sum. Still the treasury of holiness was empty. The terrestrial sources of revenue being exhausted, the celestial remained. Tetzel, a Dominican monk, was commissioned to offer seats in paradise to the highest bidder. With boundless impudence, partly constitutional, partly official, and partly the result of confidence in the bottomless credulity of the German people, he offered his goods openly in churches, public squares and taverns, with huge parade. The market was fair, and for a time a smart traffic went on to the great content of the Dominican order, which pocketed a handsome commission, and to the rapid accumulation of Peter's pence. But as the goods became shop-worn, the tradesman had to fall back on his eloquence, which was of the auctioneer's quality, not refined; he insinuated, he ranted, he cried up his wares in the most approved style of the auction block, peppered and sugared his lies, drew on his fancy for inducements, threw sulphur and turpentine at discretion into the furnaces, burnished up his tarnished images of felicity, increased the number of penalties to be compounded for, swelled the list of sins to a ruinous dimension, multiplied the candidates for perdition, caught people figuratively by the hair of the head, held them over the pit, and, when they writhed and screamed in terror, quietly remarked, "Well, the door of escape is open; pay the price, cash down, and you are free."

A prospectus of these public sales, signed and guaranteed by the Archbishop of Mentz, whom the Pope had made superintendent of the saintly lottery, fell under the eye of the monk Luther. He was struck with amazement, but not dumb. A remonstrance to his own Bishop of Brandenburg had no effect. The bishop merely advised him to hold his tongue, or he might get himself into trouble. A respectable remonstrance addressed to the Archbishop of Mentz, accompanied by a list of propositions which he offered to maintain against Tetzel and his practices, brought no reply; and on the 31st of October, 1517, the indignant monk nailed a copy of the propositions to the church door of Wittemberg Castle. The propositions are too many to quote here in full. Here are a few of them: —

"Christians should be taught that, if the Pope were made acquainted with the extortions of the indulgence preachers, he would prefer seeing the basilica of St. Peter's reduced to ashes to building it with the flesh, fleece, and bones of his sheep."

"The Pope's wish must be, if indulgences, a small matter, are proclaimed with the ringing of bell, with ceremonial and solemnity, that the Gospel, so great a matter, should be preached with a hundred bells, a hundred ceremonials, a hundred solemnities."

"The true treasure of the Church is the sacrosanct Gospel of the glory and grace of God."

"People are given cause to hate this treasure of the Gospel, by which the first became last."

"People are given cause to love the treasure of indulgences, by which the last became first."

"The treasures of the Gospel are the nets by which the rich were once fished for."

"The treasures of indulgences are the nets with which men's riches are now fished for."

"To say that the cross placed in the Pope's arms is equal to the cross of Christ is blasphemy."

"Why does not the Pope, out of his most holy charity, empty Purgatory, in which are so many souls in punishment? This would be a worthier exercise of his power than freeing souls for money, and to what end? To build a church!"

"What means this strange compassion on the part of God and the Pope, who, for money's sake, change the soul of the impious, of God's enemy, into a soul pious and acceptable to the Lord?"

"Cannot the Pope, whose treasures, at the present moment, exceed the most enormous treasures, build a single church with his own money, without taking that of the faithful poor?"

"Christians should be exhorted to follow Christ, their head, through pains, punishments, and hell itself; so that they may have assurance that heaven is entered through tribulations, not through security and peace."

In all this we see moral indignation blasting hot, the lava stream of a volcanic heart, — nothing more. But more soon followed. Straight on the heels of the propositions came the dogmatic theses and the bold sermon in the vulgar tongue supporting them: —

"Man by his nature cannot will that God be God. He would rather himself be God, and that God were not."

"It is false that appetite is free to choose both ways; it is not free, but captive."

"There exists in Nature, before God, nothing save unclean desire."

"It is false that this desire can be regulated by the virtue of hope. For hope is opposed to charity, which seeks and desires only what is of God. Hope comes not of our merits, but of our passions, which efface our merits."

"The best, the only infallible preparation and disposition for the reception of grace are the choice and predestination of God from all eternity."

"It is false that invincible ignorance is any extenuation. Ignorance of God, of one's self, of good works, is the invincible nature of man."

This was the doctrinal basis on which the protest of conscience rested. The people leaped upon it, as if it had been the Rock of Ages. A thrill of conviction ran through them. The German mind seemed about to slide off in a mass from Italy. The propositions were printed by myriads; like falling leaves scattered by the wind, they lodged everywhere, in back-yard, on door-step and window-sill. Luther trembled at his own success. He wrote to the Pope: "Most Holy Father, I cast myself at your feet, with the offer of myself and all that is in me. Pronounce the sentence of life or death; call, recall, approve, disapprove; I acknowledge your voice to be the voice of Christ, who reigns and speaks in you." He protested that he advanced no heretical doctrine.

The story of Luther's battle with himself and the Pope does not belong here. We are concerned with Protestantism, and but incidentally with its founder. On the 10th of December, 1520, at the ninth hour of the day, at the east gate of Wittemberg, near the holy cross, the Pope's bull of excommunication, along with other of the Pope's books, was publicly burned. By that act the reformer destroyed his ships, and strode forward resolutely to his life-battle, while Europe entered on the career of controversy which soon resulted in blood.

The enthusiasm of all classes for the new religion was boundless. "Nobles and people, castles and free towns, rivalled each other in zeal and enthusiasm for Luther." His popular tracts were devoured; the sheets wet from the press were hurried to the shops and carried off at almost the same instant. The printers seemed to be disciples of the reformer to a man. They printed with the greatest care, and sometimes at their own expense, writings that favored his cause, while the Romanists found difficulty in getting any thing done, had to pay dearly for it, and obtained the poorest work even then. Not a few monks caught the fury and became colporteurs for Luther. The enemy tried desperately to stem the tide, by sowing dissensions among the German principalities, and so dividing the Protestant strength; and they succeeded so far that, in 1529, the German Diet took measures to check the movement. Then it was that a minority of the delegates remonstrated, and, remonstrance being of no avail, PROTESTED. Hence the name PROTESTANTS. So much of external history must suffice.

Now, the careful thinker asks two questions: —

I. Against what was the protest made?

II. In the name of what was the protest made?

Against what? Against the right of a majority to dictate to a minority in matters of faith; against outward compulsion in concerns of religion, whether from State or Church; against spiritual dominion of all kinds. The protesting members declared their willingness to obey the emperor in all fitting duty till death; "but these are matters that concern God's honor and the salvation of souls, and we are bound to regard Him as King and God, King of kings, and Lord of lords; and, being so bound, by baptism and by his holy word, we must consult that honor and that salvation, each one standing alone, and giving account of himself. Once for all they declare that they cannot with good conscience obey in all things the emperor, since they should falsify themselves in sight of God, were they to influence any of high or low degree to depart from the commandment of God's holy word, and bow to

a lower authority. And as for the authority of the
Church to interpret God's word, it would be time
enough to speak of that when they were all agreed
on which was the true, holy Church of Christ.
But inasmuch as on one point there is not the
least controversy, — as no precept is plainer than
the command to stand fast by God's word, — as
the holy Scripture is clear on all essential points to
Christian men, — we are minded, God helping and
instructing, to abide by it, to heed what is contained in the holy gospel of the Old and New
Testaments, and to heed nothing else; for, in thus
observing the one rule of truth, and conforming to
the only just standard of doctrine and life, no one
can err or go astray; whoever builds thereon will
prevail against the gates of hell; but they that
build upon human edicts must come to naught."

The protest, therefore, was against every kind of
outward interference in matters of faith.

In what name was the protest made? In the
name of CONSCIENCE. In the early reform literature there is no more frequent word than the word
"conscience." Luther used it repeatedly. His
followers used it; it occurs many times in the appeal which the minority made, and the pith of
which I have just condensed. *But what did these
men mean by conscience?* In raising this question,
we touch the heart of our subject. *The soul of
Protestantism was respect for conscience as the kernel
of moral personality.* That was the seat of authority within, as the Church for the Romanists was

the seat of authority without. That was the organ of faith as the Church *had been* the organ of faith; the only organ there was to oppose to the Church. The external power must be supplanted by an internal power. As Rome was objective, Protestantism must be subjective. In the name of *conscience*, Savonarola pronounced Pope Alexander an atheist, and called on Catholic Christendom to depose him; in the name of *conscience*, Luther declared Leo a blasphemer, and called on Christendom at large to throw off his yoke. Both reformers arrayed conscience against the hierarchy which, combining with state-craft, crushed religion; but neither arrayed conscience against the religion thus abused. Savonarola called himself a Catholic of Catholics, and Luther called himself a Christian of Christians. Both appealed to a new attestation of faith; neither detracted from the substance of faith. It was to save the substance that they changed the representation. It is, at least, a rhetorical exaggeration to say, as George Bancroft does: "Luther based his reform upon the simple but sublime truth which lies at the basis of morals, — the paramount value of character and purity of conscience; the superiority of right dispositions over ceremonial exactness." Neither Luther nor his friends took so natural a view of justification as this.

By conscience they meant what we mean by the "Christian consciousness," the "mind of Christ" that had been imparted by grace and by inheritance. Not the *natural* conscience; not the human moral sense; not the impulse, or the persuasion, or the conviction of right; of the natural conscience, as of other things natural, Luther had the most despicable opinion. The function of the natural conscience was simply to convict people of sin. It was no oracle, unless it were of condemnation. It revealed nothing but iniquity; it proclaimed nothing but doom. In appealing to conscience, Protestantism appealed to no human power, but to an authority above humanity, on which humanity was absolutely dependent, before which humanity must devoutly kneel. The *conscience of the believer*, the conscience enlightened and renewed by grace, furnished the new point of immediate spiritual contact with God. But the conscience of the unbeliever rendered no such divine service. What respect had Luther for the consciences of the poor peasants who, getting an inkling of natural human rights from the Bible, and interpreting justice by the awakened feeling of their hearts, rose in insurrection against their brutal lords? "I am of opinion that all the peasants ought to perish, rather than the princes and magistrates, since they take up the sword without divine authority. The peasants deserve no mercy, no tolerance, but the indignation of God and man." "The peasants are under the ban both of God and the emperor, and may be treated as mad dogs." What consideration had Luther for the conscience of the earnest and indefatigable Carlstadt, who felt himself impelled to enter the church at Wittemberg and destroy the crucifixes, images, and altars, — who, pressing the Protestant principle, as he received it, to its results, questioned the doctrine of the real presence of Christ in the Eucharist? Carlstadt was an uncomfortable fellow, but he was a true and uncompromising reformer. Does Luther deal with him as an over-zealous brother? He deals with him as a miscreant. "Pray for me, and help me to trample under foot this Satan that has arisen at Wittemberg against the Gospel, in the name of the Gospel. It will be difficult to persuade Carlstadt to give way; but Christ will constrain him, if he does not yield of himself. For *we* are masters of life and death, we who believe in the Master of life and death." "The spirit of the new prophets aspires to be the highest spirit, a spirit which has eaten the Holy Ghost, feathers and all. 'Bible,' they cry out; yes, *Bible, Bubel, Babel.*" What regard did Luther show for the conscience of the Anabaptists of Münster, — fanatical people who, doubtless with intentions as serious as his own, proposed to reconstruct society on what they held to be Gospel principles? "Is it not clear," he cries, "that the devil reigns at Münster in person, or rather that there is a whole troop of devils?" "When God in his wrath deprives us of his word, no deceit of the devil's is too gross. The best weapon against the devil is the sword of the Spirit, the word of God. The devil is a spirit, and laughs at cuirass, horse, and horseman. The devil keeps the hot soup in his mouth, and only mutters *mum, mum.* Well, devil! Mutter and spit as you list; one little word overthrows all you say."

In all this it cannot fairly be said that Luther was untrue to his principle. His principle never admitted the validity of the unregenerated conscience. In common with all the reformers who have been associated with the Protestant movement, he held as a cardinal truth the doctrine of human depravity, the vital need of supernatural grace, and the indispensable importance of faith grounded on belief, to make the grace available. There was not the faintest suspicion of Transcendentalism about them. They deemed it a holy duty to put the natural reason down. Luther, indeed, condemned resort to physical violence. He had no mind to baptize unbelievers in their own blood. "I will not," he said, "use carnal weapons to spread the Gospel." "Preach I will, talk, write; but compel I will not. For belief must be voluntary, unforced, spontaneous." Luther put his vehemence into speech; his words smote like two-edged swords; his language was a consuming fire. But the less passionate, unsympathetic, unenthusiastic Calvin burned Servetus as logically and imperturbably as Alexander burnt Savonarola, or as John burnt Huss. Toleration did not make part of the plan. It is not enough to say that they could not rise superior to the spirit of their age. They could not rise superior to their religion, and they had no wish to. Their religion was the Christianity of the Middle Ages fortified by a new guarantee.

The protest was not against doctrines, but against the external dispensation of doctrines. Could they who made it have imagined that their work would have been misunderstood as it has been, they would have remained in the Roman communion for ever.

That Luther and his disciples, near and remote, should have held fast the dogmas of the orthodox faith, trinity, incarnation, atonement, fall and redemption, is not to be wondered at. How could they have done otherwise? The time for theological doubt on these questions had not come. The point to be emphasized is this: *They did all they could to prevent the possibility of any such doubt.* They wanted to make every thing as fast as the Roman Church had made it, and faster, for they would gladly have made all things secure against a second Reformation. They had renounced one authority, but only in the hope of establishing another, equally or more stringent. They had no idea of being Godless, Christless, or churchless. Three points they insisted on: —

I. The first and cardinal point was the absolute dependence of the individual on the Almighty Power, the Eternal Will, which appoints his destiny, and determines absolutely his whole life and being. The most characteristic form of Protestantism is Calvinism; but Calvin did not surpass Luther in the force with which he laid down the doctrine of predestination by the divine decrees. The iron thread of predetermining law runs through the whole system, binding reason and will in fatal bonds. Protestantism, in its essence, *is the effort of the awakened soul to secure its salvation by uniting itself with the absolute cause of all blessedness, the infinite and eternal God.* Luther made this central doctrine the basis of his reform, laying stress particularly on the subjection of the human will; Zwingli was attracted by the other aspect of the conception, the absolute Godhead, the divine prevision; Calvin completed the dogma by developing in full proportions the principle of the eternal decrees. No one tolerably acquainted with the literature of the early Reformation has failed to observe the overshadowing importance given to this speculation, or has missed the fact that it was insisted on as a safeguard against the irruption of unregenerated nature. So long as the determining causality of God could be maintained, there was no danger from rebellion. F. C. Baur, a profound student of this whole subject, says: "That, in the entire relation between man and God, as well moral as religious, nothing proceeds from human activity, but every thing, from the apprehension of the saving truth to the blessed results thereof, every thing depends on the unconditioned will of the absolute cause, is an essential assumption of Protestantism." Equally essential, no doubt, was the assumption of freedom. Luther laid stress enough on that, when on the ground of freedom he defied Church and Papacy, and all spiritual wickedness in high places. But that freedom was simply freedom to respond to the inviting Saviour,

— freedom to embrace the Christ as freedom with the Catholic was freedom to join the Church. Neither Catholic nor Protestant called the choice of a false religion freedom; that was slavery.

II. The next point was the immediate concourse of God, in Christ, with the human soul; *immediate*, without the intervention of priests; a direct, conscious, vital communion, conditioned on faith in the Redeemer. In this union, the disciple was made partaker of the renewing life as completely as was ever claimed by subject of the Papal Church. Faith was the soul's reaction on the Saviour.

III. The third point, an indispensable one, was the sufficiency of the Holy Scriptures of the Old and New Testament, Law and Gospel. To quote Dr. Schenkel, a famous living theologian of the liberal Protestant school: " The contents of religion are in God himself; and since man is conscious of God only as God reveals himself, for man the contents of religion are in the written revelation. Most gloriously and completely has God manifested himself in the person of Christ; and the Holy Scriptures give the history of that manifestation. The Holy Scripture, as the word or revelation of God, contains the divine substance. Conscience is free; but true freedom consists in obedience to the truth. Caprice is no freedom. That only is genuinely free which is bound to God. Hence the Protestant position, while appealing to conscience, at the same time insists that conscience is bound to God's word, and can attain outside of that to nothing. It is therefore the special characteristic of Protestantism *to be the religion of the Bible.*"

Here Schenkel, writing at Heidelberg, only twelve years ago, repeats what Chillingworth said two hundred and thirty-seven years ago. Chillingworth had changed from Protestant to Catholic and back again. He was now writing against the Catholics in a strain so liberal as to offend his Protestant allies: "The BIBLE, I say, the BIBLE only, is the religion of Protestants. Whatsoever else they believe beside it and the plain, irrefragable, indubitable consequences of it, well may they hold it as matter of opinion. I, for my part, after a long and, as I readily believe and hope, impartial search of the true way to eternal happiness, do profess plainly that I cannot find any true rest for the sole of my foot but upon this rock only. Propose me any thing out of this book, and require whether I believe it or no, and, seem it never so incomprehensible to human reason, I will subscribe to it with hand and heart, as knowing no demonstration can be stronger than this: God hath said so, and therefore it must be true. In other things I will take no man's liberty of judgment from him, neither shall any man take mine from me. I will think no man the worse man, nor the worse Christian. I will love no man the less for differing in opinion from me. I am fully assured that God does not, and that, therefore, men ought not to require any more of any man than this: to believe the Scripture to be God's word, to endeavor to find the true sense of it, and to live according to it."

To the objection that Protestants do not agree in their interpretations of Scripture, and therefore some of them must miss the truth and fall into error, Chillingworth replies: "The most disagreeing Protestants that are, yet thus far agree: 1. That those books of Scripture which were never doubted of in the Church are the undoubted word of God and a perfect rule of faith; 2. That the sense of them which God intended, whatsoever it is, is certainly true; so that they believe implicitly even these very truths against which they err, and why an implicit faith in Christ and his word should not suffice as well as an implicit faith in your church, I have desired to be resolved by many of your side, but never could; 3. That they are to use their best endeavors to believe the Scripture in the true sense, and to live according to it. This, if they perform truly and sincerely, it is impossible but that they should believe aright in all things necessary to salvation." But the Scripture stands in need of some watchful and unerring eye to guard it. "Very true; but this is no other than the watchful eye of Divine Providence. God, requiring men to believe Scripture in its purity, engages himself to see it preserved in sufficient purity; and you need not fear but he will satisfy his engagement." And again (for I am anxious to make this position as clear as light, and no language is so frank as Chillingworth's): "The promise of Divine assistance is twofold, absolute or conditional. That there shall be by Divine Providence preserved in the world, to the world's end, such a company of Christians, who hold all things precisely and indispensably necessary to salvation, and nothing inevitably destructive of it; this, and no more, God hath promised absolutely. But a further assistance is conditionally promised, even such an assistance as shall lead us, if we be not wanting to it and ourselves, into all, not only necessary, but very profitable truth, and guard us from all, not only destructive, but also hurtful errors."

In 1863, the archbishops and bishops of the Church of England, in their protest to Bishop Colenso, affirmed: "All our hopes for eternity, the very foundation of our faith, our nearest and dearest consolations are taken from us, if one line of the Sacred Book be declared unfaithful or untrustworthy." And Colenso had merely called in question the Old Testament arithmetic!

From all this it appears that Protestantism was a system; not a movement, but a system, as fixed and determinate as that of Rome. It erected against unbelief what it considered to be impregnable barriers, and it guarded them with a mastiff's watchfulness. An inflexible creed could not be imposed, nor was it thought desirable, at least it was never entertained as feasible. There was little consistency of opinion among the reformers on speculative dogmas. They soon engaged in controversies, and fell asunder in divisions. The disputes about the sacraments were bitter, — about the fall of Adam, imputed sin and righteousness, predestination to bliss or bane. The confessions were at issue on cardinal points of doctrine. Some were compromised, others were dropped. In course of time great modifications were made in the body of the Protestant theology. Lutherans departed widely from Luther. The Lutheran Church in America deals gently with doctrinal differences; they drop the doctrine of the *real presence*, reject the authority of the Fathers, and insist only on the fundamentals, the necessity of personal union with Christ and faith in the sufficiency of the Scriptures. *But they do insist on these.* Calvinists modify materially, in some respects essentially, the beliefs held of prime moment by John Calvin, but belief in the necessity of regeneration through and by Christ, and in the sufficiency of the Scriptures, is never relaxed. The members of the Evangelical Alliance are very tolerant beyond certain limits; they talk as if they had caught the vision of the Free Religion men. But touch with your little finger the faith in the Saviour, the necessity of a vital spiritual communion with him, the miraculous character and divine authority of the Word of God, and they are as sensitive as Luther was on the point of the sacrament, or the dogma of predestination. The evangelical unions through the country seem to be very generous in surrendering unessential points; but the essential points are never qualified, or put, even by implication, in debate. A recent correspondent of the "London Spectator," a Congregationalist, old and zealous, indignantly protests against the insinuation that there is any doctrinal despotism in the churches of his connection. But he does not deny that the discipleship in Christ, and the revelation in the Bible, are as cardinal now as ever. No man says such hard things of the Protestant theology as Henry W. Beecher. If we may credit the gossips, he serves Luther as Luther served the Pope, and deals out figuratively to Calvin the measure Calvin dealt to Servetus, fastening up the fundamentals for derision, and scorching the articles with invective; but on a late occasion, when he cut himself adrift from the churches, he avowed with whimsical solemnity his faith in the necessity of personal regeneration through Christ. As the tide flows in and out of a bay, people may drift into and out of his church, yet the church consists only of those who are made one with God in Christ!

A popular Congregational preacher bestows a generous ministry on the horse. Does he despair of the Gospel, or only of the man? As St. Paul turned from the unbelieving Jews to the Gentiles, does he turn from his church-members to the quadruped? The same apostle contrasts favorably the moral condition of Turk and Hindu with that of Christians. Does he think the Hindus and Turks need no regeneration, or only that the Christians need it more? Is he eulogizing the lost, or castigating the chosen? Mr. Alanson Picton, in a note in his remarkable volume, "The Mystery of Matter," says that in England many non-conformist places of worship contain the Westminster Confession on their title-deeds. "But I know," he says, "by experience, that the assumption of office by the minister may be preceded, not by a signature of the creed, but by an express repudiation of it." He tells the story of a young student who was sent out from his college to preach at a village chapel. The man who met him at the railway station was curious to know what precise altitude of doctrine the congregation might expect on Sunday. On his part the divinity student was curious to learn how *the congregation* stood in regard to doctrine. "Well, yo' seen, sir, some on 'em likes it igh and some on 'em likes it low. I likes it middlin igh myse'n." This indicates a vast change of mental attitude since the century came in; but it is a change in regard to matters which have always been subject to change, because always in debate. Protestants have fought hard for dogmatic uniformity; but Protestantism never pledged itself to such uniformity. Protestantism pledged itself to nothing *but spiritual union with Christ through faith, and the divine sufficiency of the Word of God.* This implied many things, — the depravity of nature, the need of supernatural regeneration, the eternal distinction between the elect and the rejected. But on all these matters shades of difference were allowed that did not go the length of frittering the essential faith away.

Some will ask why the *essential* faith should not be frittered away at last; why the process of disintegration should stop where it is; how any thing can resist the course of demoralization that, setting in at the moment of Protestantism's birth, has gone on with such prodigious force ever since, and has so completely pulverized every other ecclesiastical and speculative fragment of Christian institution? I answer, *Nothing will arrest it*. The decomposition will continue till the whole mass is decomposed. In fact, the end is already reached over large tracts of Christendom. What I contend for is, that, when it is reached, *Protestantism will be dead*. Instead of gaining its last victory as some imagine, it will suffer its final defeat, involving the final defeat of the "Christian" system. For Protestantism is *intellectual*, as distinguished from *ecclesiastical* Christianity. Its faith in Christianity was and is as absolute as that of Rome; its zeal for the Christ was and is as intense; its intellectual and moral grasp was and is more convulsively tenacious. It was an effort to come to close quarters with the Gospel, to penetrate the holy of holies, to meet the Redeemer face to face, to get within the direct pressure of his arm. If it failed, the failure does not lie at its door. If it failed, it failed because it undertook the impossible. If it failed, the final effort to recover the religion which Rome was forced to let go — which the sudden cry of a single monk precipitated from its broad sides, as the avalanche slides from a mountain, and leaves it bare — is exhausted, and the system of Luther shares the fate of the system of Hildebrand.

Six years ago, Rev. Ferdinand Ewer, of Christ Church, New York, delivered a series of remarkable discourses on the " Failure of Protestantism." They were delivered in the interest of ecclesiastical Christianity, Dr. Ewer being an eloquent preacher of the " High Church" theory. His points were, and he put them with great force, that Protestantism had failed to get at the masses, and even to retain the masses it found prepared to receive it; that its logical issue is Rationalism, which is a repudiation of Christianity; that in its own provinces, where it has held exclusive sway for two and a half centuries, in Germany and Switzerland conspicuously, scepticism and disbelief, infidelity and atheism, are regularly sown and planted (he might have added by so-called Protestant preachers). The conclusion is, that Protestantism must be abandoned, — and the Church Catholic, of which the Roman Church is but a branch, must be restored to dignity and authority.

Dr. Ewer's description of the condition of Protestantism is not exaggerated in line or color. Had he written in the autumn of 1873, after the meetings of the Evangelical Alliance, he might have put in effects of light and shadow that would have made it more sombre still. The reports of the foreign delegates were cloudy with disappointment and misgiving. If their statements are credible (and certainly they would not have made such, had they been able to make others), Protestantism is rapidly declining in Germany; it makes no perceptible progress in France; in Spain and Italy it has no future. It achieves no fresh conquests, and at every point is giving way to the pressure of secular thought. The wail of Protestantism is as general as it is pathetic.

But Dr. Ewer is clearly wrong in ascribing all this ruin to Protestantism itself, — to a fatal principle which it carried in its own bosom, to the inevitable logic of its own cardinal idea. He is wrong in holding Protestantism responsible for what Protestantism could not help. If Protestantism could not preserve Christianity, neither could Catholicism. If Protestantism cannot prevent infidelity, neither could Catholicism prevent Protestantism, and to charge Parker upon Luther is as unfair as it would be to charge Luther upon Leo. Back of them both was a power which was before either, and which they were unable to resist; and that power was the HUMAN MIND, which is more than all churches and Bibles.

But has not all this ruin come about through the application of private judgment to religion? Most certainly. And is not the right of private judgment one of the cardinal principles, if not the cardinal principle, of Protestantism? No. Dr. Ewer assumes that it is, on the authority of tradition. This is one of the solemn commonplaces of Protestant talk and writing. Even so careful a thinker as John Stuart Mill speaks of the Reformation as "the great and decisive contest against priestly tyranny for liberty of thought." A great, though hardly a decisive, contest against priestly tyranny it certainly was; but I do not find evidence that it was for liberty of thought. It was for a *spiritual*, as opposed to an *ecclesiastical* faith.

But surely Luther translated the Bible into the popular German speech, in order that the humblest people might read it; he was glad to have it multiplied by the printing-press; in fact, the invention of the printing-press has been regarded as a providential aid to the Protestant religion, because it multiplied copies of the Bible. Protestantism is for ever urging people to read the Bible for themselves, is thrusting it upon people, if they will not buy it, giving it to them, without note or comment, trusting it unreservedly to their private interpretation. What does this imply, if not the fullest confidence in the private judgment, the fullest acceptance of the principle of free thought? It implies the fullest confidence in the Bible.

Luther *did* translate the Bible; but with a firm belief in its inspired and inspiring virtue, with the devoutest of devout persuasion that it was more than able to protect itself against the assaults of unhallowed reason, that the glory which gilded the sacred page would communicate itself to all who read the book. Luther supposed that the Bible would fall into the hands of believers to whom an answering faith would explain it; of scientific unbelievers he had no thought. The same sublime confidence that animated Luther to translate the Bible animates his followers to disseminate it. They have no misgivings. Their faith that the book not merely *contains* the divine word, but *imparts* it, — that it has power to teach, convince, subdue, — that no honest seeker will miss the revelation — that the immanent Christ will work wonders of conversion by means of the word, — that, being eternal, it cannot perish, — that, being the receptacle and organ of the Spirit, it will evidence and communicate the Spirit: this faith, as absolute as the Romanist's faith in his church, holds the eyes of Protestants so that they cannot see the dangers before them. They regard the prevalence of infidelity as an inscrutable dispensation, a strange phenomenon, — intended perhaps as a trial of their faith; but it never occurs to them to doubt that their faith will be justified in the end. So far from connecting infidelity with the free reading of the Bible, they are convinced that the free reading of the Bible will check infidelity. To conceive any other result is to them impossible. They could as easily conceive of God as a liar.

Private judgment with Protestants is opposed to priestly judgment; it means that the sense of Scripture comes immediately to the individual, not mediately, — just as Christ himself does; that it is each believer's own concern. It does not mean liberty to read the Bible like any other book, to try it by literary laws, to judge its contents by rational standards; but merely liberty to find the oracles of God there, — not liberty to detect error, but liberty to be personally assured of the truth. This point cannot be made sharp enough. With Protestants, the liberty of private judgment excludes doubt, implies faith to start with. To start without faith is next door to sacrilege. Protestants are fond of quoting Pastor Robinson's farewell address to the pilgrims at Delft Haven: —

"Brethren, we are now quickly to part from one another, and whether I may ever live to see your faces on earth any more the God of heaven only knows; but whether the Lord has appointed that or no, I charge you before God and his blessed angels that you follow me no further than you have seen me follow the Lord Jesus Christ.

"If God reveal any thing to you by any other instrument of his, be as ready to receive it as ever you were to receive any truth by my ministry; for I am verily persuaded the Lord has more truth yet to break forth out of His Holy Word. For my part, I cannot sufficiently bewail the condition of the reformed churches, who are come to a period in religion, and will go at present no further than the instruments of their reformation. The Lutherans cannot be drawn to go beyond what Luther said; whatever part of his will our God has revealed to Calvin, they will rather die than embrace it; and the Calvinists you see stick fast where they were left by that great man of God, who yet saw not all things.

"This is a misery much to be lamented. I beseech you, remember, it is an Article of your

Church Covenant, 'That you shall be ready to receive whatever truth shall be made known to you from the written word of God.'"

Noble words, spoken in Protestantism's noblest spirit! But note the limitations. The truth must be "made known from the written word of God." The good man's vision of new truth as "breaking forth out of God's Holy Word" did not include any new truth which might break forth outside of it. He has no thought of any new WORD. Such thought would have been blasphemy. *It was because the Bible was the divine word that more and more truth might be anticipated from its bottomless resources.* The prophecy was inspired by his confidence in the Bible, not by his confidence in the human mind. Strauss says well: "The men of the Reformation conquered for us the right of free inquiry *in* Scripture; but modern science has conquered for itself the right of free inquiry *about* Scripture."

To identify Protestantism with liberty of thought is a mistake. It has *opposed* liberty of thought as vigorously as Romanism ever did, and in the same interest. Rome did not discourage liberty of thought, so long as it did not trespass on her ground. The moment free thought trespassed on *her* ground, Protestantism objected. In what directions has Protestantism encouraged liberty of thought? Not in the direction of Scripture interpretation. Small encouragement has she given to scholars like DeWette, Schenkel, Schwegler, Colenso. Not in the direction of theological speculation. How has she treated heresy? What was her attitude towards Dr. Channing and the Unitarians? How did she receive Theodore Parker? "Oh, Lord if this man is a subject of grace, convert him and bring him into the kingdom of thy dear Son. But if he is beyond the reach of the saving influences of the Gospel, remove him out of the way, and let his influence die with him." What course does Protestantism pursue towards rationalists? Who fixed the stigma to the word "infidel"? Who gave to free thinking its bad name? In what tone do the organs of Protestantism speak of the liberal movement generally in religion? The comments of the entire Protestant press on a late convention of the Free Religious Association sufficiently prove its hostility to thought, when it passes beyond its own border line. Does Protestantism encourage liberty of thought in the direction of positive knowledge of the material universe? Ask Tyndall, ask Huxley, ask Darwin, ask Herbert Spencer. The Young Men's Christian Association of New York refused to admit to their reading-room the "Popular Science Monthly."

"But this is backsliding," you will say; "this is recreancy; this is infidelity to its first principle." Pardon me, no. It is fidelity to its first principle; it is steadfastness; it is conscientious loyalty to traditions. It is not quite true to say that Protestantism was, from the start, inconsistent with itself; that, as a complex fact, it was struck with a radical contradiction. It would have been so had it appealed to reason and encouraged free investigation; for then it would have said almost in plain language, "Be free, and remain enslaved." The magic word "liberty," which stirred the motions of nascent thought in the modern world, and at last shook the fabric of belief in pieces, was not spoken by Martin Luther. He admitted nothing contradictory or inconsistent.

Foolish persons, seeing Protestantism come in accompanied by literature, invention, discovery, the useful arts, civil liberty, popular movements of reform, the industrial advance of the common people, talk as if it called them all into being! You might as well say that the sail of a ship causes the wind, that the mowing-machine calls into existence the prairie, or that the telegraph wires cause electricity. After hearing the pastor of a Unitarian church ascribe the post-office to Christianity, nothing surprises me; that pious people should give Protestantism credit for the printing-press and the submarine cable seems rational. The same folk believe that Tenterden steeple was the cause of Goodwin Sands, and that thunder is the cause of lightning. Athanase Coquerel gives Protestantism credit for three things: 1. *Spiritual liberty*, including a full sense of private responsibility; 2. *The family spirit*, as opposed to the monkish; 3. *The independence of the laity*. But spiritual liberty, in our sense of the term, she never gave. The family spirit was native to the Germans, who first gave

Protestantism a home. The independence of the laity became inevitable when the priesthood was abolished; but it was postponed and prevented and thwarted by the prophetic spirit, which stepped into its place and has not even yet resigned it. The secular elements of the world have not much to thank Protestantism for.

There is a superstition that Protestantism waked the human mind from a sleep of ages. Does the opening eyelid of the child create the morning? Accepting the illusion, it is singular that Protestantism should so soon have discovered that it had roused the wrong passenger, and done its best to put him to sleep again, as the nurse tries to abolish the morning by soothing syrup.

Protestantism was an indication that the human mind was beginning to stir; it was a convulsive twitching of the giant's eyelids. The huge creature had turned and stretched before. Arnold of Brescia, Giordano Bruno, Huss, Savonarola, Wycliffe, were heavings of the monstrous frame. It was the human mind that shook Rome as Enceladus shook Etna. It burst out with a great cry in Martin Luther. It set Protestantism against itself; it fell upon the dogmas one by one and pulled them about till not one of them can be recognized in its tattered garb. It took the printed Bible, read it, studied it, sifted it, proved it uninspired, adopted it among the products of literature, and passed on to find other words of truth. It showed the eternal Christ to have been a man, the primeval Adam to have been a myth, the tempter to have been a teacher, and the fall to have been a rise. It dashed idol after idol, and at every stroke said, "Nehushtan," mere brass. It took personality from the Holy Ghost, reducing it to an influence. The stage properties of the drama of Redemption it remanded to the lumber-room; and now it smiles when the mile-stones it has passed boast of having impelled its progress along a road of their building.

Dr. Ewer calls Protestantism a pestilent heresy, and warns us to go back to the Church. But the Church could not hold the human mind *three hundred years* ago, when it was an infant as compared with its present growth. Protestantism proved that the hierarchy was a pestilent heresy. They are now both heresies to human thought, which throws them off as the serpent sheds his skin.

The word Protestantism will outlive the thing; the name always survives the faith. Already it is borne by many who have discarded the religion it stood for. Unitarians, Universalists, Transcendentalists, Rationalists, call themselves Protestants, even Protestants eminently and characteristically, Protestants of the Protestants; though they have no sympathy whatever with the Protestant idea. The Protestant camp swarms with these traitors disguised as friends. Men hate to drop respectable uniforms. The whole Protestant army will go over at last to the enemy, of course, without knowing it, simply because they wear the old badges and carry the old flag. Judge the power of Protestantism by the spread of its name; it looks immense. Judge of it by the vitality of its spirit, and it shrinks within a small compass. For its breath is well-nigh spent. Liberty of thought has proved too much for it. What seemed a terminus proves to be a way-station. The swift mind has struck another track, and presently not even the station-signal will be visible.

LIBERTY AND THE CHURCH IN AMERICA.

By John W. Chadwick.

In this essay I am to speak on the subject of those relations which subsist, or should subsist, between American citizens, as such, and Religion in its organized capacity,—the Church, as we say, but not quite correctly. We have churches in America, but no Church. By some among us this is regarded as a bad arrangement, and proposals have been offered for a change which will make the government itself a sort of Church, and secure to us a State religion. I do not apprehend that any such change will be brought about at an early or even at a distant day, and have counted the proposals that have been made to this effect as rather a piece of good fortune than otherwise, furnishing as they do, in connection with other proposals and events, a capital excuse for the re-opening of questions somewhat prematurely closed, and a discussion of them which must inure to the advantage of right principles, and a more rational and vital appropriation of ideas which heretofore have been the objects of a somewhat lazy acquiescence. It is the duty and the privilege of each new generation rationally to consider, and accept or reject, the institutions and the customs that have come down to it from the past. We should be ashamed either to fail or flourish upon the wisdom of the fathers or the gracious orderings of tradition. We should prove all things, and hold fast to that which is good. So doing, I am persuaded that the people of America will not only earnestly endorse the framers of the national Constitution in their absolute separation of the State and organized religion, but proceed to harmonize all special legislation with the organic law of the nation. It will be seen that our safety for the future depends, not on the repeal of that law, but on its more absolute enforcement, the removal from all national and local legislation of every statute, and from all educational arrangements of every particular method, which is not in accordance with that pattern of entire religious freedom which the framers of the Constitution saw in their mount of vision.

Between the State and organized religion three different relations are possible, and have been amply illustrated in the history of Christianity alone. The State can be subjected to religion, or religion can be subjected to the State, or the two can "sit apart like Gods." We can have a State religion, or an ecclesiastical government, or the State and Church existing apart, and exerting only a moral influence upon each other. It is a significant fact that the last of these relations has been characteristic of the most vital hours of Christianity. Certainly nothing in its history is so remarkable as the progress which it made in the first three centuries of its existence, when it was entirely independent of the State, save as an occasional object of its persecution. Well may Dr. Newman, referring to the Christianity of that early period, speak of "the joyous swing of her advance," and quote in her behalf the words, *Incessu patuit Dea*, "the goddess was known by her step." We speak of Constantine as the first Christian emperor, but every student of history knows that in that fatal alliance Christianity lost more than it won: it was far more paganized by Constantine than Constantine was Christianized by it.

The next great period of the Church's growth and distinction was when the force of circumstances had broken up this wicked alliance, when Church and State again stood separate, and often pitted against each other. Such progress as there was during the whole middle age was the result of that separation and antagonism. Meantime Mohammedanism, that had started with so many appearances of victory, found too late that they were omens of defeat. There the union of Church and State was complete, and neither was subordinate; and the result is that both Church and State have been involved in a great common ruin. All the worst evils of Mohammedan rule can be traced to the admixture of ecclesiasticism, and all the worst evils and defeats of the religion to its connection with the State. Pius IX., in his famous

Encyclical, did not overstate the evils of a purely national administration of religion. Luther gave the Reformation its worst blow when, in an evil hour, he committed it to the care of the German princes. By that arrangement Protestantism was hopelessly fettered, and German unity infinitely delayed. In Russia, national religion shows its usual fruits of mediocrity and subserviency. In all her history not one really great name has been produced, — so vast the premium upon fools and sycophants. The National Church of Sweden can rehearse a similar tale of nerveless languor and respectability, which only rouses itself for an occasional act of base intolerance. If any further proof is wanted of the quality of national religion, let England furnish it, — England, whose Established Church has been the grave of all enthusiasm, of all progress, of all earnestness. It has steadily allied itself with tyranny and oppression: it has endorsed every outrage which the government has committed; it has been saved from utter death and absolute corruption only by the whip and spur of great outlying organizations, such as Puritanism and Quakerism and the Methodist revival of the eighteenth century, which put her somewhat on her metal and her good behavior, as Luther's courage knocked at the heart of Loyola. If to-day she feels the stirrings of a mystic energy, it is because the tie between her and the State is chafed almost to breaking, and she foretastes the joy of perfect liberation.

The subordination of religion to the State is mainly hurtful to religion. The opposite relation is mainly hurtful to the State, but hardly less so to religion. The later papacy is its most striking illustration, and perhaps it would not be extravagant to say that the government of God's vicegerent was the worst government upon the face of the earth. "God save us from infallible rulers," any people might well say, "if this is a sample of their government." The less the government that is haggled for, the worse for the religion. "Foxes are so cunning because they are not strong." The weakness of the temporal power has nursed the craft of Jesuitism till it can no farther go.

It would seem that this record by itself would be sufficient to deter any intelligent citizen of America from embarking, ever so cautiously, on a voyage having for its object to obtain the golden fleece of an ecclesiastical government, or a State religion. We are assured that these expressions do not fairly represent the nature of the thing attempted; but this disavowal pales before the calls for various conventions and the utterances of the most intelligent exponents of "the new departure." These earnest people do not seem to appreciate, even if they consider, the signs of the times. Everywhere in Europe the old relations between Church and State are being weakened or completely broken up. But is there properly no relation between them? Indeed there is,—the most vital relation. If the State is the appointed guardian of man's dearest interests, it must be somehow the guardian of religion, his dearest interest of all. And, above all, it must guard it from the faintest semblance of government interference or control. It must do this once and for ever in its organic law. It is the merit of our national government as it is at present organized that it does this. It does it not, as has been charged, by some dreadful oversight, but because of a superior insight. The men who framed our Constitution saw that the life of religion consists in its absolute freedom. They saw that only harm had come to it from government interference and control. They saw that the union of Church and State was prejudicial to both parties. They had two great examples to instruct them, — Rome and England. In Rome the ecclesiastical power was uppermost, in England the political. The papal government was beneath contempt; the State religion of England was a dull and passionless conformity. In our day both of these alliances are breaking up. The temporal power of the Pope, so long misused, has finally been taken from him. The Roman populace can do honor to their dead Mazzini, and no one shall say them nay. For political purposes the Pope is twice as dead as Mazzini, who, being dead, yet speaketh, and all Europe hears his voice. In England the disestablishment of the Established Church is only a question of time. And shall America, in the very hour when Europe is waking from her nightmare sleep of centuries, drug herself with the same poison that has worked in Europe's veins such brooding terrors, such sluggishness, such fierce, wild hate and cruelty? I have no fears that she will do so. But so she has been earnestly advised.

The proposed Religious Amendment to the Constitution invites us to introduce into the preamble of that Magna Charta the following words: "Humbly acknowledging Almighty God as the source of all authority and power in civil government, the Lord Jesus Christ as the ruler among the nations, his revealed will as the law of the land, in order to constitute a Christian government." Possibly the leaders of this movement might consent to change the wording a little; but as it stands at present it would commit the nation, first, to a belief in God, then to the lordship, messianic office and deity of Christ ("his revealed will" most certainly implying this), then to the establishment of a Christocracy. Reasons of various force and character are offered in behalf of this stupendous change in the organic law of the nation. Some of them are too trivial to receive a moment's serious attention.

The class of arguments mainly relied upon is that which goes to show that the government has always been implicitly theistic and Christian, wherefore it should be so explicitly. There is a good deal of truth in the premises, but the conclusion does not follow. Certainly the government ought to be explicitly what it is implicitly, but this harmony can be brought about by changing the implicit part as well as by changing the explicit. If the appointment of congressional and army chaplains, and the appointment of Thanksgiving and Fast days, implies that we have a Christian government, might it not be better to surrender these things than to harmonize the Constitution with them and accept the necessary consequences of such action? Fast days on which nobody fasts are dishonest excuses for an extra holiday. Thanksgiving Day is indispensable, but we could have it just the same or all the better without the government's appointing it. Should the government withhold its hand, navy and army chaplains might still be provided, and religion not be insulted by any one's being *obliged* to attend upon their services. Congressional chaplains might be elected and enjoyed by those who feel the need of them in their individual capacity, and no one would be outraged or committed, though it may well be doubted whether one less dishonest law was ever passed by any legislative body on account of the preliminary intercession. When even the excellent chaplain of the Massachusetts House of Representatives, meaning to pray, makes stump speeches to the Almighty on railroad bills and woman's suffrage, it becomes a question whether religion is not really a loser by this conventional arrangement. Still I am unable to see why any public officer has not a right to express his personal religious sense in a public document, and can but feel that only bigotry and narrow-mindedness can take umbrage at any such expression. If it is a duty never to offend by the expression of our religious opinions, it is a higher duty never to be offended by the expression of another man's, if the expression is sincere and natural. The assumption that our government is implicitly theistic or Christian or Biblical, in view of the administration of oaths and the manner of their administration, has some force in it; but here, again, the custom had better conform to the Constitution than the Constitution to the custom. Our Quaker friends do not, I imagine, perjure themselves oftener than other people, but they never take an oath. The discontinuance of this custom is not something to be deprecated, but a consummation devoutly to be wished. The custom is a premium upon everyday lying. It cheapens ordinary veracity. A man's word ought to be as good as his oath. Indeed, we have Jesus himself with us in this matter. "Swear not at all," he said. And in nine hundred and ninty-nine cases out of a thousand the way in which oaths are administered is not very solemn or impressive. Religion and piety are degraded every time an assessor or attorney rattles off or mumbles over that little formula, and every earnest person, when subjected to it, must wish the land well rid of such an idle superstition.

That our government is in some things implicitly Christian and Biblical is therefore no reason why it should be so explicitly in all things, because the implicit things are either not indispensable, or can be procured in other ways. The question still remains: Not being formally and explicitly a theistic or Christian government, ought it to be made either or both by the insertion of a clause to that effect in the preamble to the Constitution?

This question naturally divides itself into two others: What right have we to do this? What good would come of it? First, what right have we to do it? As much right, perhaps, as we have to tell any other falsehood, for falsehood it would be, unless at the start we resign the idea that the government represents the nation. The nation does not acknowledge the substance of the proposed amendment. There are thousands of men who are vital members of the nation who could not, without perjury, express allegiance to the Constitution so amended. Of the six men who have done most to make America the wonder and the joy she is to all of us, not one could be the citizen of a government so constituted; for Washington and Franklin and Jefferson, certainly the three mightiest leaders in our early history, were heretics in their day,— Deists, as men called them, — and Garrison and Lincoln and Sumner, certainly the three mightiest in these later times, would all be disfranchised by the proposed amendment. In vain do those who have this thing at heart protest that it would disfranchise nobody. It may do very well for a religious denomination to put a creed-let into its constitution, and then put in another article declaring that it is binding only upon those who believe in it. But governments do not act in that way, nor do I hear that any supplemental article is intended, declaring that the proposed amendment expresses the opinion of the majority. No self-respecting man who does not believe, not merely in God, but in the lordship and deity of Christ, could ever pledge his fealty to this government so amended. Lincoln could not have taken his oath of office had such a clause been in the Constitution. If as a nation we stand for any thing, it is for "equal rights for all;" not for "all white men," not for all Christians, not for all theists even, but for all. To make the Constitution theistic even would be to expatriate some of the best men in the country; not men who are atheists, but men who think they are, because they cannot accept any of the popular definitions of God, or cannot even define Him to their own satisfaction. There are men thus minded who are among the best in the community, second to none in their enthusiasm for every thing that looks to the improvement of society. They have as good a right to their position as the bluest Calvinist that can be found. There is more genuine religion in their silence and reserve than in the latter's furious boast. I do not suppose that such men would be driven out of the country bodily, though I think I know of some of them who would rather rehearse the part of Robinson Crusoe than remain with us physically when spiritually cut off, — with us, but not of us. Equal rights for all,— that is the American idea, and there is no other right so sacred as the right to one's own thought upon the highest themes.

But the wrong that would be done by the proposed amendment only appears when we remember that it proposes, not only to make the nation formally theistic, but also formally Christian, and not merely formally Christian, but formally evangelical. There are few men who think themselves atheists, less who are so in reality (at least among those who are so professedly). But there are many who think themselves non-Christian, although these too, in many cases, seem to me Christian in the highest sense of all. There are thousands of Jews among us, and not a few persons representative of other great religions. There are men who have been Christians, driven by the tenderness of their consciences and the force of private reasons to give up the Christian name. There are thousands more who call themselves Christians, and yet do not believe that the Bible is "the revealed will" of Jesus, nor, as this implies, that he is God. Taking all these together they form a numerous class, who heretofore have been American citizens by right, but would be only by sufferance if this amendment should prevail. Nay, they would not be *citizens* at all, but only *inhabitants*. But why stop at evangelical Christianity? Why not make the government Calvinistic, or Methodist, or Baptist, or Roman Catholic? The logic of the enterprise demands that every sect shall try to outwit all the others, and if possible get its peculiar creed foisted upon the Constitution. And if "equal rights for all" is a principle to be discarded, the Roman Catholics have as good right to make the nation Roman Catholic, *if they can*, as the Christians have to make it Christian. If might makes right, then any sect has a right to do any thing with the government it can do. If non-Christians have no rights that Christians are bound to respect, simply because Christians are in the majority, then, the majority being the other way, what might Christians reasonably expect? "But there is no danger," you say. Truly there is very little. But when Jesus said, "Do unto others as you would that they should do unto you," he did not add, if I remember rightly, "unless you know that you will always have the upper hand."

There are reasons peculiar to America why there should be no constitutional preference for any particular opinions. De Tocqueville remarks that there is always a tendency in forms of government and forms of religion occupying the same territory to find the same level. The free institutions of America have fostered freedom of thought and ensured a much greater diversity of opinion than exists anywhere else. And what right have we to foster this diversity by the main tenor of our institutions, and then by special enactment make it a crime against the State? And if, here in America, the tyranny of the majority is getting to be quite unbearable, that only shows that in some way minorities must be represented; and when minorities have their rights in politics there will be less color for the maxim that religious minorities have no rights which religious majorities are bound to respect. The only justification of the proposed amendment resides in a belief in the sacredness of majorities, which is getting largely undermined and will soon be thoroughly exploded. "Government of the people, by the people, and for the people" does not mean "government of all the people by the majority and for the majority."

We have no right then, because the nation is not actually so, to make the government formally theistic or Christian or evangelical. If we had, what good would come of it? No good whatever. Because "In God we trust" is stamped upon some of our coins, has that phrase any alchemy to convert their copper into gold? Does any grocer give better sugar for them, any milkman better milk? By no means. And by stamping God or Christ upon the Constitution we shall not make the nation more godly or more Christian. Nominal theism, nominal Christianity, does not amount to much. The worst crimes that have ever been committed have been committed in the name of God and Christianity. King Olaf put a pan of live coals upon Eyvind's naked flesh until it broiled beneath them, and then asked, without a thought of incongruity, "Dost thou now, O Eyvind, believe in Christ?" When Rome was one great sink of horrible debauchery, there was no lack of nominal religion. Incestuous popes denied not God or Christ. There was never more formal recognition of God than in the time of George II. of England; never less vital recognition of his justice and his truth. Public documents were sprinkled thick with compliments to him: public life and private were sprinkled thicker with all possible forms of vice. History will bear record that in our civil war the South was seemingly much more pious than the North. It was always calling upon God. It could quote Scripture by the yard to justify its slavery and its secession. General Lee, for all his treachery and cruelty, considered himself a Christian, and nominal Christians in the North allowed his claim.

But why multiply examples? We might formally acknowledge God and Christ in the Constitution, and not a man, woman, or child would believe or trust in either any more afterward than before. Nay, some would believe less and trust less, for real sanctities are always jeoparded by insisting upon things as real and important which are not so. From the top of a new Sinai I seem to hear the old commandment thundered with a new meaning and a higher than it had of old, "Thou shalt not take the name of the Lord thy God in vain." It *would* be taking it in vain to put it into the Constitution, there to be exhibited, like a fly in amber, — a striking curiosity, but very useless, very dead.

But it is only fair to ask what good the persons in charge of this matter expect to be derived from it. We are told then, in the first place, that "it will be a becoming act of homage to God." It may well be doubted whether "acts of homage" are so highly valued by the Almighty as some would have us to believe. The phrase is somewhat redolent of anthropomorphism in its grosser forms. Then, too, the desired amendment could not represent the nation, but only those in favor of it. To offer it to God or man as representative of the nation would be a lie. It would never represent any more than those accepting it at any given time, and those would need no such representation. Meantime our sister nations will judge us, not by our professions, but by our actions. They will not go to our Constitution to find out what manner of men we are, but to our particular laws and customs, to our treaties and our trade: were the Constitution already Christian, they would think just the same of our claim for consequential damages, thrust into the Washington treaty like the cup into Benjamin's sack.

But though it is asserted, when convenient, that the new amendment is to be only a King Log, and therefore quite harmless, as soon as its movers begin to show what good will come of it, King Log becomes King Stork right speedily. Not as an act of homage, but as "a legal basis for all Christian laws," it is particularly desired. It is something to have it acknowledged that these so-called Christian laws have at present no legal basis in our national government. What is now really desirable is to take from them whatever legal basis they have in the various States of the Union. For what are these Christian laws and institutions for which a legal basis is demanded in the Constitution? An advocate of the amendment answers, "Prayers in our legislatures, occasional days of fasting and thanksgiving, the maintenance of chaplains in our army and navy, in prisons and asylums, the use of the Bible in our public schools, the religious ordinance of the oath, laws guarding the sacredness of the Sabbath, enforcing the Christian law of marriage, and suppressing blasphemy and licentiousness." Some of these points we have already considered, and found that the Constitution is nearer right than the customs for which legal support is demanded. A similar conclusion will be forced upon us if we turn to any of the others. What, for example, is the Christian law of marriage that it should have a legal basis in the Constitution? We are referred to the New Testament. But to what part of the New Testament? To Paul's writings? Then marriage is permissible only as a safety-valve for passion. To the words of Jesus? But, if he is reported correctly, marriage is for the weak and passionate only, not for the strong and pure. Do we want a legal basis for such Christian laws as these? But by the law of marriage the law of divorce is possibly meant, which, in the New Testament, is that, save for adultery, no man shall be divorced. Do we want a legal basis for such a provision as that? Does profane swearing call for a constitutional amendment? How much of it could be reached by legal enactment? Is it not rather a sin against taste and culture than against religion, — a vulgarism rather than a crime? To punish it legally would be to provoke it to new and grosser exhibitions.

Sabbath laws and laws concerning the Bible in the public schools remain to be considered. So far as the first are concerned, the demand which is made for them is but an eddy in a current whose general flow is all the other way. On every side Sabbath laws are becoming less stringent or are less and less regarded. Public libraries are being opened, travel is being less curtailed, there is more out-of-door exercise and enjoyment. Is this as it should be, or is it all wrong, and must it be opposed by legislative enactment that has its roots in constitutional law? If the appeal to the past were final or specially significant, it might be shown that the Puritan Sabbath is itself an innovation; that the Christian Sunday and the Jewish Sabbath are two entirely distinct institutions; that for hundreds of years after the birth of Christianity work was continued on the seventh day, and that, for long after the discontinuance of work, amusement shared with worship the privileges of the day. But our appeal is not to the customs of the past, but to the needs of the present. Those needs point to a Sunday free from all government restraints. The day cannot be desecrated by work so much as work is desecrated by Sabbatarian distinctions. Long may the day survive and be held sacred to rest from ordinary cares, to earnest thought and tender recollection, to pure and simple joys. But let us carry its foundations down below the sandy soil of superstition and tradition, and base them upon common needs and aspirations and mutual respect and kindliness. Let its consecration no longer be the desecration of the week, nor Sunday idleness be esteemed a holier thing than Monday labor.

By far the most vital problem in connection with our general theme is that relating to the presence of the Bible in our public schools. The amendment movement was a very feeble spark until the Bible-in-school question fanned it into a flame. During the war there was a convention somewhere, and it was agreed that God was sore displeased with America. But why? Because of human slavery (they did see that that had something to do with it), but more especially because there was no mention of him in the Constitution. There and then this movement originated, but not much came of it till the Bible question poured its volume into it as the Missouri pours the volume of its muddy waters into the Mississippi. The proposed amendment will give the Bible a foothold in the organic law of the nation. The next thing would be to make education national, and then require reading of the Bible in every school-house in the land. This sounds remote, certainly, but it were better not to wait for it to get any nearer before going out to meet it.

The principal argument against the exclusion of the Bible from the public schools is that the Roman Catholics demand it. "Shall we be dictated to by Roman Catholics?" But if they are *right* in their demand, then it is not they that dictate, but God who dictates through them. They are his mouthpiece. "But the Catholics will not be satisfied with the exclusion of the Bible. What they want is a proportionate part of the school-tax to educate their children in their own sectarian schools." Granted. And the only ground on which we can refuse them that is the exclusion of the Bible. Keep it, and their demand is absolutely just. Exclude it, and they will have no excuse for their demand. If they still have sectarian schools, it must be at their own expense.

The presence of the Bible in the public schools *must* be regarded as sectarian. It not only makes a concession in favor of Christianity, but it makes a distinction in favor of Protestant Christianity; and Protestantism is no less a sect because it is very common to talk about this matter as if the whole difference between Catholics and Protestants was the difference between the King James and the Douay versions of the Bible. But in fact it is the smallest part of it. The great bulk and weight of it is that the Catholic believes that unless interpreted by the Church the Bible is a pernicious book. He believes this honestly. In view of this belief, is it then fair to force upon him the Bible in a translation which he does not accept, without that interpretation which he believes to be essential to its usefulness?

But the amendment people do not stick at sectarianism. Why should they? If they can distinguish in favor of Christianity, why not in favor of Protestantism, or any other *ism?* The very thing they propose to do is to make the government Protestant, Evangelical, Puritan. If they are right, then the Bible should not be excluded. But then, certainly, all Catholics, all Jews, and all persons averse to the indiscriminate use of the Bible in the schools ought to be absolved from school-taxes. Thus would our common-school system be rent asunder. The amendment people cry, "It is. in danger." It is, from their temerity.

" In order to form a more perfect union," reads the first line of the Constitution. If ever the religious amendment is adopted, by all means let this first line be expunged. It would be a mockery to have it there any longer. Not to form a more perfect union would from that time forward be the object of the government, but to breed dissension and rivalry and hate. An ever-increasing multitude of persons, inhabitants of the country, but not citizens of the nation, expatriated by the new departure, would hang upon the outskirts of the body politic, nursing their sense of wrong, making it necessary for the government in self-defence to drive them from its borders.

" To establish justice " was the second object proposed by the framers of the Constitution. Let this also be expunged if ever the religious amendment is added, for after that this, too, would be a mockery. For what justice would there be in denationalizing thousands of persons on account of beliefs which they conscientiously hold? Persecution is a Proteus that can take many shapes, but its essence is the same, whether it punishes with wheel and fagot, or with civil disabilities. The advocates of this new amendment are the spiritual antitypes of Calvin and Innocent III.

"To insure domestic tranquillity," proceeds the present preamble of the Constitution. Let that, too, be expunged if ever the religious amendment is added. That, too, would be a mockery. "Whom the gods love, tranquillity," would dwell with us no longer. In short, there can be no compromise between the Constitution and the government as it is, and the Constitution and the government as it is proposed to make them. If the latter is all right, the former is all wrong. The change proposed would be nothing less than a fundamental reorganization of the government on a sectarian principle entirely foreign to that which presided over its original construction.

A government is one thing, and a nation is quite another; but the two are being constantly confounded by the exponents of the religious amendment. A government is not even an accurate standard of any sort of national growth and power. Just at present the American Constitution and the American nation are both a good deal better than the American government, — the sum-total of its official dignities. The nation is the entire mass of the people. No constitutional amendment can adequately express the amount or character of its religious life. For these are known only to the great Searcher of hearts.

To put God into the Constitution would be one thing, and to put him into the nation would be quite another. The *name* God is, perhaps, sufficiently common. The *thing* God might well be a great deal commoner. How shall we put God into the nation? How but by putting more of his truth and justice into our laws, more of his righteousness into their administration, more of his holiness into the individual life of men and women? Blessed is that nation which fulfils the threefold condition on which God incarnates himself in it, and makes it his all-glorious dwelling-place. The experience of nearly ninety years has justified the wisdom of the fathers in the general outlines of our government. Important changes have been made, and others are still necessary in their work; but in the main our admiration is continually increased for the calm judgment of those mighty men. Surely there were giants in those days. Would that the administration of the government were more nearly equal to its organic law. Here is a field for earnestness and enthusiasm and systematic reform. Not in the Bible, but in the Koran, do I find a sentence that best enunciates the great need of the hour. It reads:

"A ruler who appoints a man to office, when there is in his dominions another man better qualified for the position, sins against God and against the State."

But, after all, the great thing to be done is to sweeten the fountains of men's individual and domestic and social life. Here is the real nation. Here is the real place for the reformer's work. The laws of a nation may for a long time remain superior to the nation's average life, but the administration of those laws must pretty nearly symbolize the general moral health of the community. What we want is not a religious amendment of the Constitution, but a religious amendment of men's lives; not to acknowledge God upon parchment, but on the fleshly tablets of our hearts. Let these things be done, and he will crave no other recognition. The kingdom of heaven cometh not with observation.

> "When the Church is social worth,
> When the State House is the hearth,
> Then the perfect state is come,
> The Republican at home."

THE WORD PHILANTHROPY.

By Thomas Wentworth Higginson.

SOME writer on philology has said that there is more to be learned from language itself than from all that has been written by its aid. It is often possible to reconstruct some part of the moral attitude of a race, through a single word of its language; and this paper will have no other value than as an illustration of that process.

In the natural sciences, the method is familiar. For instance, it was long supposed that the mammoth and the cave-bear had perished from the earth before man appeared. No argument from the occasional intermixture of their bones with man's was quite conclusive. But when there was dug up a drawing of the cave-bear on slate, and a rude carving of the living mammoth, mane and all, on a tusk of the animal itself, then doubt vanished, and the question was settled. Thoreau has remarked that "some circumstantial evidence may be very strong, as where you find a live trout in the milk-pan." These discoveries in palæontology were quite as conclusive.

Now what is true in palæontology is true in philology as well. When a word comes into existence, its meaning is carved on the language that holds it; if you find the name of a certain virtue written in a certain tongue, then the race which framed that language knew that virtue. This may be briefly illustrated by the history of the word "Philanthropy."

This word, it is known, came rather late into the English tongue. When the Pilgrim Fathers stepped on Plymouth Rock, in 1620, though they may have been practising what the word meant, there were few among them to whom its sound was familiar, and perhaps none who habitually used it. It is not in Chaucer, Spenser, or Shakspeare. It is not even in the English Bible, first published in 1611; and the corresponding Greek word, occurring three times in the original, is rendered in each case by a circumlocution. It does not appear in that pioneer English Dictionary, Minsheu's "Guide to the Tongues," first published in 1617. It does not appear in the Spanish Dictionary of the same Minsheu, in 1623. But two years later than this, in the second edition of his "Guide to the Tongues" (1625), it appears as follows, among the new words distinguished by a dagger: —

"Philanthropie; Humanitie, a loving of men."
Then follow the Greek and Latin words, as sources of derivation.

This is the first appearance in print, so far as my knowledge goes, of the word "Philanthropie." But Lord Bacon, publishing in the same year (1625) his essay on "Goodness, and Goodness of

Heart," — the thirteenth of the series of his essays, as now constituted, and occupying the place of an essay on "Friendship," which stood thirteenth in the previous editions, — uses the word in its Greek form only, and in a way that would seem to indicate, but for the evidence of Minsheu, that it had not yet been Anglicized. His essay opens thus: "I take goodness in this sense, the affecting of the weal of men, which is what the Greeks call *Philanthropia;* and the word *Humanity,* as it is used, is a little too light to express it."

The next author who uses the word is Jeremy Taylor. It is true, that in his "Holy Dying" (1651), when translating the dying words of Cyrus from Xenophon's "Cyropædia," he renders the word φιλάνθρωπος "a lover of mankind," citing the original Greek in the margin.[1] But in Taylor's sermons, published two years later (1653), there occur the first instances known to me, after Minsheu, of the use of the Anglicized word. Jeremy Taylor speaks of "that god-like excellency, a philanthropy and love to all mankind;" and again, of "the philanthropy of God."[2] The inference would seem to be that while this word had now become familiar, at least among men of learning, the corresponding words "philanthropic" and "philanthropist" were not equally well known.

---

[1] Xen. *Cyrop.* viii. 7. 25. Taylor's *Holy Dying,* c. ii. § 3, par. 2.
[2] Taylor's *Sermons,* Vol. III. Sermons 1 and 11. (Cited in Richardson's Dictionary.) In his sermon entitled *Via Intelligentiæ,* he quotes the Greek adjective, translating it "gentle."

If they had been, Jeremy Taylor would probably have used either the one or the other, in translating the words attributed to Cyrus.

So slowly did the word take root, indeed, that when so learned a writer as Dryden used it, nearly seventy years after Minsheu, he still did it with an apology, and with especial reference to the Greek author on whom he was commenting. For when, in 1693, Sir Henry Steere published a poor translation of Polybius, and Dryden was employed to write the preface, he said:—

" This philanthropy (which we have not a proper word in English to express) is everywhere manifest in our author, and from hence proceeded that divine rule which he gave to Scipio, that whensoever he went abroad he should take care not to return to his house before he had acquired a friend by some new obligement."

We have, then, three leading English writers of the seventeenth century — Bacon, Taylor, Dryden — as milestones to show how gradually this word " philanthropy " became established in our language. To recapitulate briefly : Bacon uses the original Greek word, spelt in Roman characters, and attributes it to " the Grecians," saying that there is no English equivalent; Taylor, twenty-eight years later, uses it in Anglicized form, without apology or explanation, although when quoting and translating the Greek word $\phi\iota\lambda\acute{a}\nu\theta\rho\omega\pi\sigma\varsigma$, he does not use the equivalent word in his translation. Dryden, forty years later, commenting on a

Greek author, makes a sort of apology for the use of the word, as representing something "which we have not a proper word in English to express," although he uses the English form. It is therefore clear that the word "philanthropy" was taken directly and consciously from the Greek, for want of a satisfactory English word. Men do not take the trouble to borrow a word, any more than an umbrella, if they already possess one that will answer the purpose.

Let us now consider the original word φιλανθρωπία. It has an illustrious position in Greek literature and history. It affords the key-note to the greatest dramatic poem preserved to us; and also to the sublimest life of Greece, that of Socrates. It was first used, however, in neither of these connections, but by an obscurer writer, Epicharmus, whose fragments have a peculiar historical value, as he was born about 540 B.C., and his authority thus carries back the word nearly to the First Olympiad, 776 B.C., which is commonly recognized as the beginning of authentic history. Setting these fragments aside, however, the first conspicuous appearance of the word in literature is in that astonishing poem, the "Prometheus Bound" of Æschylus, which was probably represented about 460 B.C. as the central play of a "trilogy," the theme being an ideal hero, on whom the vengeance of Zeus has fallen for his love of man. The word we seek occurs in the first two speeches of the drama, where

Strength and Hephaistos (Vulcan) in turn inform Prometheus that he is to be bound to the desert rock in punishment for his philanthropy, φιλανθρώπου τρόπου; and it is repeated later, in the most magnificent soliloquy in ancient literature, where Prometheus accepts the charge, and glories in his offence, of too much love for man, τὴν λίαν φιλότητα βροτῶν. He admits that when Zeus had resolved to destroy the human race, and had withdrawn from men the use of fire, he himself had reconveyed fire to them, and thus saved them from destruction; that he had afterwards taught them to tame animals, to build ships, to observe the stars, to mine for metals, to heal diseases. For this he was punished by Zeus; for this he defies Zeus, and predicts that his tyranny must end, and justice be done. On this the three tragedies turn; the first showing Prometheus as carrying the sacred gift of fire to men; the second as chained to Caucasus; the third as delivered from his chains. If we had the first play, we should have the virtue of philanthropy exhibited in its details; if we had the last, we should see its triumph; but in the remaining tragedy we see what is, perhaps, nobler than either, — the philanthropic man under torment for his self-devotion, but refusing to regret what he has done. There is not a play in modern literature, I should say, which turns so directly and completely, from beginning to end, upon the word and the thing " philanthropy."

Seeking, now, another instance of the early use of

the Greek word, and turning from the ideal to the actual, we have Socrates, in the "Euthyphron" of Plato, — composed probably about 400 B.C. — questioned as to how it is that he has called upon himself the vengeance of those in power by telling unwelcome truths. And when his opponent hints that he himself has never got into any serious trouble, Socrates answers, in that half-jesting way which he never wholly lays aside — I quote Jowett's translation: —

"I dare say that you don't make yourself common, and are not apt to impart your wisdom. But I have a benevolent habit of pouring myself out to everybody, and would even pay for a listener, and I am afraid that the Athenians know this." The phrase rendered "benevolent habit" is ἀπὸ φιλανθρωπίας;[1] that is, "through philanthropy;" and I know nowhere a franker glimpse of the real man Socrates.

Coming down to later authors, we find the use of the word in Greek to be always such as to bring out distinctly that meaning for which it has been imported into English. How apt we are to say that the Greeks thought only of the state, not of individuals, nor of the world outside! Yet the great orator Isocrates (born 436 B. C.) heaps praises upon a certain person as being one who loved man and Athens and wisdom, — φιλάνθρωπος καὶ φιλαθηναῖος καὶ φιλόσοφος, — a noble epitaph.

So the orator Demosthenes (born 385 B. C.) uses

[1] Plato: *Euthyph.* § 3. Jowett's *Plato*, I. 286.

the word φιλανθρωπία in contrast to φθόνος, hate, and to ὠμότης, cruelty; and speaks of employing philanthropy toward any one φιλανθρωπίαν τινὶ χρῆσθαι. So Xenophon, as we have seen, makes Cyrus describe himself on his death-bed as "philanthropic."

So Epictetus, at a later period, said, "Nothing is meaner than the love of pleasure, the love of gain, and insolence; nothing nobler than magnanimity, meekness, and philanthropy." So Plutarch, addressing his "Consolations to Apollonius" on the death of his son, sums up the praises of the youth by calling him "philanthropic,"—φιλάνθρωπος. In his life of Solon, also, he uses the word φιλανθρώπευμα,— a philanthropic act. So Diodorus speaks of a desert country as ἐστερημένη πάσης φιλανθρωπίας, — destitute of all philanthropy, or, as we should say, "pitiless," — as if wherever man might be there would also be the love of man.[1]

We have, then, a virtue called philanthropy, which dates back nearly six hundred years before our era, and within about two centuries of the beginning of authentic history, — a virtue which inspired the self-devotion of Prometheus in the great tragedy of antiquity; which prompted the manner of life of Socrates; to which Demosthenes appealed, in opposition to hate and cruelty; to which Isoc-

---

[1] Isoc. *Epist.* v. 2; Dem. adv. *Leptines*, § 165; Xen. *Cyrop.* viii. 7.25; Epict. *Frag.* 46; Plut. *Cons.* § 34, *Solon*, § 15; Diod. xvii. 50.

rates gave precedence before the love of country and the love of knowledge ; which Polybius admired, when shown toward captives ; which Epictetus classed as the noblest of all things ; and which Plutarch inscribed as the highest praise upon the epitaph of a noble youth. Thus thoroughly was the word "philanthropy" rooted in the Greek language, and recognized by the Greek heart ; and it is clear that we, speaking a language in which this word was unknown for centuries, — being introduced at last, according to Dryden, because there was no English word to express the same idea, — cannot claim the virtue it expresses as an exclusively modern possession.

It is worth noticing, that there is another use of the word "philanthropy," which prevailed among the Greeks, and was employed for a time in English. The word was used to express an attribute of Deity, as, for instance, when Aristophanes applies it to Hermes, Ω φιλανθρωπότε "O! most philanthropic" — that is, loving towards man. Paul uses the Greek word but once, and then in this same sense ; and the Greek Father Athanasius uses it as a term of courtesy, 'Η σή φιλανθρωπία "Your philanthropy," as we say to Republican governors, "Your Excellency." Young, in his "Night Thoughts," addresses the Deity, "Thou great Philanthropist;" Jeremy Taylor speaks of "the philanthropy of God ; " and Barrow, speaking of the goodness of God, says, "Commonly also it is by the most obliging and endearing name called love and philanthropy."[1] But I do not recall any recent instances of this use of the word.

And the use of this word, in this sense, by the Greeks, reminds us that the Greek religion, even if deficient in the loveliest spiritual results, had on the other hand little that was gloomy or terrifying. Thus the Greek funeral inscriptions, though never so triumphant as the Christian, were yet almost always marked, as Milman has pointed out, by a "quiet beauty." And this word "philanthropy" thus did a double duty, including in its range two thoughts, familiar to modern times in separate phrases, — the Fatherhood of God and the Brotherhood of Man.

It is to this consideration, I fancy, that we owe those glimpses not merely of general philanthropy, but of a recognized unity in the human race, that we find from time to time in ancient literature. It is hardly strange that in Greece, with its isolated position, its exceptional cultivation and refinement, and its scanty communications, this feeling should have been less prominent than in a world girdled with railways and encircled by telegraphic wires. In those days the great majority of men, and women almost without exception, spent their lives within the limit of some narrow state; and it was hard for the most enlightened to think of those beyond their borders

---

[1] Aristoph. *Peace*, 394. Paul, Titus iii. 4. Athanasius, cited in Sophocles's Lexicon. Young, Night Fourth. Taylor, Vol. III., Sermon 11 (Richardson). Barrow, Vol. II., p. 356 (ed. 1700).

except as we think even now of the vast populations of South America or Africa, — whom we regard as human beings, no doubt, but as having few habits or interests in common with our own. But every great conquest by Greece or Rome tended to familiarize men with the thought of a community of nations, even before a special stimulus was at last added by Christianity. It does not seem to me just, therefore, in Max Müller to say that "humanity is a word for which you look in vain in Plato or Aristotle," without pointing out that later Greek writers, utterly uninfluenced by Christianity, made the same objection to these authors. Thus, in an essay attributed to Plutarch on the Fortune of Alexander, he makes this remarkable statement: —

"Alexander did not hearken to his preceptor Aristotle, who advised him to bear himself as a prince among the Greeks, his own people, but as a master among the Barbarians; to treat the one as friends and kinsmen, the others as animals or chattels. . . But, conceiving that he was sent by God to be an umpire between all and to unite all together, he reduced by arms those whom he could not conquer by persuasion, and formed of a hundred diverse nations one single universal body, mingling, as it were, in one cup of friendship the customs, the marriages, and the laws of all. He desired that all should regard the whole world as their common country, the good as fellow-citizens and brethren, the bad as aliens and enemies; that the Greeks should no longer be distinguished from the foreigner by arms or costume, but that every good man should be esteemed an Hellene, every evil man a barbarian."[1]

Here we have not a piece of vague sentimentalism, but the plan attributed by tradition to one of the great generals of the world's history; and whether this was Alexander's real thought, or something invented for him by biographers, it is equally a recognition of the brotherhood of man. And the same Plutarch tells us that " the so much admired commonwealth of Zeno, first author of the Stoic sect, aims singly at this, that neither in cities nor in towns we should live under laws distinct from one another, but that we should look on all men in general to be our fellow-countrymen and citizens, observing one manner of living and one kind of order, like a flock feeding together with equal right in one common pasture."[2] So Jamblichus reports that Pythagoras, five centuries before our era, taught " the love of all to all ; "[3] and Menander the dramatist said, " to live is not to live for one's self alone ; let us help one another ; "[4] and later, Epictetus maintained that " the universe is but one great city, full of beloved ones, divine and

[1] Merivale's translation: *Conversion of the Roman Empire*, p. 64. He also gives the original, p. 203. Compare Goodwin's *Plutarch*, I. 481.

[2] Plutarch's *Morals*. Goodwin's translation, I. 481.

[3] Jamblichi de Pythag. vita, cc. 16. 33. Φιλίαν δὲ διαφανέστατα πάντων πρὸς ἅπαντας Πυθαγόρας παρέδωκε.

[4] Meineke: *Fragmenta Com. Graec.*

human, by nature endeared to each other;"[1] and Marcus Antoninus taught that we must "love mankind."[2] In none of these passages do we find the Greek word φιλανθρωπία; but in all we find the noble feeling indicated by that word; while Aulus Gellius quotes the word itself, and attaches to it the self-same meaning borne by the English word.[3]

And it is well known that the same chain of tradition runs through the Latin writers, as when Terence brought down the applause of the theatre by saying, "Homo sum; humani nihil a me alienum puto;"[4] and Cicero says, "we are framed by nature to love mankind (*naturâ propensi sumus ad diligendos homines*); this is the foundation of law;" and Lucan predicts a time when all laws shall cease and nations disarm and all men love one another (*inque vicem gens omnis amet*); and Quintilian teaches that we should "give heed to a stranger in the name of the universal brotherhood which binds together all men under the common father of Nature;" and Seneca says that "we are members of one great body," and "born for the

---

[1] Epictetus, III. 24.
[2] Marcus Antoninus, VII. 31. Φίλησον τὸν ἀνθρώπινον γένος.
[3] Aulus Gellius, XIII. xvi. 1. "Quodque a Græcis φιλανθρωπια dicitur, et significat dexteritatem quandam benevolentiamque erga omnes homines promiscuam."
[4] Terence: *Heaut*. I. 1. 25. Cicero de Legibus, I. 15, and de Repub. III. 7. 7 (fragm). Lucan: *Pharsalia*, I. 60-1. Quintilian: *Declamations*, quoted by Denis. Seneca, Ep. 95. Juvenal: *Sat*. XV. 140-2.

good of the whole;" and Juvenal, that "mutual sympathy is what distinguishes us from brutes."

Shall we think the better or the worse of the Greeks for having no noun substantive just corresponding to our word "philanthropist," whether as a term of praise or reproach? With us, while it should be the noblest of all epithets, it is felt in some quarters to carry with it a certain slight tinge of suspicion, as is alleged of the word "Deacon" or "Christian Statesman." There is a peril in the habit of doing good; I do not mean merely in case of hypocrisy; but I have noticed that when a man feels that he is serving his fellow-men, he sometimes takes great liberties in the process. It was of this style of philanthropists that old Count Gurowski spoke, when he cautioned a young lady of my acquaintance, above all things, against marrying one of that class. "Marry thief!" he said, "Marry murderer! But marry *philantrope* never-r-r!"

It is a singular fact that while the generous word "philanthropy" was thus widely used in Greek and widely spread in English, there should have been no such wide-spread word for the answering sin, self-love. The word $\phi\iota\lambda\alpha\upsilon\tau\iota\alpha$ was known to the Greeks, and a word, "philauty," was made from it, in English; and $\phi\iota\lambda\alpha\upsilon\tau\sigma\varsigma$ is used once in the New Testament by Paul;[1] but in neither language did it become classic or familiar. Minsheu has "philautie" in his second edition,

[1] 2 Timothy, iii. 2.

and Beaumont, in his poem of "Psyche;" and Holinshed, in his "Chronicle" (1577), speaks of philautie " or " self-love, which rageth in men so preposterouslie." But the word is omitted from most English dictionaries, and we will hope that the sin rages less "preposterouslie" now. I once heard a mother say that if she could teach her little boy good words one-half as easily as he could learn the bad ones for himself, she should be quite satisfied. Here is the human race, on the other hand, seizing eagerly on the good word, transplanting it and keeping it alive in the new soil, while the bad word dies out, unregretted. In view of this, we may well claim that our debt to the Greek race is not merely scientific or æsthetic, but, in some degree, moral and spiritual also. However vast may be the spread of human kindliness in Christendom, we should yet give to the Greeks some credit for the spirit of philanthropy, as we are compelled, at any rate, to give them full credit for the word.

RELIGION AS SOCIAL FORCE.

By Ednah D. Cheney.

I AM to speak in this address of Religion as a Social Force, especially in relation to Philanthropy and Reform. The very utterance of my subject seems a sufficient argument; for the relation of religion to philanthropy is as natural as that of the mother to the child. How can I separate religion from life? It is everywhere, as diffusive, as necessary as the air that we breathe. Religion is our word for the relation of the mortal to the immortal, of the finite to the infinite, of the human to the divine. It is the essence and mainspring of life, and must be the moving, vital power in all love of men, which is philanthropy, and all desire of progress, which is reform. As well might we expect all this fair work of nature — every tree and shrub putting forth into new life and beauty — to be accomplished without looking upwards to the sun, and drinking in his warmth and light, as imagine that humanity will bud and blossom without constant influx from its Divine Centre.

Religion is the very spirit of our daily life, animating all that we are and do. The ancients rightly used the term " pious " alike to express the reverence given to human beings and that due to the gods. Every hero of humanity believes himself to be inspired by Divine light and protected by Divine power, and there is no great movement in history which does not find in religion its source and guide. Pious Æneas went forth from Troy into Latium, trusting in the protection of the gods, even as Abraham went from the land of Ur into Canaan at the command of the Lord. This is the grand idea of Hebrew legislation, which gives to every rule of life the sanction of Divine authority. The sanitary measures rendered necessary by their climate and mode of life had to the Jews the force of Divine command.

The day of rest for man and beast was so guarded by this sanction that three thousand years have hardly lessened its authority, and reason has a hard struggle even now against the tyranny of its superstitious observance. The same religious sanction, modified according to the genius of the people, made the authority of Greek, Roman, and Mohammedan power. The Turk believes that the prayer of the faithful must be perpetual; that if a moment passes in which the word "Allah" is not breathed out into the air with pious fervor, the reign of chaos will come again, and "all this goodly frame, the earth, this most excellent canopy, the air, this brave, overhanging firmament, this majestical roof fretted with golden fire, will become a foul and pestilent congregation of vapors."

The Turk is right: there is no safety for the

outward world, none for the State, none for society, or our daily household life, but in religion, — that is, in the constant relation of every thing human to the Divine, the perpetual refreshment and recreation from the source of all life. Like the air, religion must be always a new and living force, never cut off from its primal source, but always renewed by free access to the whole unlimited range of Divine life. "Get religion," and bottle it up : it is stale as the air which is confined without renewal.

And yet religion, the great conserver of life and humanity, is also the great iconoclast and destroyer. It is a flaming fire which burns up whatever has not living force within itself to withstand it. Again, it is like the air, the breath and life of whatever is living and growing, the great destroyer of all that is dead. It will suffer nothing useless or stationary under its influence : it will make either better or worse all that is submitted to its action. Religion, which is the very breath of life to true humanity, to real progress, is the radical foe of all old idols and dead traditions. Like life, it is constantly expressing itself in forms, but yet ever freeing itself from them.

Hence it is, that while every one accepts the religious origin and basis of reforms in the past, the reformer finds no enemy so bitter, no *inertia* so sluggish, no resistance so obstinate as that from organized ecclesiasticism. It is the history of all reform from the prophets stoned in Judea and the martyr crucified on Calvary, from Socrates drinking the hemlock in prison to Lovejoy murdered in Alton, that it must contend to the death with the old and traditional church.

It is here, then, that we claim the superiority for the free religious movement in its relation to reform. It is religion restored to its native freedom, answerable to its own consciousness of God alone, unfettered by tradition, unrestrained by formulas and creeds, able to expand itself to its utmost limits, free to flow into every channel that is open to it, gathering help and counsel from all, binding chains upon none. It is religion, like Pegasus unharnessed from the yoke, that must inspire us with new life and strength to battle against the forces of evil, the great army of negation, embodied in corrupt and oppressive institutions.

Free religion can accept this work, because she has no hindrances in the way. She has no old institutions venerable in their decay, which will crumble into dust at the movement of reform. The ecclesiastical historian, Eusebius, allows that he only mentions what will reflect credit on the martyrs, and Millner makes the same confession in regard to the Church; but free religion is no hired advocate with a cause to defend. She can rejoice in a brave deed done anywhere, and accept the truth by whomsoever spoken. So her armory against evil is rich in weapons, forged by all true souls of whatever name, and she is never afraid that they will be turned against herself; for she is baptized all over in the waters of immortality, and has not even a vulnerable point in her heel where the arrows of truth can wound her.

I shall speak now of only two points in which free religion has a special advantage and superior power over the old organized forms of religion in promoting reform and doing the work of philanthropy. It must be the task, not of a brief half-hour, but of many years of thought and study, to apply it wisely to all the varied demands of life and society.

First, free religion has an infinite faith in humanity. It sets no bounds to the possibilities of the human race here and now on this very planet. It knows man only as the child of God, partaker of his spirit, and heir to his infinite resources. Glorying in all the past achievements of the mighty leaders of the race, it accepts none as the Ultima Thule of progress beyond which humanity cannot go. It is enough for it to know that a thing is good, to be sure that it must be possible. It knows no

>"fallen Adam there, —
>A red clay and a breath,"

but a new-born babe full of the spirit of its maker, and capable of infinite progress in intelligence and goodness. It recognizes evil, not as a vital force, coequal with God, but as delay and hindrance, negation and darkness, to be overcome only with superabounding light and love and life. It accepts, therefore, the means of reform which are all ready for its use. It asks only man with God, the Divine man, one with the Father, and one also with all humanity, to do God's work on this planet. It demands no miraculous power: it finds power and love enough incarnated in humanity to redeem and advance the world. It sees in man the very agent God has created for this very purpose, to organize and develop the life of humanity on this earth; and it believes that only faithful use of the powers implanted within us is needed to accomplish all that we ask for in our wildest dreams or our highest prayers. Swedenborg says, " The very heavens are in the form of a man," and all that we need ask for earth is, that man should rise up to his true stature, and live out in its utmost fulness the life that is possible for him here upon earth.

How perfectly does this apply to the reform which we have seen begun and nearly accomplished, the abolition of negro oppression, and to those which so imperatively demand our attention now in America, — the Indian and Chinese questions. The moment the full recognition of the negro's manhood was accomplished, the work was done; and the same will be the case with the Indian and the Chinese.

And here is the meeting-point of free religion with true science, which brings me to my second statement.

Baron Quetelet, of Belgium, one of the ripest scholars and profoundest students of statistical science (I quote from the Journal of the American Social Science Association for 1870), says:

"The more intelligence increases, the nearer we approach the beautiful and the good. The perfectibility of the human species results as a necessary consequence of all our researches."

Free religion is therefore specially adapted to the work of philanthropy and reform by its cordial alliance with science. Reading by the light of ecclesiastical history, what a strange proposition is this, — religion and science one! Was not Anaxagoras exiled in the name of religion, and Galileo put under the tortures of the Inquisition? Did not the gentle Cowper scoff at the researches of geology? and does not every scientific treatise feel bound to justify itself against the charge of conflicting with the dogmas of the popular religion? Are we not again and again warned against the pride of intellect, and taught that it is only by unquestioning faith that we can receive the spirit of God?

But looked at from the centre of things, in the light of reason and common-sense, what is more obvious than the unity of religion and science? Religion is the relation to God in the inward heart, through love and faith. Science is the inquiry into God's methods of action in the outward world, the world which we believe he has created, and of which he is the vital essence and sustaining force. What do we fear to find there? That our Father has blundered and failed, or has wilfully done evil instead of good? What faith would that be in a human friend which led us to shun investigation into his words and deeds lest perchance our love and faith should be destroyed?

Free religion is not afraid of the truth. It has no pet dogmas to defend, nor old traditions which must not be shaken. It is not disturbed, though the earth has rolled on in space for ten millions of years instead of six thousand: it knows it has always rolled under the guiding hand of its infinite and perfect Creator. It does not shudder if science teaches that it is gradually approaching the sun, and will finally be absorbed into that great luminary. It knows that it will only be in accordance with the same Divine Law, and that the welfare of all will be secured amid the great conflagration, if such is to take place.

And much as science needs the inspiring power of religion to keep it broad and sweet and sane, always loyal and true to its Divine Centre, just as much does religion need science to guide its hand, and show it how to accomplish the good which love prompts it to desire. Free religion will return to science the service she receives from her. As Pythagoras said, "Divine Wisdom is true science," so the conscious intuitions of religion will give that guiding light to science which she needs. Faith will assure us of the grand harmony which must exist in creation, and will not suffer the intellect to rest until it proves the law, and justifies clearly to all men that which religion had discerned spontaneously for itself. Thus we find that many of the grandest discoveries of science have been foreshadowed and predicted by religious men who welcomed the truth of God in their souls before they read its confirmation in his works. When the marriage between religion and science is acknowledged, and the couple are admitted into good society, we may hope for yet richer fruits from their union.

Never was the need of this union more clear than now. We have arrived at the point where we cannot rest in the unconsciousness of ignorance. The childhood of the world is past. We must study the laws of nature and of social life, to maintain society in a sound and healthy condition. Life has become rich and complicated, full of difficult problems. The simple wish to help and bless others is not enough to save us from doing incalculable mischief, unless we have profound wisdom to guide our action.

The philanthropist leaves large sums of money to feed the poor, and builds up a pauper settlement which is the curse of the country for miles around. Science should have ploughed his money into the ground, and enabled the people to feed themselves.

The great questions which agitate us to-day are not merely questions of good and evil dispositions. The temperance question, the labor movement, the woman question, the sanitary reforms, the treatment of crime, pauperism, — all demand the most thorough and scientific knowledge to save us from the gravest errors. The saint accepts the saying of Jesus, "The poor ye shall always have with you," and believes it a Divine provision for enabling him to exercise the virtue of giving alms, and so securing a higher seat in heaven. But the reformer asks, Why must ye always have the poor with you? Why should not society be so organized that every human being shall have a fair chance for his share of this world's goods? — and he turns to science to help him to solve this question. Social science says, The alms-giving of the church has been the fruitful source of pauperism, and hence of intemperance, vice, and crime. You have no right to gratify your own benevolent impulses by this indiscriminate giving; you are bound to seek out causes. You have no right to keep pet beneficiaries for the luxury of bestowing charity, as the English lords preserve their woodcocks for the pleasure of hunting them: you are bound to teach them to help themselves, and to raise them to your own level of independent freedom.

A pious Spanish poet says, that sickness is the sign of God's love. I give a part of the quaint translation: —

> "This frame so weak,
> Sharp sickness' hue,
> And this pale cheek
> God loves in you.
>
> "More faltering speech
> And weary days
> Than beauty's blaze
> His heart will reach."

Mr. Emerson says, "Sickness is felony." Is he not right? Have you any right to let your arms rust when God wants you to fight the battle of life? any right to come with broken tools to work in his vineyard? any right to waste in a year what should serve for a life? Which spirit will be most likely to establish the board of health and clear out the foul alleys in our cities? Let Spain and New England test the question.

Again, how does the old ecclesiasticism speak of death? —

> "As for man, his days are as the grass;
> As a flower of the field, so he flourisheth:
> The wind passeth over it and it is gone."

And a familiar Wesleyan hymn thanks God,

> "whose wise, paternal love
> Hath brought my active vigor down."

This spirit is not confined to Christianity. We find the same wail and contempt of life in much of the heathen poetry and philosophy, in all religion which is introspective and partial, instead of round and whole. Superstition and piety alike regard premature death either as a cruel fate or as an arbitrary exercise of God's inscrutable will. But social science says, "The first great object of sanitary organization should be to watch the death rate," and it conclusively proves that nothing is more entirely under the control of law than human mortality; and every instance of increased care, in obedience to the Divine laws of health, clearly reports itself at once in the percentage of mortality.

Nothing can be more holy and tender than Jesus'

attitude towards the fallen woman; but the Christian religion has struggled in vain for eighteen centuries against the great social evil. How to prevent it is still the great unsolved problem, which religion and science must work out together. Neither can do it alone.

Again, the labor question cannot be solved by religion without the aid of science. The capitalist may shorten the hours of labor, and increase the rate of wages; but he will not put any more bread into the mouths of the hungry million, unless science steps in and shows him how to apply the forces of nature so that eight hours may do the work of twelve, and an acre of ground well tilled and well harvested may produce the food of three.

The Quaker says these desires after beautiful things cannot be satisfied without injuring your fellow-beings. Your white paint is poisonous: your dyed garments are unhealthful. He cuts them off, preserving his own sense of right, but impoverishing the world of grace and beauty. Science combined with religion says, " The resources of God are infinite. He has given us these longings for beauty and comfort; there must be innocent means for gratifying them: let me go to work and seek them out." It substitutes zinc for lead, and the paint becomes harmless; and it will some day find that it may dye green gauze as innocently as spring decks the meadows and fields without the aid of arsenic.

Religion will not let us rest, while our enjoyments and comforts are purchased with the debasement and degradation of a human being: science must furnish new means by which the abundance of good things shall be multiplied, so that all may partake of them. Will it be the millennium when the nobleman takes his turn at delving with the spade, and the peasant sits upon the throne? No; but when labor is made so noble and its rewards so rich, that the misery of idle luxury will become too heavy to be borne. But to accomplish this work science must be free, — the friend and partner of religion, not her slave.

If religion says to science, "Seek and find, but find nothing but what I bid you," her freedom and power are gone. And this has been the attitude of ecclesiasticism toward science. "You may teach that the earth moves round the sun, but you must not refuse to teach that Joshua commanded the sun and moon to stay their apparent motion and remain to give light for his victory over the enemies of Israel." "You may teach the law of gravitation, and demonstrate to your pupils that its operation is universal, and that by its unerring force and constant action the whole machinery of the heavens is kept in harmony and order; but you must not suffer them to doubt that this beneficent law was suspended that Peter might walk upon the waves to meet his Master." Science thus held in fetters cannot do its legitimate work. It must speak the bidding of its master, not follow out the guidance of truth.

But free religion is not fettered to any such formulas. It does not even feel itself bound to protect and patronize God. If the sincere student comes to it and says, "I have searched through nature, I have penetrated into the heavens with my telescope, and have traced out the law which binds star to star, even to the remotest verge of the Milky Way; I have turned my microscope upon the minutest insects that crowd a drop of water, and traced out their nervous organizations in their little bodies, but nowhere can I find your God," — free religion does not answer him with contempt or anathema. But she replies, "Search on, my friend: tell us what you do find. Your gaze will not drive God out from the world which he has created. You will not deprive me of the joy of his presence if I find him and you cannot. But you will find many and precious truths; you will find power, harmony, and beauty; you will find deep meanings and wonderful illustrations. You may call the power law or chance or what you will, only seek honestly, and tell me plainly what you do find; and it shall be my own fault if I cannot relate it to any higher truth than I think has been given me to hold." She says with Plato, "While truth leads the way, we can never say that any band of evils follows in her train." The present revelations of science as of religion may be partial and erroneous, but as long as they are sincere and progressive, they will lead to good; for in the universe of God every path leads to the centre, if only steadily followed.

This attitude of free religion to science makes our work the most eminently practical one. We are not seeking merely speculative freedom, or intellectual culture. We are trying to clear the ground of the old rubbish of tradition and formula; we are striving to let in the free air and warm sunlight upon the germs of life with which it is filled, so that these shall quicken and fructify and bear fruit, and "the leaves shall be for the healing of the nations."

Religion means to us warmth and life and love and growth, — what the sun is to the plant, what the dew is to the grass, what the air is to our lungs, — its native atmosphere into which we are born, — from which we need no protection, — into which we can open out our whole natures, and receive it in that we may expand and grow into the full stature and bloom of humanity. We strive to prune away the dead wood, not because it has not served the growth of the past year, but because it is in the way of the living shoots of this year. We know that even the decay of the past may become living nourishment for the present, if only the free forces of nature be allowed to play upon it, so that seeming to be destroyed it shall really be taken up anew into the current of life.

Free religion does not at this moment tend to express itself in finer cathedrals or sweeter litanies or more glorious anthems. All these are good. We must have religion expressed in art; or, rather, it cannot help so expressing itself when it is full of rich, bounding, joyous life, as it should be. But it may be long ages before we surpass the forms of art which the past has bequeathed to us.

For us to-day the work is eminently a practical one. Our art must be the art of life. Religion wedded to science must give us bread for all, shelter for all, health, freedom, education for all. Religion must inspire us with the love to pour itself out in good to others, and to ask for them all that we would ask for ourselves. Science must be the hand to execute her will, to search out causes and to devise remedies, and to found the good that we ask for on the eternal rock of Divine and Immutable Law.

Do not fear that life thus developed will become hard and unlovely: when the heart and the head work together, when wisdom does the bidding of love, when religion and science, the love and knowledge of God, have worked out their appointed results, what can the product be but immortal good and beauty?

VOICES FROM THE FREE PLATFORM.

[EXPLANATORY NOTE. — One purpose of this volume is to give an answer to the question, now not infrequently asked, What is the meaning of the Free Religious Association? It is one of the objects of that Association to encourage and to bring before the public just such discussions of religious problems as this book contains. It aims to discover and to establish truth in religious matters by the method of intelligent free inquiry. Lectures, Conventions, and Publications are its instrumentalities: and this volume is made up chiefly of Essays and Addresses that have appeared upon its platform. In addition to the foregoing more elaborate essays, it has been thought advisable to append some selections from the less formal discussions which have occurred in the annual meetings of the Association, and have been preserved in its Reports. The following extracts, made entirely from these annual pamphlets, will show what a variety of representative voices have been heard in the Conventions of the Association, and indicate somewhat the range of topics which have been touched. It will be perceived that the organization represents certain principles and tendencies, and not any new creed or jointly subscribed system of faith. These principles and tendencies are perhaps best suggested by the title of the book, "Freedom and Fellowship in Religion," — Freedom of inquiry and opinion, and yet Fellowship in spirit and aim. And they are expressed in the two chief articles of the Constitution as follows: —

"I. This Organization shall be called the Free Religious Association, — its objects being to promote the practical interests of pure religion, to increase fellowship in the spirit, and to encourage the scientific study of man's religious nature and history; and to this end all persons interested in these objects are cordially invited to its membership.

"II. Membership in this Association shall leave each individual responsible for his own opinions alone, and affect in no degree his relations to other associations; and nothing in the name or Constitution of the Association shall ever be construed as limiting membership by any test of speculative opinion or belief, — or as defining the position of the Association, collectively considered, with reference to any such opinion or belief, — or as interfering in any other way with that absolute freedom of thought and expression which is the natural right of every rational being."

Should any readers wish to know more of such an Association, the first of these selections may meet their desire. — W. J. P.]

VOICES FROM THE FREE PLATFORM.

AIMS OF THE FREE RELIGIOUS ASSOCIATION.

As one who from the outset was especially interested in the formation of this new Association, the Secretary may here be allowed to put on record the statement, that, so far as he is aware, there was on the part of no one of those having the like interest any desire or thought of forcing into a compact organization, and into a strict community of purpose and action, the various representative religious elements to which they made their appeal for a public meeting; much less did they presume to control, through any formal, mechanical contrivance, the progressive religious spirit of the age, and think to turn it into some special channel. On the contrary, the first premise of all their thinking and acting was, that this spirit must be left perfectly free and untrammelled in order to work out its proper results; and their sole aim was to form some simple plan of association which should represent and give expression to this perfect religious freedom; not prematurely to hasten, nor artificially to shape, any natural religious movements that are in progress, but to provide an organism — itself a natural result of these movements — for religious elements that are spontaneously attracted more or less strongly to each other, and that are already prepared for some kind of combination and fellowship, — an organism that should enable these elements the better to define and express themselves in public sentiment in their united force, and at the same time leave the largest liberty to individual opinion and utterance.

. . . .

The *objects* of the Association are succinctly stated in the first Article of the Constitution. We are organized, according to that Article, "to promote the practical interests of pure religion, to encourage the scientific study of theology,[1] and to increase fellowship in the spirit." But we fail to perceive the full bearing of this language, unless we note that this statement of purpose is introduced by the title of the Association, which is "*Free* Religious," and is followed by an invitation to "*all persons* interested in these objects" to become members. The basis of the Association, therefore, is broader than any thing before attempted in the way of organization in religious history. It goes below any one specific form of religion, and seeks to find the common ground on which all religions rest, or more properly religion itself rests, and plants itself there. It contemplates the ultimate union, not simply of all sects in Christendom, but of all religions, Christian and non-Christian. It looks beyond "Christian" limits for its fellowship. Nor is this aim, even thus early, only ideal. As the meetings last year and this both testify, it is in a measure already realized. And this fact, with what it involves, is the most distinguishing feature of the Association. "With what it involves;" for the important

---

[1] This phrase has been since amended so as to express the idea more clearly thus: "Scientific study of man's religious nature and history."

thing is not so much the fact that the Association brings different sects and religions together on one platform, as the principle underlying that fact. This principle is, that in this Association these various religious opinions and faiths meet and mingle *on perfectly equal terms,* no one claiming for itself what it does not cordially accord, by courtesy and by right, to every other. For the first time in religious history, not only representatives of differing Christian sects, but people of all religious names and of no religious name, are invited to come together as equal brothers, and confer with one another on the highest interests of mankind. Most of us here are probably, by reason of birth and education, counted in the census of the world's population as "Christian," whether we make any other claim to the name or not. But on the platform of this Association we do not obtrude that title. We agree here to listen to what our Hebrew friend may have to utter, or to what our India brother may write to us of their respective religious faiths, with the same candor and the same integrity and openness of judgment that we accord to a "Christian" speaker. A believer in the Christian system of religion may, if his conscience so dictate, use his right to speak on the platform of this Association with the purpose of proving the claims of his particular faith paramount to all others, and of converting non-believers to his views; but if he does so, that very act commits him to hear impartially the same claims made for any other faith. One who should come here simply to speak with dogmatic and sectarian arrogance for his own belief, and not cordially to listen to what might be said in behalf of another belief, would not come certainly in the spirit of the constitution of this Association.

Yet this is not to say that the Free Religious Association takes the ground that one form of religion or of faith is as true and good as another. It simply does not determine the claims of any specific form of faith, or assume the claims of any to be determined. It declines to consider it a closed question that the claims of any religion are to be regarded as finally established, and gives a fair, open field for the establishing of any religion, or of so much of any religion as can prove itself to be true. Christianity, thus far, has attempted to convert all other religions to itself. The Christian missionary goes to India and says to the natives there, "You must be converted to my faith, or there is no hope of your progress to any thing better in this world, or of your happiness in the world to come." This Association says to these native religious devotees, "Let us see what is true in your religion, and what is true in this and that other form of faith, and be ready to accept the true from any quarter: and, meantime, let us put our heads together and see if we cannot contrive some better and worthier ways of living." The Free Religious Association simply does not accept any instituted form of religion as necessarily a finality. It admits the possibility of advance in religious truth beyond any present religious system. It plants itself on *Truth-seeking*, and does not claim to have found a finality in religious faith and practice.

On this broad basis, with this declaration of equal religious liberty and rights, the Free Religious Association is organized; and it is evident that the specific objects of the Association, as stated in its constitution, must take direction and shape from these fundamental principles. The Association aims "to promote the interests of pure religion," without stamping those interests with any special name, or seeking to build up any sectarian form of faith and worship. It aims "to encourage the scientific study of theology," — not fearing to trust reason and free inquiry on all fields of thought, not recalling them when they reach the limits of the "Christian" or any other special confession of faith, but striving to apply a more truly rational and scientific method of investigation to all problems of religious experience and history. It aims "to increase fellowship in the spirit," — defining that fellowship as nothing narrower than the brotherhood of man, and making it rest on the aspirations and strivings of our common humanity after higher truth and life. — *Executive Committee's Report*, 1868, *by the Secretary.*

RELIGIOUS NEEDS OF THE AGE.

I THINK the necessity very great, and it has prompted an equal magnanimity, that thus invites all classes, all religious men, whatever their connections, whatever their specialities, in whatever relation they stand to the Christian church, to unite in a movement of benefit to men, under the sanction of religion. We are all very sensible, it is forced on us every day, of the feeling that the churches are outgrown; that the creeds are outgrown; that a technical theology no longer suits us. It is not the ill-will of people, — no indeed, but the incapacity for confirming themselves there.

The church is not large enough for the man; it cannot inspire the enthusiasm which is the parent of every thing good in history, which makes the romance of history. For that enthusiasm you must have something greater than yourselves, and not less.

The child, the young student, finds scope in his mathematics and chemistry, or natural history, because he finds a truth larger than he is; finds himself continually instructed. But, in churches, the healthy and thoughtful mind is likely to find itself in something less; it is checked, cribbed, confined. And the statistics of the American, the English, and the German cities, showing that the mass of the population is leaving off going to church, indicate the necessity, which should have been foreseen, that the church should always be new and extemporized, because it is eternal, and springs from the sentiment of men, or it does not exist. One wonders sometimes that the churches still retain so many votaries, when he reads the histories of the church. There is an element of childish infatuation in them which does not exalt our respect for man. Read in Michelet, that in Europe, for twelve or fourteen centuries, God the Father had no temple and no altar. The Holy Ghost and the son of Mary were worshipped; and in the thirteenth century the First Person began to appear at the side of his son in pictures, and in sculpture, for worship, but only through favor of his son. These mortifying puerilities abound in religious history. But as soon as every man is apprised of the Divine presence within his own mind, — is apprised that the perfect law of duty corresponds with the laws of chemistry, of vegetation, of astronomy, as face to face in a glass; that the basis of duty, the order of society, the power of character, the wealth of culture, the perfection of taste, all draw their essence from this moral sentiment, then we have a religion that exalts; that commands all the social and all the private action.

What strikes me in the sudden movement which brings together to-day so many separated friends, — separated but sympathetic, — and what I expected to find here was, some practical suggestions by which we were to reanimate and reorganize for ourselves the true church, the pure worship. Pure doctrine always bears fruit in pure benefits. It is only by 'good works, it is only on the basis of active duty, that worship finds expression. What is best in the ancient religions was the sacred friendships between heroes, the sacred bands, like the relations of the Pythagorean disciples. Our masonic institutions probably grew from the like origin.

The close association which bound the first disciples of Jesus is another example; and it were easy to find more. The soul of our late war, which will always be remembered as dignifying it, was first, the desire to abolish slavery in this country, and secondly, to abolish the mischief of the war itself, by healing and saving the sick and wounded soldiers, — and this by the sacred bands of the Sanitary Commission. I wish that the various beneficent institutions, which are springing up, like joyful plants of wholesomeness, all over this country, should all be remembered as within the sphere of this Association, — almost all of them are represented here, — and that within this little band that has gathered to-day should grow friendship. The interests that grow out of a meeting like this should bind us with new strength to the old eternal duties. — *Ralph Waldo Emerson.*

LIBERTY AS CONDITION.

It is said that liberty is only a condition. True, but it is a vital condition. A man with his feet tied is in the condition of being bound; untie his feet, and he is only in the condition of being unbound; but that condition is the essential condition of all his progress. In the one case, he cannot move a step; in the other case, he walks whithersoever he will. We admit that freedom is a condition, but we say it is a necessary condition of progress. When we mention the word "liberty," we account for all that has been done in modern science, modern art, modern literature, and modern life. Our American civilization turns upon this one pivot of liberty. Our people are free. All the power there is, is represented by man. All the power there is, is in human nature. There is no power outside of man. Power becomes strong when it becomes incarnate in man. There are infinite resources and possibilities of power; but there is no force, even of divinity, until it is made human force; and the only condition on which that human force can be developed, can expand, and find application, is the condition of absolute freedom. Not simply freedom of discussion, not freedom of debate, freedom of quarrel; we do not open a gladiatorial arena; we would put an end to all that. There is fighting enough now; there has been fighting enough before. Freedom of *discussion* implies partial freedom. When people are only free enough to be able to come with their swords and clear a little place about them, where they can stand face to face with their adversary, and fight on equal terms each fighting for life, that is but partial freedom. But when there is no opprobrium, no reproval cast upon any, no ill word spoken of any; when one is as free to avow himself an Atheist as a Theist, a Materialist as a Spiritualist, a Christian as a non-Christian or an anti-Christian; when one is perfectly free to sit down with any company, — with publicans and sinners if he will, without having any ugly name of "Atheist" or "Infidel" flung in his face, then we have freedom, — freedom of contribution; polemics are no more; debate is disarmed; controversy is at an end; we are not enemies; we have nothing to do with swords and pistols; we are friends; we take each other by the hand; we open our arms for all to come in; we say, "You shall have as much right as we have. We are brothers. Let us each add his mite to the general fund of knowledge and cheer and inspiration, and then we shall get all the power there is, losing no atom of it." — *O. B. Frothingham.*

SPIRITUAL LIBERTY.

For myself, I belong to a sect. I love it and I honor it. I believe its history to be one of transcendent glory. I believe that the brave men and women who have belonged to it in different ages and in different lands have stood in the front rank of those who have demanded "soul-liberty;" and at the stake, at the whipping-post, in the prison, everywhere by their blood they have sealed this precious testimony. But I am sometimes afraid that my sect, having passed out from under the harrow of persecution, being no longer a scorned and outcast people, and having grown to magnificent proportions of strength, of culture, of education, of wealth, and of power, are beginning to forget the glorious lessons of the past, and are tempted to build up simply an ecclesiastical structure, and to put their hand of power upon those who to-day wish only to repeat the announcements which our ancestors so gloriously and so bravely made. All church history is but a repetition of this experience, and, therefore, it comes to pass that in every age this battle must be fought over again. Through eighteen long centuries, now in this land and now in that, now by this people, now by that people, now by a resistance to civil tyranny, now by a protest against ecclesiastical despotism, this assertion of the liberty of every man to believe for himself, answering only to God, and not to human tribunals, has been made again and again. I believe that it is made here to-day, not in any spirit of wild enthusiasm or distorted fanaticism, but in a calm, earnest, studious, and honest way.

Now, in this land, which we call free, in this age, which we call glorious, we need, not so much, perhaps, for our own sakes as for the sake of those who shall come after us, to assert the principle which more than two long centuries ago was the very axiom of Protestantism, — the absolute right of every human soul to interpret for itself the whole word of Scripture. True, the age of outward persecution is past. No longer do the thunderbolts forged at the Vatican, and hurled by the angry hand of the Pope, excite alarm, but merriment only, on the part of those against whom they are directed. The horrid chambers of the Inquisition are deserted, the dreadful mechanism of torture lies idle and rusted, the whipping-post and the scaffold to-day claim no victims to religious bigotry; but there is a more subtle, and, if possible, a more accursed persecution, which to-day, even, is employed by too many who vainly dream they are doing God service. It is the persecution which seeks to brand with odium and write "outcast" upon brave and honest souls, who simply differ from their fellows on questions of intellectual interpretation or doctrinal statement, while their behavior and lives are on the side of justice, of brotherhood, and of love. I think, therefore, that we need to take to ourselves the lessons which are so beauteously illustrated in the life and behavior of Jesus; that it is not what a man says he *believes* that makes him either to be accepted or to be rejected, but it is what a man *does*. A life of justice, a life of purity, a life of chasteness, a life of temperance, a life of benevolence, a life that puts out its hand of defence over the weak and the oppressed, a life that dares to defy wealth and power, even, if they are upon the side of wrong, — is not such a life a life of unquestioned righteousness? For myself, I hold it to be a cardinal and vital dogma, that Jesus of Nazareth is the Saviour of the world. I believe him to be God incarnated, manifested in flesh. When I look upon him stretched upon the Cross of Calvary, when I behold that crown of thorns, those wounded hands and feet, that side pierced by the cruel foeman's spears, my soul sees there my vicarious atonement and sacrifice, and by the shedding of that blood I believe my sin to be pardoned. That to my soul is a profound, deep, earnest, and absorbing belief. But if any other man judge differently, I am not constituted an ecclesiastical tribunal to try him, or to pronounce a verdict of condemnation against him. I think of what Paul said, " Who art thou that judgest another man's servant? To his own master he standeth or falleth." I recollect that the severest and bitterest rebukes which passed the lips of the gentle Nazarene were those which were hurled at the scribes and pharisees who sat in Moses' seat, who wore broad phylacteries, who loved the uppermost seats in the synagogue, who paid tithes of mint, anise, and cummin, and yet who devoured widows' houses, and forgot the wider law of justice and of love. I transfer that lesson to to-day, and think that it is not the outward ecclesiastical relationships which men hold that will save them, or cause them to perish, but that vital communion between God and their own souls is the one thing necessary to salvation.— *Charles H. Malcom.*

LIBERTY SAFE AND CONSERVATIVE.

A DEFINITION of liberty will not supply the place of liberty. We must have the thing itself, nor fear to confront the spirit which our fathers evoked. It is not from the free-born that come the excesses that have darkened the pages of history, but from bondmen who have broken loose. Impose restraints, and you shall have rebellions. Withhold rights, and the State shall be convulsed with the earthquake throes of revolution.

The yearning for liberty is ineradicable, but it may be repressed till it becomes a blind instinct, bursting all barriers, scorning all restraints; a Samson, reckless of consequences, so it can bring to their overthrow the ponderous walls of old abuse. Liberty is conservative; it builds up; it is like the sap of the oak that courses to every twig and root, creating as it goes new germs, developing ever more perfect forms, ever greater strength. License is liberty made insane, the household fire become a conflagration. The Church points to the French Revolution and the Reign of Terror as an illustration of too much liberty. She does not hint that the force of the recoil of that outraged humanity was precisely the measure of the outrage it had suffered. Revolution is the asphyxiated heart in the spasm of recovery. In the crypts of the Church the atmosphere had grown poison by centuries of confinement, and when Voltaire and his fellow-mockers let in a little fresh air from the outer world, the restorative breath excited convulsion terrible to behold, but an evidence of returning health.

The breath of life in the human soul is love of liberty. All progress is from less to more freedom; from ignorance and subordination to intelligent self-direction. The natural enemy of liberty is authority. This stays progress and hinders growth; and of all forms of authority that which entrenches itself behind holy names is the subtlest and most oppressive. No tyranny is so relentless as that which is exercised in the name of God. The despotism of mere force is comparatively harmless; but when despotism takes the form of religion, and enforces its exactions with a "thus saith the Lord," not only human rights are endangered, but humanity itself is paralyzed. To the individual soul, born to a destiny that it cannot grasp, it is of vital importance that it be left in freedom to deal as it best can with the great problem of its relations and destiny. What hope for it when authority in the name of religion seizes on every vague hope and fear, and out of these forges a chain that never clanks, but clings so closely that the victim scarcely knows where the oppression begins, nor whether his limitations are of his nature and inevitable, or the result of a usurping will? Mystery is transformed into mastery, and religion is made to rebind the soul. — *Celia Burleigh.*

HUMANITY'S DREAM.

CONCEIVE the situation of the animal man in the midst of the physical universe. What an insect, what an atomy, what an embodied insignificance he appears! Without natural clothing, without natural weapons, wanting the wing and eye of the falcon, wanting the scent, speed, and native cunning of the fox, a mere mouthful to some of his animal neighbors, feeble in instinct, delicate in digestion, more sensitive and susceptible of pain, and less provided by nature with ready-made supply, than any other creature, — he exhibits the maximum of want and the minimum of resource. What can he do but tug and sweat under the whip of his own necessities? Lorded over by the immense system of the world, what sentiment can he have but that of his own littleness, subjection, and insignificance? When the thunder breaks, when the storm roars, when the sea rages, when the earth shakes, when the elements are at their huge horse-play, what is he? The grass beneath his foot grows fearlessly when his knees are knocking together. The pines lift their proud heads to wrestle with the tempest when he dives for an uncertain security into a hole in the earth.

Nature overlies him with all its weight; what shall lift it off, lift him above it, and enthrone him in a sense of the sovereign significance of his own being?

It is to be done by a peculiar resource within himself; by somewhat, which, in allusion to its ethereal nature, I shall at present call the immanent dream of the human soul, — a dream that stands in perpetual, defiant contrast with his outward experience. The forces of the world enslave him; he dreams pure freedom, absolute and immortal. All things around him change, and helplessly he changes with them; he dreams a conscious poise and comprehension, that mutation cannot invade. Time sweeps past with its succession of days, and on the wings of the days his life flies, to disappear as they do; he dreams the conscious eternal. The world affronts him with hard, material, impenetrable fact; insolently independent of him; owing nothing, as appears, to any principle in his breast: he dreams the primacy and universality of thought, holding the solid universe in solution for ever. In the physical world, force is the be-all and end-all; he dreams the conscious right, commissioned with authority to judge reality by ideal standards, and renew it in an ideal image. All that he beholds partakes of imperfection; he dreams the perfect, — beauty and good without flaw and without instability.

This dream, moreover, is *humanity itself*, the essence of its nature. All the distinctive genius of man is in it; all his high performance comes out of it. It enters into his contemplation of the forms of nature and life, and makes poetry and art; into his regard of nature assumed to be the embodiment of thought, and makes science; into the eye, with which he reads the significance of his own being, considered as universal truth, and makes philosophy; into his sense of relation to his fellow, and makes morality, civil and social order; into his self-recognition, and makes the aspiration to liberty; it hovers before him as an ideal, and makes the impulse, the guidance, and the goal of progress. — *D. A. Wasson.*

INNER MEANING OF RELIGION.

What a word that is, — " Religion "! How deep it lies in the whole history of man! How, in all the efforts that men make to escape from the bondage which has been connected with it, they cannot get away from the thing itself! A friend of mine, recently returned from England, said that, among intelligent and cultivated men whom he met there, he found that religion was utterly given up; "but," he said, "they are men who hold fast, with true loyalty, to moral principle." "Then," I said, "that is their religion." And that is the religion of multitudes, who, either from want of an original constitution of sentiment, or disgusted by the false exhibitions of devout sentiment, turn away from the whole emotional side of religion, but place their feet firm on the rock of righteousness, right doing, obeying the divine law, — a sacred principle itself, consecration itself, therefore itself a religion: though I should not say the whole of religion, for religion, covering the whole of man, is the idea of truth with reason; it is a righteousness of law in his conscience; it is an inspiration and an affection in the heart. We want to plead for all these things: we find room for them all in our freedom. Our freedom does not release us from the attractions of any one of them; we do not in our liberty go off into space: but we find within ourselves those sacred divine laws — a reality of experience — which bind us, in every direction, to the true, to the right, to the beautiful, to the loving. A sentiment so deep in man's soul is not going to pass away: it is only the transient forms which pass away, when sometimes men are wrenched from their old beliefs, and seem to be set afloat; when they are ready to believe that, because they have been deceived under the guise of sentiments called religious and emotions called devout, there is no such thing as true, devout feeling. What we want to get at, on every side, is reality, — facts: facts of physical nature, and of the spiritual world; facts of the emotions; facts of the soul. . . . We want to be uplifted at times from things visible into things invisible, and to know that in our life, which is passing away and in its nature perishable, there is a reality which constantly passes on, through ways of change, itself unchanged, and to lay hold of this reality through the ideal faculty of our souls. That is Religion.

What is aspiration after perfection but the action of the ideal element in us, seeking a better than we have ever seen, not contented with the facts that are, but knowing that there are greater facts beyond? A reality we want our religion to be in its freedom: freedom from superstition; freedom from external authority. Not that we may stand still, but that we may grow in every direction; that we may fill out towards every point; that we may receive, from all quarters, light and truth and peace and strength and inspiration, — a feeling that there is something above ourselves, — name it as you may, state it as you may, — a feeling of something above ourselves and yet akin to ourselves, for ever drawing us on by an attraction which we could not resist if we would, and would not if we could in our best moods, and hemming us in, not letting us go from it, because it is the law of our own life, — that life within us which is akin to God; which enables us to say, with all the liberty of thought as well as the emotion of feeling, "Our Father," since it is this kindred with the Infinite that we mean when we say, "Father." — *Samuel Longfellow.*

THE PERMANENT AND THE TRANSIENT IN RELIGION.

FORMS, the determinate mould in which ideas of God and worship are cast, may change or perish, and yet religion in its essence remain unharmed, untouched. Flesh and blood cannot inherit the kingdom of God. The task set to man, and especially to man of this generation, is to purify his worship, to purge it of the sensuous element. As there is a destructive force, a power disintegrating, tending to break down, to corrupt, to kill, so also there is a vital force, a power industrious to build up, to enlarge, exalt, and free. There is this vitality in the soul. It seeks to resist and surmount the degradations of sense, to raise the spirit to pure thought and liberty. The battle is as old as history, and there are shown to have been substantial conquests won. From the low fetich-worship there has been an advance to a partially finer and better in nature-worship, prostration before gods grotesque enough, dwelling in dark abodes, but less material, invisible. The outer image gave way before an inner image; the idol of wood or of stone was broken to be succeeded by a conception in thought, a conception gross and very anthropomorphic indeed, but still finer, less unworthy than that represented in wood. Polytheism was exchanged for monotheism, the divine was unified, the many melted into one. The grosser personal conceptions were laid aside; corporeity, physical organs, as eyes, ears, hands, dwelling in special place, or locality, the anthropomorphic ways of seeing, knowing, doing, &c., — these, in the course of ages, in good degree have passed away.

Other work remains to be done, till there be in our conception of the divine a complete separating away of every thing that even in thought involves outer or personal limitation.

In this thorough elimination is the idea of *person* to be laid aside? Perhaps so, since it is so hard to hold by person and escape the anthropomorphic conceptions. "In the idea of person," says Fichte, in his sublime invocation, "there are limitations; how can I clothe thee with it, without these?" In attempting to disengage and lay hold of the content of pure thought, the intuition within us, it is difficult to say where we may or must stop. Our idea is conditioned by form, and yet form limits the idea. All unconsciously men borrow from the sensuous fancy what they suppose to belong to the spiritual intuition. Professor Martineau, as indeed do generally the theologians who appeal to intuition for support of their views, deems that in that content are given, not only the divine existence, but personality, and will, works, ways, very much after the human cast. Very hard it unquestionably is, as we speak of the Highest, to escape the necessity of impersonation. And yet, doubtless, the thought is to clear itself more of the personal determination as we attempt to reach pure view of God.

But, not to dwell upon this subtle question, which might involve us in debate as protracted and unsatisfactory as that which afflicted the schoolmen upon the subject of Universals, we may say that religion will come more and more to centre in those ideas which, present ever in consciousness and intelligible to the simplest understanding, are yet so ethereal that they pass beyond the range of the loftiest thought, and represent to us well the conditions of the infinite; ideal Truths, — ideas so substantial and enduring they are the reality of Truth itself, — truths so transcendent, superlative, everlasting, they are pre-eminently ideal. Justice, Truth, Beauty, Excellence, — these are some of the names we call them by; and, under whatever name, they hint the illimitable. Do we seek terms comprehensive, most deeply significant? There are no words so broad and inclusive as they. Do we seek that which conveys omnipresence, eternity, the majesty of wisdom and power? There is nothing which so finely fulfils the conditions of spirit as the reality which they symbolize. They veil and they reveal, temper the light to our mortal eyes, and express in sublimest, fittest speech we know, the One inexpressible. Here is shrine for worship, altar for sacrifice, temple for aspiration and prayer. Here is fane where idolatry cannot enter, an object we may adore without possibility of unworthiness or any excess, a beauty, a Madonna, we may love without degradation or effeminacy. Much as we sip and quaff, we can never exhaust the sweet; freely as we may partake, we can never cloy of the possession.

Religion thus becomes the pure worship of Truth and Reality, the largest, noblest fact possible to our being. It is *sobriety*, holding every thing at its worth, reading all aright, suffering never any intoxication, exaggerating never the present, pursuing nowhere unduly whatever may be grateful or desired. It is *activity*, wakeful energy, deep interest, constant doing, finding stakes to be contended for in this world of time, and willing to sacrifice all for their winning. It is *repose*, keeping ever the poise, no heat even in the thick of the battle, remembering the to-morrow after to-day, and resting in perfect trust. It is *dedication* to the highest, wedding Virtue, embracing Truth and Excellence. It is *invocation* to the finest and the best; it says to great Propriety, —

> "Be thou my pattern, thou my guide,
> O'er every thought and step preside."

"I invoke and I worship benevolence, purity, and a worthy life," says a Persian prayer, coming down mayhap from the days of Zoroaster. So the soul shall say, "I invoke and I worship the ideal perfect. Oh! mould thou me, and assimilate to thy complete image; make me to be like thyself." — *C. D. B. Mills.*

RELIGION AS EFFORT TOWARD SELF-PERFECTION.

IF I find that religion reduced to its lowest terms, to its simplest expression, is simply the effort of man to perfect himself, does that seem to be an inadequate, poor, and empty conception? Does it seem to exclude the Infinite? No; far from that. You cannot travel the road towards perfection without very soon discovering that you cannot attain it step by step. The path to infinity is not a ladder. You cannot complete your search, and gain its object. You feel that you have entered upon a quest which is infinite, endless, — not possible to be ended, even in an eternity of time. The very thought of progress presupposes a goal: the very thought of progress, again, implies the impossibility of a goal. You go from less to more and from more to most, but you still have an infinite stretch of space beyond; and the very fact that you are thus travelling onward into space gives you an idea of the infinite space in which you live, and move, and have your being. Many a man starts out on this road towards perfection, fired by a deep hunger and thirst for the ideal, but not knowing whither it shall lead him, or what thoughts it shall give birth to in his own soul. But I believe that, if he travel that road persistently, he will find himself accompanied by a growing consciousness of the infinity of the universe in which he dwells, the infinity of the Power which has made him and makes all the infinity of this Nature which he inhabits. Nature herself is the effort of the Infinite to express its own perfection. The very thought of infinite perfection is implied in the effort to perfect one's self. The thought of our own perfection implies the thought of that infinite perfection of which ours is but the feeblest imitation and copy. So, although I admit that many a man may be a religious man in having this deep thirst for the ideal, and in putting forth the effort to create and perfect it in his own life, and yet be technically and in his own thought an atheist, I do believe that this effort to reproduce voluntarily within himself the unity of the universe and to help carry forward its laws and powers to their highest evolution in his own soul, has a direct tendency towards what I should name Theism, were I called upon to describe it by the fittest term. The Atheism which starts out with devotion to any idea must logically end, I think, in the simplest, the fairest, the noblest, the highest form of Theism. That is the reason why I feel so much sympathy for men like George Jacob Holyoake, of London, a man who is conscientiously atheistic, who has written the most touching, tender, and heart-probing book, perhaps, that was ever penned, "The Trial of Theism." I never in my life felt a more earnest religious spirit in any book than in that. And yet he denies a personal God, denies God in every sense in which he can be defined in words, and declares himself to be a simple atheist, — a "Secularist." There is nothing in all literature more deep, tender, and earnest than the spirit that pervades that book. I feel myself infinitely more in sympathy with that atheist than I do with thousands and thousands of men who call themselves religious, and lift their hands in horror up to God, as if I turned my back upon Him.

This is the religion that I believe in, — a religion which is consistent with perfect freedom, and presupposes it; nay, a religion that aims directly at freedom as part of the ideal itself. This religion, once planted in the human heart, must grow. It is a vital seed, which cannot be suppressed or killed out. No drought will kill it; no flood will kill it. Nothing will kill it but the extinction of the soul itself. So long as that hunger after the ideal survives, you have the very spirit, the very essence and epitome, of all religions. That is enough. Leave it to grow as Nature wills; leave it to develop as human nature shall direct; and when it comes to its natural growth, depend upon it, it will be something most fair, beautiful, and lovely to behold. We need not fear that any monster or any baneful Upas-tree will come from it. No, it is the divine seed; the seed of truth, the seed of beauty, the seed of happiness, the seed of love, the seed of every thing that can sweeten, and enlarge, and beautify life. — *Francis E. Abbot.*

REASON AS GUIDE.

Who shall guide man in this path to perfection? How are we to distinguish the universal from the temporal or local stand-point, God from the gods, justice from compacts of selfishness? History itself as little as the Bible can guide us in this matter, for they contain both the ideal and the history of development towards it, the universal and all particular stand-points, truth and the various shades of aberrations. If the Bible is to guide, what are we to do with its immoral incidents, the unreasonable tales and myths, the local or temporal presentations of Deity? The religious sentiment called faith cannot guide, for it is evidently uncertain. Whence the various and contradictory views of the Christian sects, all claiming the guidance of faith, if it is reliable? By faith, crusades were organized, inquisitions instituted, *autos-da-fé* celebrated, tens of thousands were massacred. How could faith be a good guide? Imagination cannot invent a doctrine revolting to reason and conscience, which, at one time or other, has not been adopted by faith as a divine precept. By faith, all sorts of superstitions and barbarities have been preached, believed, and practised. Faith is not our proper guide. The ethical sentiment, conscience, must guide, it may be maintained; but this is also an unsafe guide. Conscience, too, has misguided, and does misguide individuals and nations. The conscience of those parents who drown their new-born daughters because they cannot afford to give them the proper education and outfit; and of those barbarous sons who kill their feeble and aged parents, because they are burdensome to themselves and others; the conscience of fanatics and enraged mobs, of despots and their obedient coadjutors, is human conscience. Conscience, clearly, is an unsafe guide.

Reason, the understanding, is THE guide which God has given us; the highest and last arbiter in all matters, human and divine. Reason is the supreme authority; and there is no appeal from its decisions. By reason we distinguish correctly the true from the false, right from wrong, the universal from the particular. Faith, conscience, history, and Bible must submit to reason. This is the touchstone to distinguish gold from brass, the precious metal from the dross. Whatever cannot stand the test of reason is worthless, and to be cast away. This was the case in all ages of history, and will be so for ever. With the progress of reason, faith and conscience are purified, humanity is elevated, and the ethical feeling sanctified. Truth is the only Messiah. Reason, says a Jewish authority, is the angel (the mediator) which stands between God and man. Reason has redeemed the human family from barbarism, and will complete the work of redemption. If I speak of reason as the highest authority, I do not mean my reason or your reason ; I mean reason itself, universal and eternal, in which and through which the human family is a unit, and God is revealed to man. Reason must distinguish the universal stand-point from the particular ones in the Bible and elsewhere. Truth is the seal of God. Reason is the connecting link of God and man, — like the rays of light that connect the earth with the sun. Therefore science, the favorite mistress of reason, is the ally of religion and truth. Research, criticism, inquiry, and all other exertions of reason, are divinely appointed means for the progress of humanity to its lofty ideals of God, truth, and happiness. — *Rabbi Isaac M. Wise.*

UNITY IN RELIGIOUS SENTIMENT.

Religious controversy seeks agreement and mutual understanding. It invites the development of individual views, in the interest of a final reconciliation whose harmony is preluded and prepared by musical dissonance. Only masters possess the idea of this symphony of many minds in which all severalties conduce to the common and final consent. Not once in a hundred years is a true symphonist born. So rare is his power, that his works increase in recognized value and authority long after the term of his mortal life. Remote generations seek to interpret his high meanings, and flatter themselves that they understand him when their homage flatters him no longer. Rare as is a symphonist in music, a symphonist in morals is far more rare. Few of us have that fine sense of the one in the many, and the many in the one, which enables a man, by one golden thread of doctrine and example, to draw all men unto him. The religious spirit in man is the spirit which in the master awakes, and in the multitude responds to this sublime invitation. The consideration of supreme subjects may promote diversity of opinion, but will lead to unification of sentiment. To attain this desirable end, each and all should be mindful of individual limitations, and of the oneness of truth. Every pair of antagonist minds should see between them the infinite, which the finite of neither can possess. Then will arise a noble emulation, not of self-illustration, but of mutual help. Then, however one may pray and the other respond, Amen will be a clause of peace.

The religious progress which I desire and expect lies in this direction. The absolute religion, as I understand it, is not a featureless abstraction. It is not a belief without a church, a soul without senses. It is the reality of faith which underlies and includes all sects and all creeds. Not as if all were alike in value and merit. For, while we grant one origin to all religions, we cannot insist that all shall have the same issue. The primal source of Philip II.'s bigotry and of Channing's liberalism was the same, — the religious element in man. The difference of result makes one a poison, not yet worked out of Europe, the other a medicine not yet worked into America. Our absolute religion must first formulate what shall be called religion in spirit and in action. When it recognizes this, it says, "This is religion. This man is or was religious." Where it recognizes the most of this, it says, "Here is the most."

Religion does strangely include and govern the whole man. It is imagination, it is energy. It is zeal, it is charity, it is love and aversion. It is intellection and enthusiasm. It is all of these, and none of them singly. And as it is composite of these various elements, those who specially represent one of them must show appreciation, not disrespect, to those who represent the others. The world-church is a divine body from which no member can be spared. The happiest lesson of my later life has been this, — that all true souls can agree in supreme things, that what is religious in the intolerant sects is civilizing, energizing, and reformatory, as well as in the tolerant ones. Where the religious persuasion accompanies the larger intellection, it removes the barriers of prejudice and superstition. The truly liberal build no citadel for themselves. They only patrol and keep the streets of the free city. — *Julia Ward Howe.*

NATURAL RELIGION UNIVERSAL AND SYMPATHETIC.

I THINK we have disputed long enough. I think we might now relinquish our theologic controversies to communities more idle and ignorant than we. I am glad that a more realistic church is coming to be the tendency of society, and that we are likely one day to forget our obstinate polemics in the ambition to excel each other in good works. I have no wish to proselyte any reluctant mind, nor, I think, have I any curiosity or impulse to intrude on those whose ways of thinking differ from mine. But as my friend, your presiding officer, has asked me to take at least some small part in this day's conversation, I am ready to give, as often before, the first simple foundations of my belief, — that the Author of Nature has not left himself without a witness in any sane mind; that the moral sentiment speaks to every man the law after which the universe was made; that we find parity, identity of design, through nature, and benefit, to be the uniform aim; that there is a force always at work to make the best better, and the worst good. We have had, not long since, presented to us by Max Müller, a valuable paragraph from St. Augustine, not at all extraordinary in itself, but only as coming from that eminent Father in the Church, and at that age in which St. Augustine writes: "That which is now called the Christian religion existed among the ancients, and never did not exist from the planting of the human race until Christ came in the flesh, at which time the true religion, which already subsisted, began to be called Christianity." I believe that not only Christianity is as old as the creation, — not only every sentiment and precept of Christianity can be paralleled in other religious writings, — but more, that a man of religious susceptibility, and one at the same time conversant with many men, — say a much-travelled man, — can find the same idea in numberless conversations. The religious find religion wherever they associate. When I find in people narrow religion, I find also in them narrow reading. Nothing really is so self-publishing, so divulgatory, as thought. It cannot be confined or hid. It is easily carried; it takes no room; the knowledge of Europe looks out into Persia and India, and to the very Caffirs. Every proverb, every fine text, every pregnant jest, travels across the line; and you will find it at Cape Town or among the Tartars. We are all believers in natural religion; we all agree that the health and integrity of man is self-respect, self-subsistency, a regard to natural conscience. All education is to accustom him to trust himself, discriminate between his higher and lower thoughts, exert the timid faculties until they are robust, and thus train him to self-help, until he ceases to be an underling, a tool, and becomes a benefactor. I think wise men wish their religion to be all of this kind, teaching the agent to go alone, not to hang on the world as a pensioner, a permitted person, but an adult, self-searching soul, brave to assist or resist a world; only humble and docile before the source of the wisdom he has discovered within him.

As it is, every believer holds a different creed; that is, all the churches are churches of one member. All our sects have refined the point of difference between them. The point of difference that still remains between churches, or between classes, is in the addition to the moral code, that is, to natural religion, of somewhat positive and historical. I think that to be the one difference remaining. I object, of course, to the claim of miraculous dispensation, — certainly not to the doctrine of Christianity. This claim impairs, to my mind, the soundness of him who makes it, and indisposes us to his communion. This comes the wrong way; it comes from without, not within. This positive, historical, authoritative scheme is not consistent with our experience or our expectations. It is something not in nature: it is contrary to that law of nature which all wise men recognize; namely, never to require a larger cause than is necessary to the effect. George Fox, the Quaker, said that, though he read of Christ and God, he knew them only from the like spirit in his own soul. We want all the aids to our moral training. We cannot spare the vision nor the virtue of the saints; but let it be by pure sympathy, not with any personal or official claim. If you are childish and exhibit your saint as a worker of wonders, a thaumaturgist, I am repelled. That claim takes his teachings out of logic and out of nature, and permits official and arbitrary senses to be grafted on the teachings. It is the praise of our New Testament that its teachings go to the honor and benefit of humanity, — that no better lesson has been taught or incarnated. Let it stand, beautiful and wholesome, with whatever is most like it in the teaching and practice of men; but do not attempt to elevate it out of humanity by saying, " This was not a man," for then you confound it with the fables of every popular religion; and my distrust of the story makes me distrust the doctrine as soon as it differs from my own belief. Whoever thinks a story gains by the prodigious, by adding something out of nature, robs it more than he adds. It is no longer an example, a model; no longer a heart-stirring hero, but an exhibition, a wonder, an anomaly, removed out of the range of influence with thoughtful men. I submit that, in sound frame of mind, we read or remember the religious sayings and oracles of other men, whether Jew or Indian, or Greek or Persian, only for friendship, only for joy in the social identity which they open to us, and that these words would have no weight with us if we had not the same conviction already. I find something stingy in the unwilling and disparaging admission of these foreign opinions, — opinions from all parts of the world, — by our churchmen, as if only to enhance by their dimness the superior light of Christianity. Meantime, observe, you cannot bring me too good a word, too dazzling a hope, too penetrating an insight from the Jews. I hail every one with delight, as showing the riches of my brother, my fellow-soul, who would thus think and thus greatly feel. Zealots eagerly fasten their eyes on the differences between their creed and yours, but the charm of the study is in finding the agreements, the identities, in all the religions of men.

I am glad to hear each sect complain that they do not now hold the opinions they are charged with. The earth moves, and the mind opens. I am glad to believe society contains a class of humble souls who enjoy the luxury of a religion that does not degrade; who think it the highest worship to expect of Heaven the most and the best; who do not wonder that there was a Christ, but that there were not a thousand; who have conceived an infinite hope for mankind; who believe that the history of Jesus is the history of every man, written large. — *Ralph Waldo Emerson.*

MISSION OF JESUS.

It seems to me, that the nearer we come to the spirit of Christ, the nearer we shall come to those who appear not to wish to assert that name of Christ respecting themselves; that those who are the most Christian in spirit will say the least about it. For I suppose that Jesus Christ did not come to preach Christianity. Christianity, the Church, no doubt, was the result of Christ's preaching; but he did not come to preach it. He came to preach the truth; and we shall be nearest to him, not when we preach Christianity, not when we preach the Church, not even when we preach Christ, but when we preach Christ's preaching, which he made as broad as the truth. The Church was the result; but it was a result, as many things are results, of causes which it did not resemble. You may have been in some great cavern, and seen the sparkling, beautiful-shaped, finger-like stalactites that hang on the roof of the cavern; but from the droppings from these beautiful, sparkling, crystalline stalactites, there is formed a dark, amorphous, yet somewhat interesting mass, called the stalagmite. The original truth is the stalactite; and the Church is the dark, amorphous stalagmite. We are not to preach that stalagmite of the Church, but to preach the truth as Christ preached it, or in the spirit in which he spoke.

Christ is regarded as a mediator between God and man. A mediator undoubtedly he became between God and man. He has been such to millions. But the office of a mediator is to introduce; that is, Christ introduces you to God. Certainly, then, like any other introducer, doing his office generously, he leaves you to private conversation with the Being to whom he introduces you. You may have been present on some great occasion, when hundreds or thousands of persons were introduced by one man — the mayor of a city, perhaps — to some great author, general, or president; but the moment a man was introduced, the mediator stood aside, and let the man speak for himself to the person to whom he was introduced. So, I think, the office of mediator, so far as Christ exercised it, was simply to bring us into immediate relation with God. That is the true mediation.

Once more. I think Jesus came simply to be the

voice of the moral sentiment. He refers you back to the moral sentiment; and is the voice of that; and only in the strength of your own moral sentiment can you understand one word that he says.

I think if the two sides would look at these three principles, — that Jesus came, not to preach Christianity, but truth; that he came, not to be a mediator, but to bring us into immediate relation with God; and that he came, not to be, and never pretended to be, the author of the moral sentiment, but only its voice, — I say, if the two sides would look at these three principles, they would find themselves more agreed than perhaps they imagine. — *C. A. Bartol, D.D.*

DEATH A NATURAL LAW OF LIFE.

When Death calls, he neither deprives us of the virtues, nor suddenly relieves us of the vices, of which he finds us possessed. Both go with us. The moral, social, and intellectual qualities which may have distinguished us in this world, will be ours in another, there constituting our identity and deciding our position. So also of the evil. That dark vestment of sin with which, in a man's journey through life, he may have become endued, clings to him through the death change close as the tunic of Nessus. He, too, retains his identity; his earthly shortcomings determine his spiritual state.

I believe, then, that the spirit of man passes the ordeal without other metamorphosis than that which its release from the fleshy envelope and its acquisition of clearer perceptions effect: undimmed now, unobscured by the heavy veil of the material, gradually relieved from the weight of bodily grossness and physical infirmity; a great gainer, too, by this, that, through the agency of the spiritual senses, there is opened up a wider and more luminous horoscope; and thus drawn closer to the great Source of Wisdom; yet essentially the same spirit still. It changes there, indeed, but not by miracle. It changes, even as now it does, by the intervention of motive presented, by the agency of will, by the influence of surroundings; but of surroundings better and nobler than those of earth. It changes, as it changed here, by its own aspirations. It inhabits a world of progress still; a world of active effort, not of passive beatitudes, nor yet of irrevocable doom. While there is life there is hope, and there is life beyond the veil.

The Christian world has been, and still is, blighted with false conceptions of Death. Death is not, as Plato taught, the opposite of life. He is life's best friend; a friend through whose agency life is embellished, ennobled, perpetuated. To Death, at the close of a life well spent, man owes Paradise. Yet Orthodoxy has taught us to think of this greatest of benefactors and reformers as the requiter of sin, the Avenging Angel, the fell destroyer. Men robe themselves in black when he appears; mourners go about the streets. The great punishment, the evil of evils, the primeval curse, declared to have been entailed on man by Adam's fall, is held to be that summons which calls him hence. Yet, under Omniscient Goodness, nothing so universal, so inevitable as death, ever was, or ever can be, essentially evil. — *Robert Dale Owen.*

TRUTH IN OBSOLETE DOGMAS.

Have you ever heard a noble musician take some very simple theme which to you a few notes or words would represent, and, sitting down before his instrument, begin to dream away upon that theme, until, as the moments passed, it turned into great orchestras of sound, and tides of fresh meaning that you had known nothing of come rolling in towards you, and you felt a freshening from your little theme that you never believed was in the words or the thought? Somewhat so, I think, these old dogmas of the recent Christian past come freshening with full tides of meaning to the thinker of to-day. Let me instance one, — and yet I hardly dare to, — not a doctrine but a practice, but you know practice is underlaid by doctrine: the vital and the inevitable act, as I think it is, of prayer. People say to us, "With your idea of God, with your idea of the relation between yourself and God, what is prayer to you?" As if in the act one stopped to analyze the experience. But when one does stop to analyze the experience, and recognize it in all its new relations to the thought of God and of ourselves, then he sees, of course, that the old meaning of prayer is dissolved out of his mind. But is there nothing abiding and growing in its place? The old thought of petition, — and that to most minds, to most Orthodox minds, at least, seems to be the essence of "prayer," — that thought has absolutely gone; and has nothing remained? Has nothing come up to larger meaning? Why, every thing! The man who trusts absolutely does not beg. The man who *knows* he is forgiven does not entreat forgiveness. The shame itself is pledge of that. The very feeling that when you are praying you are not praying *to* a person, but *with* a person; the very thought that the prayer comes from the One who answers it; the very thought that the "Thou" and the "I" are one in that act, — is not that a nobler, a sweeter, a deeper, a higher inspiration, than the old thought, even to those who value the old thought most? That is only one illustration, and I have phrased it very poorly. It is hard to say what one thinks, he hardly knows all he thinks, about such an act as that.

Take that word "Incarnation." Do you know a holier thought than comes into your mind when you say that word? The divine opening in the human; the divine implanted in the human, from the foundation of the first things, pressing upwards into visibility all the time; pressing up in the individual, pressing up through the race until a higher individual is formed; pressing up from the poor savage, pressing up from the lowest sinner, into the greatest being. What tides of religious meaning come swelling into that old word "Atonement"! It is almost the butt of some schools of religious thought. Do you know a more true law of the universe than that law of atonement? Not concentrated into one man's history, or found only in that man's life and death, but a law going through and through the life of every creature on the earth; the law of a force which lifts us by the sufferings of others; the law of a force which lifts others by our sufferings. And so about all the other doctrines. The meaning glows within them, until the old words seem the veriest last year's husks to the great resurrection that we begin to recognize. — *William C. Gannett.*

RADICAL FAITH AFFIRMATIVE.

It is a mistake for any of us believers in natural religion to allow ourselves to be betrayed, for a moment, into a negative position; to allow, for an instant, that the burden of proof is on our side. The burden of proof is on the other side. It is we who have the positive, and the sects the negative; it is we who have the affirmation, and the sects the denial. Each little sect builds its little wall, and encloses its special atom of God's truth. It denies all outside of the wall, and then when we sweep that wall away, charges us with denial. Our answer to them all must be that the church of freedom and philanthropy is older, larger, and grander than they. As Luther said, we say, but in a wider spirit, " We are the Church," because we represent no platform narrower than humanity itself. Religion is the natural instinct of the human soul; this and this only lies behind all these petty organizations, and gives them their being; and when we push them away, and come down to God's solid foundation, it is no denial, but affirmation. That is the only assertion; it is that which gives the believer in natural religion strength, not alone for himself, but to labor for others; because he represents, not this or that conventicle, but the central spirit which they all embody, the love of God and man, by which alone they live. Take away from them what is superficial, and they are all alike. Take away a few ceremonies from the Catholic and the Protestant, a few technical phrases from the Trinitarian and the Unitarian, and they are one and the same. Take away from the Jew and the Mohammedan these separating forms and dogmas, bring back each one to what makes his manhood, and they are all the same. Behind the highest utterances of the world, of the Vedas, of Epictetus, of Marcus Antoninus, and of Jesus, — behind them all, and greater than all, is the eternal aspiration of humanity to the absolute truth of God. It is that truth to which the radical is pledged, because it is natural religion which he recognizes. He it is who affirms, and leaves each little sect of each little religion to do its own denying.

Look into your books of piety, and see the unity of the great expressions among all peoples! Look into your hymn-books, and you see that the hymns which come nearest to every religious soul are the hymns which are not sectarian, which were not written by sectarians, which were written, in many cases, by persons cast out by the churches. Those hymns which are most immortal in the hymn-books are often those which the churches borrowed from poets whom they left outside. Who wrote, "While thee I seek, protecting Power," that perfect utterance of the last triumph of religious trust? Helen Maria Williams, the friend and imitator of Mary Wollstonecraft. You may still find her branded as a heretic in the biographical dictionaries. Who wrote, "Nearer, my God, to thee"? It was Sarah Flower Adams, the friend and disciple of William J. Fox. In her lifetime, she would have been disowned by the very churches which now cannot draw near to their God without borrowing her wings to fly with. And so, through piety as through morality, you find that all forms are superficial, and all souls are saved by that simple religious sentiment which lies behind all creeds. . . .

It is the affirmation of the free religious movement that makes it strong. An affirmation that takes in not only one man's belief, but all men's belief, — is not that a positive faith? Here, let us suppose, is an organization that has met this week somewhere, and every man who comes upon its platform comes with his religion stereotyped into some creed; and every thing else is shut off that platform. That is affirmation, is it? Yes: it is the affirmation of one thing, and the negation of every thing else. And when the old religious teacher and his opponent come together on this platform, and each in turn speaks his mind freely, you call that denial. We call the other the denial, and this the affirmation. The affirmation that recognizes not only one creed, but the dignity, value, and worth of all; that is what is recognized here as religion. I do not understand it when I am told that my attitude is that of denial only, while I find that that which shuts me out of the churches is not so much that I deny some little things which they believe, as that I believe whole centuries of history, and whole races of humanity, that they all deny; while they shut themselves into their little tabernacle, and say only one creed has any foundation in it. I am not separated from evangelical religion because it attributes the divine inspiration to Jesus, but because it denies it to all others. It is their denial, not their affirmation, which separates me from them. When they tell me Jesus taught a gospel of love, I say I believe it. Plato taught a gospel of love before him, and you deny it. If they say, "Jesus taught it is better to bear an injury than to retaliate," I say, "Yes: but so did Aristotle, before Jesus was born. I will accept it as the statement of Jesus, if you will admit that Aristotle said it too." I am willing that any man should come before us and say, "Jesus taught that you must love your enemies: it is written in the Bible;" but if he will open the old manuscript of Diogenes Laertius, he may there read, in texts that have never been disputed, that the Greek philosophers, half a dozen of them, in words as well authenticated as any literature can be, said the same before Jesus was born. The brotherhood of man is a sacred thing to think of, — a sublime thing to teach. When the Greek tragedians taught the brotherhood of man before the Christian dispensation, was it less sacred than it became after Jesus came on earth and repeated it? There is this difference between the attitude of natural religion and the attitude of any sectarianism, even the widest Christian sectarianism, that, while natural religion recognizes every voice of God that ever spoke through the soul of man, Christian sectarianism only admits the utterance of one pure soul to be divine.

Affirmation! There is no affirmation except the belief in universal natural religion; all else is narrowness and sectarianism, though it call itself by the grandest name, compared with that. It impoverishes a man; it keeps his sympathy in one line of religious communication; it takes all the spiritual life of the race, and says, "All of this that was not an effluence from Jesus, you must set aside;" and so it makes you a member in full standing of some little sect, all of whose ideas, all of whose thoughts, revolved in the mind of some one narrow-minded theologian who founded it. It shuts you up there, and you die, suffocated for want of God's free air outside.

Therefore, I say, it is an affirmative position that is

to rule the world; it is this large affirmation of universal religion, bringing a person into contact with the natural instincts of the human heart, that enables him to deal with that heart in all its wanderings, to reach the conscience, however degraded, and to raise and strengthen and encourage man as no gospel of narrowness or despair ever can do. I do not believe, any more than you do, that the mere theology of a few dry metaphysicians or pedants is sufficient to move the world. Whether they are radical or conservative, they will equally fail. The theology that is to move the world has got to have heart and impulse and faith in it, as well as mere intellect. The religion that is to move the world must be such a religion as the mother can feel by her baby's cradle, and the child at his mother's funeral. I have heard theologians quarrel about texts; I have heard scholars debate among themselves these petty questions, "Who was it first taught these doctrines? Can we fix the year and the day when somebody came into the world and wrote in some books the golden rule, or the principle of love to God and man?" and I have thought to myself, "Stop your discussion, and go home and take counsel of your own little child." Of what importance is it who first wrote into a book the golden rule, when you may go into your own nursery and find your little girl, two years old, acting the golden rule by her own lovely, childish impulse, before she has ever seen the inside of a Sunday-school? Talk of putting the thing into words! There was never a generous-hearted child, there was never a tender sister, who did not enact the principle of love to enemies long before anybody thought of making a book, — before this world was burdened

with any such thing as learning. The child teaches
the lesson to its mother, to its father; God sends the
child into the world with the lesson already in it ; and
the bigot goes home from his parchment of doctrine,
and finds a holier gospel which his little girl teaches
him as she springs into his arms; she, in her unconscious
innocence, has a universal religion, and he is nothing
but a bigoted sectarian by her side. . . . I have lived
for months among an ignorant and degraded people,
whose religion was of the lowest type of Christianity,
still bearing those fruits which all sincere religion will
bear. I lived for two years among those who had
spent their lives in the darkness of slavery, and had
only so much of Christianity, in any form, as their
masters had chosen to give them. I saw the results of
this religion among them, but I never saw a man among
them whom the simplest truth of natural religion could
not reach. I never had occasion to wish for any of the
tools the churches give. I never saw reason to oppose
or alter the opinions that the Southern negroes under
my charge held, but did I ever for an instant believe
that their Christianity, ignorant and lowly as they
were, was a better thing even for them? that it had
more affirmation in it than the natural religion which I
held? Never! Of all the religions to live by and to
die by; of all forms of religious opinion to carry to the
sinful and the suffering, and bring them back restored;
of all the forms of religion to give renewed hope, to
relieve despair, and to enlighten ignorance, — I believe
that natural religion stands at the head. I ask no more
than that with which to reach the sinner or the suffering;
and, if I cannot reach him with that, it is my fault, and
not the fault of the instrument; and, thank God! there

are plenty of others who can. And we, who owe so much, all our life long, to the gradual swelling, in this community, of a religious impulse which is greater than any in the past, because it is affirmative, are grateful to bear testimony to its power. We can never own it as negative. It has nothing to regret, nothing to apologize for. It is to us as much the hope of the world, as the religion of the Roman Catholic, the Protestant, or the Mohammedan is so to him; and it is greater than any of them, because it includes them all; and a day is coming, when even what we call the great religions of the world shall show themselves but sects, and when all these little sects shall be united in one vast religious assemblage, which shall march into St. Peter's, and all the great old-time cathedrals of the world, shall take possession of them all, and shall celebrate in them a religious ceremonial as much grander than any that Rome can now witness, as the dome of the sky is grander than this petty building which contains us here. — *T. W. Higginson.*

SOLIDITY AND POSITIVENESS OF RADICAL FAITH.

I was severely pitied by an old friend this morning, because I was coming here to take my stand upon "that rickety platform of radicalism." Now that I am here, it seems to me that I am as safe as I am in any place in God's universe. Underneath the platform of radicalism on which I stand this morning, I find the whole of past time, I find all the great natures of all the great men who have ever lived, who have ever spoken or sung a word for God or for humanity. There is such a phrase as the "Rock of Ages," as applied to the infinite wisdom and strength. Underneath the platform of these religious ideas, I feel the Rock of Ages; because I find that every age has contributed its stratum and deposit to build it, and that, standing here to-day, I stand upon the most positive place I can find upon the earth, since I stand in the last moment of time, upon the last deposit that God has made in it, mixed, as it is, with the human nature of the present, and with all its needs and contingencies, and growing, as it does, out of the human nature of the past, with all its circumstances and its prophecies, as the tree grows from a root, for the express purpose that it may free itself from the ground beneath, where it is dark, and spread its full mass of foliage into the light and air and rain of the ever-present God. And if I undertake to scrape off from that tree its bark and tetter of supernaturalism, if I venture to say that the grain of the tree is supremely good and sound and sweet, without taking with it every accretion and parasite of the past which has made its home upon the outside of it, I do so, that in my way, with these my brethren who believe in Radicalism, I may be able to show you what a grain, capable of what a polish, what an exquisite beauty and durability, has been concealed underneath that bark and the thin crust of mythologizing that has gathered around it.

I never felt in such a positive place in all my life as I do now. I never felt a plank beneath my feet that was so thick, so deep. Thousands of years deep is the wood of which this plank is made; hundreds of thousands of years, with their rings of daily pleasure and of daily sweetness, and the presence of the Divine Mind, and the smiles and tears of all the men and women who have ever lived, have gone into the depth of the plank of this platform; and you are called here this morning, that we may come to meet you, and to look you in the face and say to you, that nowhere else can you find a work so positive, upon material so durable, with thoughts and feelings so far-sighted and so prophesying. For we have beneath us the idea of the Infinite God, Father of all men and women, the infinite, ever-present, ever-creating Providence, who works for our behoof, and for the cause of his laws and of his truths, by laws. I feel beneath me that vital and irresistible tendency which no denomination, no creed, no man, no sect can stifle or can put aside, — the mighty desire that lives in all hearts to know how it is that God, the infinite Father, brings his truths to pass, and makes every day, and day after day, a perpetual revelation and expression of his presence. Beneath me, I feel your desire, and the desire of all mankind, to understand God's presence upon the earth, in every righteous cause, in every central truth, in every tendency that sweetens and harmonizes, in all social and philanthropic science, in that which drains and irrigates and defecates infected districts, in that which saves men and women from miasma and cholera, that brings pure air, clean quarters, and a great margin of space for comfort to all mankind, however miserable they may seem to us to be to-day. I feel beneath me the irresistible desire of all men's hearts for permanence and continuance of living, either within or without a body, — the old, primeval rock of personal immortality. Is there any thing more positive than that? What will you bring me? What will you bring into this hall to-day that will compare with the positiveness of the presence of the infinite God and of his truths in the heart of mankind, and the desire of men and women for personal continuance of existence for the sake of the infinite truths of God?

Somebody said to me, also, as I came here, "Your ideas are very fine, and we can detect them scattered all over the world, like gold which, the most widely distributed of minerals, crops out upon the surface everywhere. Your ideas are beautiful; they may be what you call central and organizing ideas, but you have left all the heart out of the concern. You have got a few very superfine speculations about the Divine Mind and human nature, but you have omitted all the tenderness and pathos, all the sweet smiles and delights of human existence, all the yearning, all the longing, all the filial clutching for the Divine Hand, all the trust in Providence, and all the sweet content which makes one day succeed another, keeps all men and women alive and prevents them from committing suicide. It has all gone overboard. You have emptied the baby out with the bath."

I should like to know what is meant by the word "heart." It seems to me when people use the word "heart" in this connection, that they want to have a monopoly of Providence; that they would like to have a channel of Divine Providence within their house, on tap, where they can turn it on like gas or water. They are not content with trusting to the infinite laws which are inevitable and irrepressible, whatsoever we may say or think about it; and every one of them is constructed for our supremest good, and with reference to our best advantage; so that, as the Scripture says, not even a sparrow falls to the ground without his care.

But it falls, and it cannot help falling. It is hard for the sparrow to drop; perhaps it twitters a continual dread of falling, or desire that it may be saved from falling. But shall a man twitter too, and try to bribe the Infinite Law with prayers, and to besiege the Infinite Presence with supplications that this thing or that thing may come to pass, that this or that may not occur, or that he may be saved from any thing, whether more or less piteous and grievous, while all the time one thing is pleasure and another thing is pain, that is joy and this is grief, all the time there is law, Providence, the Infinite Presence? The manliest heartfulness that I can conceive of is that of the person who throws himself directly into the bosom of the Infinite Presence, and says to it, "Come what may, let what will happen to my house, to my family, to my children, to my office, to my future, I will not be so mean as to expect from thee comfort merely, to derive from thee immunity, to claim a share in providence. I want to be built by thy providence; to be organized by that which thou shalt send me. Here I am. Take me; take the whole of me, — my heart, my soul, my emotions, my intelligence, — take my soul and body into thyself, and let me be, in deed and in truth, the gentle and filial and trusting subject of thy law." That is what I mean by having a heart towards God.

And we have a heart towards man. Do you tell me that when Radicalism takes its stand upon the platforms of America, by the side of the negro, and insists upon his rights, upon his suffrage, upon his immunities, and upon the opportunities that we ourselves so love and enjoy, and so confide and place our future in, — that we have no heart? Do you tell me that when we take up the cause of woman, and desire to see her educated like ourselves, and standing, if she can, where we stand, and doing, if she can, what we do, — at any rate, *doing what she can*, — when we seek to give her that greatest of all boons that can be given to God's children, *opportunity*, that we have no heart? I tell you, my radical friends and listeners, that in America, *heart* is belief in the moral law. Yes, it is belief in justice, it is belief in equality. *Heart?* It is the brotherhood of man! — *John Weiss.*

THE TRUE TEACHER IN RELIGION.

Do you remember that story in the life of Theodore Parker? When he was a little boy, coming home from the field, one day, he saw a little animal by the wayside, and raised his stick to smite and kill it; but something, he said, distinctly bade him stay his hand, and he let the little creature live. When he got home, he asked his mother what it was that told him, when he wanted to strike the animal, he must not do it; and his mother took him reverently on her knee, and said to him, "Some people call it conscience; I call it the voice of God; and if you always listen to it, you will always know what is right, and you will never need to go wrong." From that reverent teaching came such a man as Theodore Parker. It is the same thing that Socrates meant by his "demon;" it is the same thing which, in every true soul, impels to noble deeds, or restrains from those which are wrong.

We come into the world, I believe, every one of us,

with all that is needful in ourselves, if we will only trust it, — all that is needful to help us on and up to the very highest heights to which a human being can ever climb; but we have covered it over by dogma and creed and sectarian theory, and by our own misdeeds, until these angel voices that are in us cease to be heard, — not totally cease, I do not believe they ever totally cease, but they become less and less audible to us. But if we learn to heed their faintest whisper, reverently and obediently, I believe that there is no path where the soul asks you to go that you may not safely tread. It may carry you to the burning, fiery furnace, but you will come out, and the smell of fire even will not be on your garments. It may compel you into the lion's den, but the wild beast's mouth will be shut. You may walk where scorpions are in the way of duty, and you will not be hurt. It is this "inner light;" it is not a text, it is not a creed, but it is this in ourselves which, if trusted, will lead us into all truth.

I said I did not believe this voice was ever lost in the human soul. I do not forget that men grow very wicked, and women, too, for that matter; I do not forget that men and women sometimes appear to us so lost and fallen that it seems as if no power in themselves, or any human power, could help them up; and yet, to these worst men and women, in some hallowed moment, is the word given, "This is the way: walk ye in it." And if, at the side of this man or woman, at that very moment, is some helping hand, some voice wise enough to counsel, he or she may be started to walk in that way. . . .

I do not believe that our present way of teaching

religion is the true way. I know this platform will help it; I know the lives of all good men and women help it; and yet, after all, I believe that the world's true teacher, in all that pertains to the soul and its duties, has not been found. I believe she sits in every household, and by the side of every cradle, and that the true priest and the true religious teacher is the mother. I know how, from the earliest time, woman has been in bondage; that the things which go to help all other human beings in growth and symmetry and beauty have always been withheld from her: but, after all, I believe that all the healing, the helping, and the building-up, comes through woman. "The seed of the woman shall bruise the serpent's head." I believe that she who should, by divine right, be the religious teacher above all others, is to take her place as such. There comes up, to-day, a voice asking that Harvard College shall be opened to women; that schools of science, and whatever else will give breadth of being, shall be open to her; that no field of activity shall be denied to her, if she can occupy it. I believe that all the signs of the times point to woman's freedom; and, when she is free, as every thing else in nature finds its place, so will she; and the woman who, by God's appointment, inevitably takes her place beside the world's cradle, will sit by the world's altar; and when the Theodore Parkers that are to be, ask counsel from her lips, the answer will not be unwise or ignorant or irreverent; but the mother, herself developed and taught, will be able to be herself a priestess to the little one at her side, and teach him that, as he grows up, he shall be his own priest, his own lawgiver, and that the holiest oracle is in his own soul. We shall not see this ourselves, because it is so far in the future. As are the ages behind us which have dragged woman down, so many years will it take to build her up to the place where she shall occupy her real throne; and then, with her sons and daughters, as she herself, "but little lower than the angels," extending helping hands to whoever needs, aspiring toward all that is noblest and best in character, reaching after those infinite fields of knowledge which the heavenly Father spreads everywhere, the world itself will be so changed that it will be "Paradise regained."— *Lucy Stone.*

THOUGHT AND DEED.

I HAVE seen many charmed days, and shared a sublime hope; but this, of all days which I have yet seen, is the most sublime; because it not only speculates in the most transcendent way, and absorbs all thought, and all peoples, and all races, and all bibles, but it looks to practice; and you will all be disappointed if it end merely in convention after convention, annual meeting after annual meeting. You say: "Work, work, work! Work lovingly, work deliberately, not wilfully." You say that. Therefore I shall look for the next step to be declared hereafter for action. Let not the accusation be made any longer, my friends, that we are mystics, that we speculate, that we have delicious and delightful thoughts, but we do nothing. A friend said to me to-day: "Mr. Emerson! Oh, yes, a lovely man, but what has he done?" *Who brought us here?* Who is the father, or, if not the father, the cousin, at least, of the thought that brought us here? You know who, so far as any one person is concerned. This meeting is transcendentalism. This is the fruit of forty years of earnest, private, self-respecting modest thought. Therefore, I say, the more modest we are, and the less we say about our religion, the more we shall possess. It is too fine a thing to talk about; it is a precious thing to live by, and to show in action. That is the jewel, is it not? Therefore, I say, not until this thing is incarnated, not only in one man, but in all of us, and we can say: "I and my Father are one;" "he that hath seen me, hath seen the Father also;"—not until we say that, not in egotism, but in the sublime and delightful and beautiful personality which makes us one with Him, is the word really spoken. So, in my judgment, my friends, we have had almost enough of talk, we want action; and as I have now but a little while to stay on any platform in this world, perhaps it will delight me as much as any one to take part in the action which must follow. So fine, so sublime a religion as ours, older than Christ, old as the Godhead, old as the soul, eternal as the heavens, solid as the rock, *is and only is;* nothing else is but that; and it is in us, and is us; and nothing is our real selves but that in the breast. That is *the* religion, and nothing else; not in the flesh, but speaking and acting through the flesh; that is it.—*A. Bronson Alcott.*

RELIGION AND SOCIAL SCIENCE.

RELIGION, while faithful to its function of affording a substantial ground and an encouraging countenance to the high spiritualities of the human race, is, and must be, concerned about labor and wages, commerce and capital, health and houses, civil rights and laws, and the like. It will be asked to give or withhold its sanction in such matters, and it will owe an answer. Now, in order to give an answer, which shall at once be good in spirit and sane in judgment, it must know, not only the sovereign claim of the soul, but *the law of outward things.* Here science is its proper eye. The spiritual consciousness knows by its own light what are rectitude and honor, holiness and heroism, adoration, charity, noble awe, the spirit of faithfulness, the spirit of truth: it does not know by its own light whether or not wine is wholesome, usury beneficial, eight hours of labor better than ten; and, in the attempt to pronounce out of hand upon these matters and the like, it has made sad mistakes. Whenever and wherever it has to decide upon outward conditions, and, therefore, to take the law of things into account, it is dependent for the sanity of its judgment upon other resources than those which are native to it. Here it must supplement its own methods by those of scientific investigation. Science, and science alone, as I think, can teach it to be practical with entire sanity. This, too, is the proper corrective of passionate reform, — which surely needs a corrective: surely it is time that for the methods of agitation were substituted the methods of growth; and for the harangue, study, and the sober conference of prepared minds. Sober, modest, temperate, capable of a wise silence, able to wait and seek, able to distinguish between partial and perfect knowledge, speaking when it does speak in the modulated tones of calm knowledge and clear intellectual conviction, science is not one of those dangerous allies which are liable at any moment to annul their services by excesses. Like religion, it subdues passion, and respects truth. A substitute for religion it can no more be than vegetable physiology can be a substitute for sunshine: the natural ally of religion, its eye for truth of the outward world, science should be. Well, therefore, may modern religion stand in the door to reach forth a cordial hand, and say to social science, " Welcome, younger brother, to an honored place in the household of faith." — *D. A. Wasson.*

PRACTICAL PROBLEMS OF RELIGION.

WHATEVER may now be our speculative opinions concerning the Trinity, the atonement, the divinity of Jesus, the authority of the Bible, or the future condition of the soul; whatever change these opinions may hereafter undergo, it is certain that the teachings of Jesus concerning love to God and love to man will never be falsified or antiquated, since they are the expression of a sentiment inborn and natural to the human heart. The sympathetic feeling of mankind responded to them when first uttered, and will always do so. They do not require the support of logic, nor of infallible authority, for they furnish their own evidence, and no miracle could make them more impressive. There have been disputes about doctrines; but these are not doctrines: they are practical statements, perceived by the intellect, but accepted by the heart. I never heard the Good Samaritan's claim to goodness denied, even by the most orthodox Hebrews.

And yet there is something peculiarly religious in this portion of the teachings of Jesus. It is not only the most undoubted, but the most affecting part of the Christian religion. It is hard to persuade ourselves, perhaps, that there is not something particularly religious in the maintenance of an opinion, though nothing can be more absurd; and so we are in the habit of speaking of a man's "religious opinions." But it is in the heart and life alone that religion manifests itself; the intellectual convictions are as nothing in comparison.

Reasoning in some such way as this, and resolutely overlooking the fact that it is opinions rather than modes of life that have been the source of religious dissensions, I have fancied that the time might come when persons of all shades of religious belief would cordially unite in works of charity and reform. And I have interpreted the word "Free," in the name of our Association as implying this liberation from the tyrannies of sectarian jealousy and dislike, rather than as indicating a particular form of belief on the part of our associates. Let us welcome to our work, as we invite to our platform, the champions of every opinion provided they are willing to labor with us for the elevation of mankind. Let the Catholic who loves God more than his creed be as welcome in our assemblies as the Jew who does the same. Let us extend to Calvinists and Churchmen, to the disciples of Wesley, of Murray, and of Channing, the same invitation; and, whether they join us or not, let us proceed to the labors before us.

It is one of the most encouraging signs of the times, that the tendency of all our religious organizations is now very strongly towards works of charity and social reform. The oldest and the newest churches feel the same impulse and obey it. This is partly because the moral evils of the time are seen to be great and growing, while the remedies which the Church has been wont to apply have ceased to be efficacious. The Labor Question, the Woman Question, the Question of Education for the poorest, of reclaiming the thief and the prostitute, of suppressing intemperance, of dealing with insanity, of diminishing pauperism, — these and a hundred other questions, derived from these or related thereto, press upon us for decision and we cannot escape them. If we have a true religious feeling, we shall not try to escape them; we shall entertain them all, and devote ourselves to those with which we can best deal. One person will teach the freedmen, others will secure them the right to vote, will visit prisons, found hospitals, open new avocations for women, proclaim a truce between labor and capital, diminish poverty, and banish drunkenness; 'and at every step of every reform, Religion will be present to give her sanction. She will not always wear the vestments of the Church, nor speak the voice of tradition, but sometimes she will do both; and she will never fail to attest the truth of Pliny's saying, "To benefit mankind is worthy of a God." — *F. B. Sanborn.*

PHILANTHROPY AND THE CHURCH.

I BEGAN life with a most profound faith in the honesty and in the efficiency of church organization. I had the most entire belief (which I did not inherit) that the Church contained all the sincere religious feeling and purpose that existed. I was bayoneted out of that conviction by experience. My eyes were opened by the facts about me; and when I began to look back, with eyes anointed by the facts of my own life, into the history of church organization, my experience seemed natural enough. For instance, the Church, as such, gave us no help in the anti-slavery effort or in any other radical movement. I do not believe that the philosophy of organization allows the possibility of a church ever helping in such an onward movement. We are not to be exacting. We are to allow, exactly, to every phase of opinion, lever of purpose, organized representative of conviction, its actual value. It seems to me that organization is a milestone which represents how far opinion had travelled when it crystallized into an organization. You cannot expect of that organization, necessarily in its shape as an organization, an acceptance of any new idea. It will discharge, unexpectedly, its full duty if it even maintains life enough bravely to represent the opinion which created it; which in seven cases out of ten it never does. It seems to me that every organization is the representation of an idea, but never can go beyond it. It never has been, or rarely has been, faithful to the application of an idea. It has fallen back into the worship of the fathers. It has limited itself by the application made by its own saints. For instance, Luther claimed the right for bodies of men to go out and represent Catholicism; but Luther did not reach the point of allowing the individual to do that; and when some of his own followers went to that extent, the public sentiment of the era being unable to bear them up, they were surged and swamped in the age, and forgotten. The age was not ready for such individuals. It could not hold them up.

Succeeding them came Congregationalism, having the idea that a church, a small collection, could assert the right of individual judgment as against a large body. That was another gain. Then came the Brownists, the Independents, and the Baptists, asserting the right of individual judgment within the line of what was considered the inspired rule of the Scriptures. That was another gain. But when the Quaker went out beyond that, and claimed the right of individual judgment, not subject to the inspiration of a book, they cried out "heretic;" they repudiated him, inevitably. Were they not all good? Yes, undoubtedly. Did not Luther do a great deal of good? Certainly. Did not the Congregationalists? Indubitably. Does not the Church of to-day do a great deal of good? Certainly it does. It takes up the admitted truths, the respectable truths; it gathers them into shape, applies them to admitted evils; cheap soup and the primer, giving away money, perhaps the tenth of your income; the duty of not allowing your neighbors in the next street to starve; the duty of sending the truth you have got to somebody else, — all good, excellent! The only weakness you find in organization is when you demand of it to walk. The fluid is a force; the solid is a weight. While the river is a fluid it moves. You must not expect motion of that which is crystallized; but it has its use. When I was on the Mississippi's banks lately, we walked across the river. The ice was useful. It was church organization. The fluid of the last summer crystallizes into a useful bridge; but if the river subsides, and leaves ten feet of vacancy below, the bridge will fall. If, with the advancing spring, the water rises, it will carry the whole Church into the ocean of absolute truth; it will carry the ice away. But you must not expect motion of the crystallized sentiment which has become a church. There was great truth in what the old Italian said in the fifteenth century : " There has not been a Christian to die in his bed for two hundred years," — that is, there had not been a real Christian man who looked about him, saw the needs and met the lessons of the actual day, with nothing in his own soul between him and God, who led a comfortable life. He must always go out with the Baptist into the wilderness. He need not, perhaps, always reproach the Church that staid at home and did its own business, — acted up to its light. It has its uses. His duty is, as it seems to me, to confess the light God gives him. As was beautifully said as I stood by the coffin of a deceased friend this week, " Her right never rebuked another's wrong." Perhaps I should vary the statement a little ; but what I mean is, there is no need, necessarily, of rebuking short-coming until it passes into dishonest antagonism; until it seeks to throw a net under your feet, and trip you up; until it thunders after you misrepresentation and scandal, and cries out, " schismatic ! " " fanatic ! " " infidel ! " As long as it can recognize its own place, and let you take yours, it is to be fellowshipped, not as a force in the movement of society, but as a breakwater and anchor to keep what we have gained. That is my idea. In the mean time, we are all to set to work and preach whatever God or man has taught us of the finest laws of the religious sentiment, and each age will see more and more of it. Luther was honest ; but Carlstadt was necessary in a certain sense, because he saw more.

The records of Christianity hold, it seems to me, a

very large measure of the lessons that social science needs. In the first place, the Christian records are principles. The Church is an alleviative. It approaches evils to alleviate them, not to cure them. That is not the New Testament method. There are two ways of touching evils. If the gas was escaping in this room, we should open the ventilators and relieve ourselves. That is *relief*. To-morrow the superintendent would send for a gasfitter, and he would stop the leak. That is *cure*. Now, as I look at it, all action of the Church approaches poverty to make it comfortable; it approaches crime to endeavor to soften it; it approaches prostitution to shield it from temptation. That is *relief*. That is opening the windows to get rid of the leaking gas. But social science and the religious philosophy of the New Testament, while they attempt all that, prescribe that the really religious intellect shall seek, not relieve, but cure. . . .

If there is any strength, God gave it in order that it might hold up weakness, supplement weakness. If there is any knowledge, God gave it that it might sit down side by side with ignorance, and put its arm around its neck, and divide. If there is any wealth, it is only a trust, and the poorest man you can find in the neighborhood is your co-trustee. That is Christianity, as I read it. That is Christianity; and, singularly enough, we generally leap right off, and say, that is the Church. But take the amelioration of punishment, for instance, as an illustration of my meaning, — the old vindictive theory of the Jews, and the European idea, that hangs a man to satisfy the passions of society. That lived a great while. Then came the exemplary idea, that I must be hung to make you better; which sacrificed me to your welfare. That held its own a great while. Those two were the pet ideas of the Christian Church. We have got a new idea now, and it is this: that the moment society has seized a man, society owes him education, moral development, protection, emolument. Having put him within stone walls for its own defence, it shall thereupon begin the duty it owed to him in his cradle, and neglected; that is, begin to educate him. Prisons are moral hospitals. God let that man commit a murder in order that society might get the right to take hold of him, and do what God holds it guilty for not doing before, — educate him. Where did you get that idea? Got it from Beccaria, got it from Voltaire, got it from Romilly, got it from Dumont, got it from Bentham, — men, who, if they ever were inside of a church door, would be held as heretics, — got it from Brougham, whom the Church denounced as an infidel. Never has there been a man in advance of the age, on this question or in any other way, who had not been driven into the wilderness by the Church of the day. But whence really came this idea of the treatment of persons, for instance? It came from the great normal root of Christianity, — the sacredness of the individual. Religion, having taken hold of a man, no longer deems him a chip of a block, a part of the government, a unit that goes to make up the State; it no longer looks at him in the mass, — a hierarchy, an aristocracy. That single unit of a soul and God, — these are the only two things in the universe, in the contemplation of religious principle. The sacredness of the individual! What right have you to hang me? Stuart Mill is the only infidel who ever failed to see this, but he is followed by nine hundred and ninety-nine out of a thousand Christians, so called. But those men called infidels studied social science; they studied philanthropy; they studied principle; they studied it in human instincts. *Called* infidels, — for there are men called infidels who really are Christians, as there are men calling themselves Christians who really are Infidels, without suspecting it. I have met in my day many specimens of both these classes. That man is a Christian whose life and ethics grow out of the central root of Christianity; no matter, if in his ignorance or his prejudice he disowns the name. That man is an Infidel who is not, with his whole heart, willing to bear his brother's burden; no matter how broad his phylactery, how regular his church-membership papers, or how loud his profession of Liberalism or Radicalism. . . .

God's method of education is to lay responsibility on the human soul. The doctors say there is electricity enough in the brain to cure any disease, if you can only rouse it. So there is moral power enough in every man to make him a man, if you could only rouse it; and responsibility rouses it. Take a girl, a mere popinjay, a toy; she gets married, and people say: "What a mere child that is to have children!" She has one or two children, and then her husband is taken from her side. How wisely she plans; how patiently she watches; how she opens careers for them; how she guards her children's interests; how she begs from one and from another, and earns from a third, the means to give that boy an education, sheltering the girl meanwhile! What a wonderful being! We never knew her. Where were all those powers hidden? How did she get them? Necessity brought them out;

God created them. If you had given her a career before, you would have seen them all. You were beginning to move in the line of God's law when you found her a widow, with those two children on her brain and heart. You had got into the line of the great necessity which God meant should unfold, educate, and lift up every human being. You did not need the magnet that a mechanic filled up with electricity — that is, a benevolent society — for her; the great natural magnetism of the earth, that is, God's law, made her gravitate towards a career and a success.

The value of social science to men of radical faith and purpose is, that it digs down to the root of principle. It does not seek alleviation merely; it does not seek what the Church can give; it faces the great problems of the hour. Negro slavery was a very great question, but still, to a certain extent, it was a limited one; it applied to a race. Its value was that it forced us, in the conflict with the Church, in the conflict with the State, to dig down to the principles which, when they grew up, covered all kindred interests.

Seek out, publish, and, as fast as possible, bring society into harmony with the laws of *justice*. This is social science. All Labor asks is *justice*, not charity; all woman asks is *justice*, not pity; all the negro asks is *justice*, not humanity. Indeed, where is the treasury full enough to pay that debt? All crime asks is *justice*, not sympathy. Who shall teach us the full meaning of this great word, JUSTICE? "*Owe no man any thing.*" When that command is obeyed, Social Science will be dazzled out of sight by the millennium. — *Wendell Phillips.*

IMPROVEMENT OF MAN ON EARTH.

I THINK there is hope when a religion is presented to the people which is not only in favor of free thought and free speech, but which endeavors also to benefit the physical condition of humanity. There never was, there never can be, such a thing as true pleasure in vice or crime; and yet the land is full of them, because, as I think, the social condition of the people is not cared for as it ought to be at the present moment. I agree with the sentiment of that great social reformer, Robert Owen, that the characters of men are formed for them, instead of by them; and consequently I think the influence of circumstances in this country, rather than any natural or inherent depravity in mankind, accounts for the degradation and vice and crime that prevail in every section of the country. Let us not, then, suppose that it is owing to any natural or inherent depravity that this state of things exists, but only in the fact that the true remedy for social evils has not yet been put into practice; but when the remedy is applied, the reform will be complete. And it is a great sign of the times, that radicals and liberals and free-thinking men are doing what lies in their power for the promotion of this great reform.

Let men, if they can do no better, dream of a hereafter, to which I have no kind of objection; but the hereafter must be according to the present, and if people live well in the present, they have the best preparation for the future. But to go into the future unprepared by the present may, perhaps, for any thing I know to the contrary, be the same routine over again.

But be that as it may, I am getting beyond my depth; I do not know any thing about these matters; I do not pretend to know. Being finite, frail, and imperfect, I do not presume to understand the infinite, and therefore I confine my thoughts here; for I think there is enough to do in this world, and more than enough, to occupy all our time in improving the condition of the people here. And those who believe in the hereafter should not object to the doctrine, because he who is right to-day will probably be right to-morrow. That there are those in the community who entertain these aspirations, and are endeavoring by the aid of social science to improve society and even religion itself, is one of the hopeful signs of the times. — *Horace Seaver.*

ESSENTIALS OF FAITH.

As regards the subject upon which so much has been written of late, the importance of faith in a personal God, we shall be content to let our limited knowledge remain where it is, while we have all that science can reveal, both that which is self-evident, which is natural, which is spiritual, and that which belongs to outward nature, — which it needs not that I enlarge upon, ignorant as I am, after all that has been said. But I think that this shall be found to suffice, and, as has just been expressed, that it shall pervade the universe of God, and bring us into the kingdom, which is nigh even at the doors; and that we need not enter into any speculations as regards the future, as regards immortality, but that we all shall learn to rest content with the limited knowledge we have, and be confident, by fulness of faith, that that which is best for us shall and will be ours, while we do not endeavor by our speculations to make out or build up a heaven. I remember, when Dr. Channing, years ago, at our house, attempted to advocate his views, and to show what everlasting progress there would be in the hereafter, I told him it was as interesting to me as any speculation to which I had ever listened on the subject, but he must allow me to say that it was speculation still. I want we should tread under foot our speculations, and every thing that will mingle aught that is uncertain with the religion which we have heard presented to us to-day, — which is certain, which is sure; for that which is self-evident needs no argument. And so we come near to the beautiful truths and testimonies that rise out of this pure religion and undefiled, that need no scholastic learning, that need no pulpit explanations. They are clear truth, justice, love, — highest, noblest, finest instincts of the human heart and mind, which we are to apply to all that we can imagine of the unseen and unknown. That divine power will be ours, if we seek it; and when these principles are stated they are self-evident; they need no learned oratory, and it is not employed in regard to them. You do not hear, in any of the pulpits, a definition of what love, and justice, and mercy, and right are. You know, and all know, that they are innate, self-defined. Therefore, I say, preach your truth; let it go forth, and you will find, without any notable miracle, as of old, that every man will speak in his own tongue in which he was born. And I will say, that if these pure principles have their place in us, and are brought forth by faithfulness, by obedience, into practice, the difficulties and doubts that we may have to surmount will be easily conquered. There will be a power higher than these. Let it be called the Great Spirit of the Indian, the Quaker "inward light" of George Fox, the "Blessed Mary, mother of Jesus," of the Catholics, or Brahma, the Hindoo's God, — they will all be one, and there will come to be such faith and such liberty as shall redeem the world. — *Lucretia Mott.*

MESSRS. ROBERTS BROTHERS'
NEW BOOKS

IN PREPARATION FOR THE AUTUMN OF 1875.

I.

JEAN INGELOW.
FATED TO BE FREE. A Novel. By JEAN INGELOW. With numerous Illustrations by G. J. PINWOOD. One volume, 16mo. Uniform with "Off the Skelligs."

II.

LOUISA M. ALCOTT.
EIGHT COUSINS; or, The Aunthill. By LOUISA M. ALCOTT. With numerous Illustrations by ADDIE LEDYARD and SOL EYTINGE. One volume, 16mo. Uniform with "Little Women," "Little Men," "An Old-Fashioned Girl."

III.

SUSAN COOLIDGE.
NINE LITTLE GOSLINGS. By SUSAN COOLIDGE. With Illustrations by J. A. MITCHELL. One volume, square 16mo. Uniform with "The New Year's Bargain," "What Katy Did," "What Katy Did at School," "Mischief's Thanksgiving."

IV.

PHILIP GILBERT HAMERTON.
ROUND MY HOUSE: About the Neighborhood where I live in Peace and War Time. By PHILIP GILBERT HAMERTON. With Illustrations by C. O. MURRAY. One volume, square 12mo. Uniform with "The Intellectual Life," &c.

V.

NEIL FOREST.
MICE AT PLAY: "When the Cat's away, the Mice will play." A Story for the whole Family. By NEIL FOREST. With Illustrations by SOL EYTINGE. Square 12mo.

VI.

P. THORNE.
JOLLY GOOD TIMES; or, Child Life on a Farm. By P. THORNE. With Illustrations by ADDIE LEDYARD.

VII.

JULIANA HORATIA EWING.
SIX TO SIXTEEN. A Girl's Book. By JULIANA HORATIA EWING, author of "The Brownies." One volume, 16mo.

MESSRS. ROBERTS BROTHERS
HAVE JUST PUBLISHED:

By the Author of " Christian Art and Symbolism."

OUR SKETCHING CLUB: Letters and Studies on Landscape Art. With an authorized Reproduction of the Lessons and Woodcuts in Professor Ruskin's "Elements of Drawing." By R. St. John Tyrwhitt. 8vo. $2.50.

This book is in the form of a narrative, and is the doings of a supposed Sketching Club, their letters, talks, and essays on various art subjects, — nearly all practical ones, — such as would be likely to be exchanged between fairly good critics and well-educated men and women. It is a handsome 8vo volume, with numerous illustrations.

By the Author of " The Intellectual Life."

HARRY BLOUNT: Passages in a Boy's Life on Land and Sea. By Philip Gilbert Hamerton. With Frontispiece Illustration. 16mo. $1.50.

Mr. Hamerton has successfully accomplished a difficult task, and "his book for boys reaches the standard of a first-rate one," says the *London Academy;* and the *Spectator* says, " Harry Blount is a fine fellow, and we are glad to see him safely through his perils."

By the Author of " The Old Masters " and " Modern Painters."

MUSICAL COMPOSERS AND THEIR WORKS.
By Sarah Tytler. 16mo. $2.00.

"Distinctively gossipy and very entertaining. Lovers of music, who read for entertainment, wi l heartily enjoy these bright and minute sketches of the great composers; in point of readableness they are not surpassed by any similar sketches in recent literature," says *The* (Boston) *Literary World.*

PARAGRAPH HISTORY OF THE UNITED STATES, from the Discovery of the Continent to the Present Time, with Brief Notes on Contemporaneous Events. By Edward Abbott. Square 18mo, flexible cloth covers. 50 cents.

A pocket *vade mecum* of great value at this interesting period. It will be published on the Centennial Anniversary of the Battle of Lexington and Concord.

THROUGH THE YEAR. By Rev. H. N. Powers, D D., Rector of St. John's Church, Chicago. 16mo. $1.50.

A collection of serious and religious papers suited to the seasons of Nature and of the Church.

A SHEAF OF PAPERS. By Thomas G. Appleton. 16mo. $1.50.

Bostonians in particular, and lovers of good things in literature in general, will be glad that the author of these Papers, the rich and ripened fruits of his intellectual labors, has been induced to gather them into a Sheaf for publication. A few of them only have been previously printed.

MADAME RÉCAMIER AND HER FRIENDS.
From the French of Madame Lenormant, by the translator of "Memoirs and Correspondence of Madame Récamier." 16mo. $1.50.

Madame Lenormant's previous volume contained the memoirs of Madame Récamier, and the correspondence of her friends. The present volume is the complement of the first, and contains her Friendships and her Private Correspondence.

THE DEFENCE OF GUENEVERE AND OTHER POEMS. By William Morris. Crown 8vo. $2.00.

The author of "The Earthly Paradise" has been induced to reprint his earlier poems, now for a long time out of print. The volume was never published here, and is therefore entirely unknown to the numerous admirers of Mr. Morris's poetry in America.

FREEDOM AND FELLOWSHIP IN RELIGION.
A Collection of Essays and Addresses. Edited by a Committee of The Free Religious Association. 16mo. $2.00.

MESSRS. ROBERTS BROTHERS' PUBLICATIONS.

MEET FOR HEAVEN.

A STATE OF GRACE UPON EARTH THE ONLY PREPARATION FOR A STATE OF GLORY IN HEAVEN.

BY THE AUTHOR OF "HEAVEN OUR HOME."

Crown 8vo. Cloth, extra. Price $1.25.

OPINIONS OF THE ENGLISH PRESS.

"This forms a fitting companion to 'Heaven our Home,'— a volun e which has been circulated by thousands, and which has found its way into almost every Christian family." — *Scottish Press.*

"What we shall be hereafter, — whether our glorified souls will be like unto our souls here, or whether an entire change in their spiritual and moral condition will be effected after death, — these are questions which occupy our thoughts, and to these the author has principally addressed himself." — *Cambridge University Chronicle.*

"The author, in his or her former work, 'Heav n our Home,' portrayed a social heaven, where scattered families meet at last in loving intercourse and in possession of perfect recognition, to spend a never-ending eternity of peace and love. In the present work the individual state of the children of God is attempted to be unfolded, and, more especially, the state of probation which is set apart for them on earth to fit and prepare erring mortals for the society of the saints. . . . The work, as a whole, displays an originality of conception, a flow of language, and a closeness of reasoning, rarely found in religious publications . . . The author combats the pleasing and generally accepted belief that death will effect an entire change of the spiritual condition of our souls, and that all who enter into bliss will be placed on a common level." — *Glasgow Herald.*

"A careful perusal of this book will make it a less easy thing for a man to cheat himself into the notion that death will effect, not a mere transition and improvement, but an entire change in his moral and spiritual state. The dangerous nature of this delusion is exhibited with great power by the author of 'Meet for Heaven.'" — *Stirling Observer.*

"This, like the former volume, 'Heaven our Home,' by the same anonymous author, is a very remarkable book. Often as the subject has been handled, both by ancient and modern divines, it has never been touched with a bolder or a more masterly hand." — *John O'Groat Journal.*

LIFE IN HEAVEN.

THERE, FAITH IS CHANGED INTO SIGHT, AND HOPE IS PASSED INTO BLISSFUL FRUITION.

A New Work by the Author of "Heaven our Home" and "Meet for Heaven."

Crown 8vo. Cloth, extra. Price $1.25.

This new work is a companion volume to "Heaven our Home," and 'Meet for Heaven," and embraces a subject of very great interest, which has not been inclu'ed in these volumes.

The two works above mentioned have already attained in England the large sale of 100,000 copies.

MESSRS. ROBERTS BROTHERS' PUBLICATIONS.

REV. C. A. BARTOL'S NEW BOOK.

RADICAL PROBLEMS.

By REV. C. A. BARTOL, D.D.

CONTENTS. — Open Questions; Individualism; Transcendentalism; Radicalism; Theism; Naturalism; Materialism; Spiritualism; Faith; Law; Origin; Correlation; Character; Genius: Father Taylor; Experience; Hope; Ideality.

One volume, 16mo. *Cloth.* *Price* $2.00.

PROFESSOR PARSONS'S NEW BOOK.

THE INFINITE AND THE FINITE.

By THEOPHILUS PARSONS.

AUTHOR OF "DEUS HOMO," ETC.

One neat 16mo volume. *Cloth.* *Price* $1.00.

"No one can know," says the author, "better than I do, how poor and dim a presentation of a great truth my words must give. But I write them in the hope that they may suggest to some minds what may expand in their minds into a truth, and, germinating there, grow and scatter seed-truth widely abroad. I am sure only of this: The latest revelation offers truths and principles which promise to give to man a knowledge of the laws of his being and of his relation to God, — of the relation of the Infinite to the Finite. . . . And therefore I believe that it will gradually, — it may be very slowly, so utterly does it oppose man's regenerate nature, — but it will surely advance in its power and in its influence, until, in its own time, it becomes what the sun is in unclouded noon."

Sold everywhere. Mailed, post-paid, by the Publishers,

ROBERTS BROTHERS, BOSTON.